"Stylistically fluid and finely detailed...Santiago's auto-biographical account cinematically recaptures her past and her island culture. What is particularly appealing about Santiago's story is the insight it offers to readers unaware of the double bind Puerto Rican Americans find themselves in: the identity of conflict. Is [she] black or white? Is she rural or urban? Even more importantly, is she Puerto Rican or is she American? A reader can only be grateful that Esmeralda Santiago has chosen to explore her culture and share what she has found."   —*Los Angeles Times Book Review*

"*When I Was Puerto Rican* is the bittersweet story of a young girl trapped between two cultures...filled with coming-of-age anecdotes and sweet memories of family. Brothers, sisters, neighbors, aunts and uncles are delightfully woven into the fabric of the book."
—*Boston Globe*

"In the tradition of *A Tree Grows in Brooklyn* and *Call It Sleep*, Esmeralda Santiago's *When I Was Puerto Rican* tells the American story of immigration, this time with a unique Latin flavor. Santiago has sent a package to the world about her voyages, [and] her travelogue is now our bounty."   —*Washington Post Book World*

"A moving narrative, lyrically written. Generously, Esmeralda Santiago shares with the reader her memories of her Puerto Rican childhood and her bewildering years of transition in New York City. I admire the courage it took to make that journey—and then to write about it with such a clear eye. Always, her view of her past is affectionate, spirited and unromantic. The Puerto Rican landscape is alive in this book, in rich, evocative detail."
—Bobbie Ann Mason, author of *Feather Crowns*

"Read her book....You will see how one particular woman's journey from a rippled metal shack in a Puerto Rican countryside barrio becomes a story rich in reverberations about all those who have made a transforming physical and spiritual journey in life."   —*San Juan Star*

Esmeralda Santiago

WHEN I WAS PUERTO RICAN

Esmeralda Santiago's work has appeared in *The New York Times*, *The Boston Globe*, *The Christian Science Monitor*, and *Vista* magazine. She is a graduate of Harvard University and has an MFA from Sarah Lawrence College. With her husband, director Frank Cantor, she owns CANTOMEDIA, a film production company. They have two children, Lucas and Ila. This is Ms. Santiago's first book. She continues the story of her life in *Almost a Woman*.

WHEN I WAS PUERTO RICAN

Esmeralda Santiago

VINTAGE BOOKS

A Division of Random House, Inc.

New York

FIRST VINTAGE BOOKS EDITION, AUGUST 1994

Copyright © 1993 by Esmeralda Santiago

Excerpt from *Almost a Woman* by Esmeralda Santiago
reprinted by permission of Perseus Books, 1998. All rights
reserved. Copyright © 1998 by Esmeralda Santiago.

Library of Congress Cataloging-in-Publication Data
Santiago, Esmeralda.
When I was Puerto Rican / Esmeralda Santiago.
p.   cm.
ISBN 0-679-75676-0
1. Santiago, Esmeralda—Childhood and youth.   2. Puerto Ricans—
New York (N.Y.)—Biography.   3. Puerto Rico—Biography.
4. New York (N.Y.)—Biography.   I. Title.   II. Series.
[F128.9.P85S2718   1994]
974.7'1004687295'0092—dc20
[B]   94-11467
CIP

Manufactured in the United States of America
C987654

for Mami

CONTENTS

El bohío de la loma,
bajo sus alas de paja,
siente el frescor mañanero
y abre sus ojos al alba.
Vuela el pájaro del nido.
Brinca el gallo de la rama.
A los becerros, aislados
de las tetas de las vacas,
les corre por el hocico
leche de la madrugada.
Las mariposas pululan
—rubí, zafir, oro, plata. . .—:
flores huérfanas que rondan
buscando a las madres ramas. . .

Under its palm frond wings, the little house on the hill senses the freshness of morning and opens its eyes to the dawn. A bird flies from its nest. The rooster jumps from his branch. From the nostrils of calves separated from the cows runs the milk of dawn. Butterflies swarm—ruby, sapphire, gold, silver—orphan flowers in search of the mother branch.

from "Claroscuro"
by Luis Lloréns Torres

PROLOGUE: HOW TO EAT A GUAVA

Barco que no anda, no llega a puerto.

❧❧

A ship that doesn't sail, never reaches port.

There are guavas at the Shop & Save. I pick one the size of a tennis ball and finger the prickly stem end. It feels familiarly bumpy and firm. The guava is not quite ripe; the skin is still a dark green. I smell it and imagine a pale pink center, the seeds tightly embedded in the flesh.

A ripe guava is yellow, although some varieties have a pink tinge. The skin is thick, firm, and sweet. Its heart is bright pink and almost solid with seeds. The most delicious part of the guava surrounds the tiny seeds. If you don't know how to eat a guava, the seeds end up in the crevices between your teeth.

When you bite into a ripe guava, your teeth must grip the bumpy surface and sink into the thick edible skin without hitting the center. It takes experience to do this, as it's quite tricky to determine how far beyond the skin the seeds begin.

Some years, when the rains have been plentiful and the nights cool, you can bite into a guava and not find many seeds. The guava bushes grow close to the ground, their branches laden with green then yellow fruit that seem to ripen overnight. These guavas are large and juicy, almost seedless, their roundness enticing you to have one more, just one more, because next year the rains may not come.

As children, we didn't always wait for the fruit to ripen. We raided the bushes as soon as the guavas were large enough to bend the branch.

A green guava is sour and hard. You bite into it at its widest point, because it's easier to grasp with your teeth. You hear the skin, meat, and seeds crunching inside your head, while the inside of your mouth explodes in little spurts of sour.

You grimace, your eyes water, and your cheeks disappear as your lips purse into a tight O. But you have another and then another, enjoying the crunchy sounds, the acid taste, the gritty texture of the unripe center. At night, your mother makes you drink castor oil, which she says tastes better than a green guava. That's when you know for sure that you're a child and she has stopped being one.

I had my last guava the day we left Puerto Rico. It was large and juicy, almost red in the center, and so fragrant that I didn't want to eat it because I would lose the smell. All the way to the airport I scratched at it with my teeth, making little dents in the skin, chewing small pieces with my front teeth, so that I could feel the texture against my tongue, the tiny pink pellets of sweet.

Today, I stand before a stack of dark green guavas, each perfectly round and hard, each $1.59. The one in my hand is tempting. It smells faintly of late summer afternoons and hopscotch under the mango tree. But this is autumn in New York, and I'm no longer a child.

The guava joins its sisters under the harsh fluorescent lights of the exotic fruit display. I push my cart away, toward the apples and pears of my adulthood, their nearly seedless ripeness predictable and bittersweet.

JÍBARA

Al jíbaro nunca se le quita la mancha de plátano.

❧❧

A jíbaro can never wash away the stain of the plantain.

We came to Macún when I was four, to a rectangle of rippled metal sheets on stilts hovering in the middle of a circle of red dirt. Our home was a giant version of the lard cans used to haul water from the public fountain. Its windows and doors were also metal, and, as we stepped in, I touched the wall and burned my fingers.

"That'll teach you," Mami scolded. "Never touch a wall on the sunny side."

She searched a bundle of clothes and diapers for her jar of Vick's VapoRub to smear on my fingers. They were red the rest of the day, and I couldn't suck my thumb that night. "You're too big for that anyway," she said.

The floor was a patchwork of odd-shaped wooden slats that rose in the middle and dipped toward the front and back doors, where they butted against shiny, worn thresholds. Papi nailed new boards under Mami's treadle sewing machine, and under their bed, but the floor still groaned and sagged to the corners, threatening to collapse and bring the house down with it.

"I'll rip the whole thing out," Papi suggested. "We'll have to live with a dirt floor for a while. . . ."

Mami looked at her feet and shuddered. A dirt floor, we'd heard, meant snakes and scorpions could crawl into the house from their holes in the ground. Mami didn't know any better, and I had yet to learn not everything I heard was true, so we reacted in what was to become a pattern for us: what frightened her I became curious about, and what she found exciting terrified me. As Mami pulled her feet onto the rungs of her rocking chair and rubbed the goose bumps from her arms, I imagined a world of fascinating creatures slithering underfoot, drawing squiggly patterns on the dirt.

The day Papi tore up the floor, I followed him holding a can into which he dropped the straight nails, still usable. My fingers itched with a rust-colored powder, and when I licked them, a dry, metallic taste curled the tip of my tongue. Mami stood on the threshold scratching one ankle with the toes of the other foot.

"Negi, come help me gather kindling for the fire."

"I'm working with Papi," I whined, hoping he'd ask me to stay. He didn't turn around but continued on his knees, digging out nails with the hammer's claw, muttering the words to his favorite *chachachá*.

"Do as I say!" Mami ordered. Still, Papi kept his back to us. I plunked the can full of nails down hard, willing him to hear and tell me to stay, but he didn't. I dawdled after Mami down the three steps into the yard. Delsa and Norma, my younger sisters, took turns swinging from a rope Papi had hung under the mango tree.

"Why can't they help with the kindling?" I pouted.

Mami swatted the side of my head. "Don't talk back," she said. "You girls keep away from the house while your father is working," she warned as we walked by my sisters having fun.

She led the way into a thicket behind the latrine. Twigs crackled under my bare feet, stinging the soles. A bananaquit flew to the thorny branch of a lemon tree and looked from side to side. Dots of sun danced on the green walls of the shady grove above low bushes weighted with pigeon peas, the earth screened with twigs, sensitive *morivivi* plants, and french weed studded with tiny blue flowers. Mami hummed softly, the yellow and orange flowers of her dress blending into the greenness: a miraculous garden with legs and arms and a melody. Her hair, choked at the nape with a rubber band, floated thick and black to her waist, and as she bent over to pick up sticks, it rained across her shoulders and down her arms, covering her face and tangling in the twigs she cradled. A red butterfly circled her and flew close to her ear. She gasped and swatted it into a bush.

"It felt like it was going right into my brain," she muttered with an embarrassed smile.

Delsa and Norma toddled through the underbrush. "Mami, come see what I found," Delsa called.

A hen had scratched out a hollow and carpeted its walls and floor with dry grass. She had laid four eggs, smaller and not as white as the ones our neighbor Doña Lola gave us from time to time.

"Can we eat them?" Delsa asked.

"No."

"But if we leave them here a snake will get them," I said, imagining a serpent swallowing each egg whole. Mami shuddered and rubbed her arms where tiny bumps had formed making the fine hairs stand straight up. She gave me a look, half puzzled, half angry, and drew us to her side.

"All right, let's get our sticks together and bring them to the kitchen." As she picked hers up, she looked carefully around.

"One, two, three, four," she chanted. "One, two, three, four."

We marched single file into our yard, where Papi stacked floorboards.

"Come look," he said.

The dirt was orange, striped in places where crumbs had slipped through the cracks when Mami swept. Papi had left a few boards down the center of the room and around his and Mami's bed, to stand on until the ground was swept and flattened. Mami was afraid to come into the house. There were small holes in the dirt, holes where snakes and scorpions hid. She turned around swiftly and threw herself off balance so that she skipped toward the kitchen shed.

"Let's go make supper!" She singsang to make it sound like fun. Delsa and Norma followed her skirt, but I stared at the dirt, where squiggly lines stretched from one wall to the other. Mami waited for me.

"Negi, come help in the kitchen."

I pretended not to hear but felt her eyes bore holes in the back of my head. Papi stepped between us.

"Let her stay. I can use the help."

I peered between his legs and saw her squint and pucker her

lips as if she were about to spit. He chuckled, "Heh, heh," and she whirled toward the kitchen shed, where the fire in the *fogón* was almost out.

"Take these boards and lay them on the pile for the cooking fire," Papi said. "Careful with the splinters."

I walked a broad circle around Mami, who looked up from her vegetable chopping whenever I went by. When I passed carrying a wide board, Mami asked to see it. Black bugs, like ants, but bigger and blacker, crawled over it in a frenzy.

"Termites!" she gasped.

I was covered with them. They swarmed inside my shirt and panties, into my hair, under my arms. Until Mami saw them, I hadn't felt them sting. But they bit ridges into my skin that itched and hurt at the same time. Mami ran me to the washtub and dunked me among my father's soaking shirts.

"Pablo!" she called, "Oh, my God! Look at her. She's being eaten alive!"

I screamed, imagining my skin disappearing in chunks into the invisible mouths of hundreds of tiny black specks creeping into parts of my body I couldn't even reach. Mami pulled off my clothes and threw them on the ground. The soap in the washtub burned my skin, and Mami scrubbed me so hard her fingernails dug angry furrows into my arms and legs. She turned me around to wash my back and I almost fell out of the tub.

"Be still," she said. "I have to get them all."

She pushed and shoved and turned me so fast I didn't know what to do with my body, so I flailed, seeming to resist, while in fact I wanted nothing more than to be rid of the creepy crawling things that covered me. Mami wrapped me in a towel and lifted me out of the tub with a groan. Hundreds of black bugs floated between the bubbles.

She carried me to the house pressed against her bosom, fragrant of curdled milk. Delsa and Norma ran after us, but Papi scooped them up, one on each arm, and carried them to the rope swing. Mami balanced on the floorboards to her bed, lay me beside her, held me tight, kissed my forehead, my eyes, and murmured, "It's all right. It's over. It's all right."

I wrapped my legs around her and buried my face under her chin. It felt good to have Mami so close, so warm, swathed by her softness, her smell of wood smoke and oregano. She rubbed circles on my back and caressed the hair from my face. She kissed me, brushed my tears with her fingertips, and dried my nose with the towel, or the hem of her dress.

"You see," she murmured, "what happens when you don't do as I say?"

I turned away from her and curled into a tight ball of shame. Mami rolled off the bed and went outside. I lay on her pillow, whimpering, wondering how the termites knew I'd disobeyed my mother.

❧ We children slept in hammocks strung across the room, tied to the beams in sturdy knots that were done and undone daily. A curtain separated our side of the room from the end where my parents slept in a four-poster bed veiled with mosquito netting. On the days he worked, Papi left the house before dawn and sometimes joked that he woke the roosters to sing the *barrio* awake. We wouldn't see him again until dusk, dragging down the dirt road, his wooden toolbox pulling on his arm, making his body list sideways. When he didn't work, he and Mami rustled behind the flowered curtain, creaked the springs under their mattress, their voices a murmur that I strained to hear but couldn't.

I was an early riser but was not allowed out until the sun shot in through the crack near Mami's sewing machine and swept a glistening stripe of gold across the dirt floor.

The next morning, I turned out of the hammock and ran outside as soon as the sun streaked in. Mami and Papi sat by the kitchen shed sipping coffee. My arms and belly were pimpled with red dots. The night before, Mami had bathed me in *alcoholado*, which soothed my skin and cooled the hot itch.

"*Ay bendito*," Mami said, "here's our spotty early riser. Come here, let me look." She turned me around, rubbing the spots. "Are you itchy?"

"No, it doesn't itch at all."

"Stay out of the sun today so the spots don't scar."

Papi hummed along with the battery-operated radio. He never went anywhere without it. When he worked around the house, he propped it on a rock, or the nearest fence post, and tuned it to his favorite station, which played romantic ballads, *chachachás*, and a reading of the news every half hour. He delighted in stories from faraway places like Russia, Madagascar, and Istanbul. Whenever the newscaster mentioned a country with a particularly musical name, he'd repeat it or make a rhyme of it. "*Pakistán. Sacristán. ¿Dónde están?*" he sang as he mixed cement or hammered nails, his voice echoing against the walls.

Early each morning the radio brought us a program called "The Day Breaker's Club," which played the traditional music and poetry of the Puerto Rican country dweller, the *jíbaro*. Although the songs and poems chronicled a life of struggle and hardship, their message was that *jíbaros* were rewarded by a life of independence and contemplation, a closeness to nature coupled with a respect for its intractability, and a deeply rooted and proud nationalism. I wanted to be a *jíbara* more than anything in the world, but Mami said I couldn't because I was born in the city, where *jíbaros* were mocked for their unsophisticated customs and peculiar dialect.

"Don't be a *jíbara*," she scolded, rapping her knuckles on my skull, as if to waken the intelligence she said was there.

I ducked away, my scalp smarting, and scrambled into the oregano bushes. In the fragrant shade, I fretted. If we were not *jíbaros*, why did we live like them? Our house, a box squatting on low stilts, was shaped like a *bohío*, the kind of house *jíbaros* lived in. Our favorite program, "The Day Breaker's Club," played the traditional music of rural Puerto Rico and gave information about crops, husbandry, and the weather. Our neighbor Doña Lola was a *jíbara*, although Mami had warned us never to call her that. Poems and stories about the hardships and joys of the Puerto Rican *jíbaro* were required reading at every grade level in school. My own grandparents, whom I was to respect as well as love, were said to be *jíbaros*. But I couldn't be one, nor was I to call anyone a *jíbaro*, lest they be offended. Even at the tender age when I didn't yet know my real name, I was puzzled by the hypocrisy of celebrating a people everyone looked down on. But there was no arguing with Mami, who, in those days, was always right.

∾ On the radio, the newscaster talked about submarines, torpedoes, and a place called Korea, where Puerto Rican men went to die. His voice faded as Papi carried him into the house just as Delsa and Norma came out for their oatmeal.

Delsa's black curly hair framed a heart-shaped face with tiny pouty lips and round eyes thick with lashes. Mami called her *Muñequita*, Little Doll. Norma's hair was the color of clay, her yellow eyes slanted at the corners, and her skin glowed the same color as the inside of a yam. Mami called her *La Colorá*, the red girl. I thought I had no nickname until she told me my name wasn't Negi but Esmeralda.

"You're named after your father's sister, who is also your godmother. You know her as Titi Merín."

"Why does everyone call me Negi?"

"Because when you were little you were so black, my mother said you were a *negrita*. And we all called you *Negrita*, and it got shortened to Negi."

Delsa was darker than I was, nutty brown, but not as sun ripened as Papi. Norma was lighter, rust colored, and not as pale as Mami, whose skin was pink. Norma's yellow eyes with black pupils looked like sunflowers. Delsa had black eyes. I'd never seen my eyes, because the only mirror in the house was hung up too high for me to reach. I touched my hair, which was not curly like Delsa's, nor *pasita*, raisined, like Papi's. Mami cut it short whenever it grew into my eyes, but I'd seen dark brown wisps by my cheeks and near my temples.

"So *Negi* means I'm black?"

"It's a sweet name because we love you, *Negrita*." She hugged and kissed me.

"Does anyone call Titi Merín Esmeralda?"

"Oh, sure. People who don't know her well—the government, her boss. We all have our official names, and then our nicknames, which are like secrets that only the people who love us use."

"How come you don't have a nickname?"

"I do. Everyone calls me Monín. That's my nickname."

"What's your real name?"

"Ramona."

"Papi doesn't have a nickname."

"Yes he does. Some people call him Pablito."

It seemed too complicated, as if each one of us were really two people, one who was loved and the official one who, I assumed, was not.

⮞ The day he was to put in the new floor, Papi dragged our belongings out to the yard. Mami's sewing machine, the bed, her rocking chair, the small dresser where Papi kept his special things, baked in the sun, their worn surfaces scarred, their joints loose and creaky. A stack of new floorboards was suspended between cinder blocks near the door. Mami asked me and Delsa to find small stones to plug the holes in the dirt inside the house, so that snakes and scorpions wouldn't get out and bite us.

"Let's go see if the hen laid more eggs!" Delsa whispered.

We sneaked around the house to the path behind the latrine. On the way we picked up a few pebbles, just in case Mami asked what we were doing. A brown hen sat on the nest, her wings fluffed around the eggs. As we came near, she clucked softly.

"We'd better not come too close, or she'll beak us," I whispered.

The hen watched us, cackling nervously, and when we walked around the bush, her beady eyes followed us.

"If we keep walking around her," Delsa said, "we'll make her dizzy."

We circled the bush. The hen turned her head all the way around, as if her neck were not attached to her body. Delsa looked at me with a wicked grin, and without a word, we looped around the bush again then switched and went in the opposite direction. Possessive of her eggs, the hen kept her eyes fixed on us, no matter how fast we moved. We broke into a run. Her scared twitterings rose in pitch and had a human quality, like Mami's words when she swore we were driving her crazy. The hen's reproachful eyes followed us as we ran around the bush, her body aflutter, her head whirling on her body until it seemed that she would screw herself into the ground.

"Negi! Delsa! What are you doing back here?" Mami stood in the clearing, hands on hips.

"We were looking at the hen," I said in a small voice. Delsa giggled. I giggled. Mami didn't. The hen buried her head into her feathers the way a turtle crawls into a shell. I wanted to slide under her wings and get away from Mami.

"Get back to the front yard and let that poor animal be."

"We just wanted to see the eggs."

"You've frightened her. Now she won't give us any more eggs."

We had to go by Mami to get to the front yard. Her eyebrows were scrunched together, the eyes under them as round and black and reproving as the hen's, her lips stretched across her face so tight that all I could see was a dark line under her nose. "What are you waiting for? Didn't you hear me?" Her voice quivered with fury, her whole body enlarging with each breath.

Delsa hid behind me. I shuffled forward, and Mami stepped back to let me by. Delsa whimpered. Mami stared at me, immobile, hands on hips. I was very small. I took a deep breath, closed my eyes, and walked past her. As I did, she knuckled me hard on the head. I ran home, rubbing the bump that was forming under my hair. Behind me, Delsa screeched and ran past, covering her ear.

Papi raked the dirt in the house. He looked up when we came to the door, holding our heads and crying.

"Don't come bawling to me," he said. "You both know better than to cross your mother." He turned his back and pushed more dirt against the zinc walls.

Delsa sat on a stump and sobbed. I stared at his back, willing him to scold Mami, even though we'd done something wrong. He heaped piles of dirt into the corners of the house and hummed a song under his breath. Mami stood at the mouth of the path, her fingers laced under her belly. She looked small against the thick green behind her. She too seemed to be waiting for Papi to do or say something, and when he didn't, she walked to the kitchen shed, rubbing her stomach, a pained expression on her face.

A bubble of rage built inside my chest and forced out a scream meant for Mami's harshness and Papi's indifference but directed at Delsa who was smaller. I pushed her off the stump, sending her small body sprawling on the dirt. For a moment she looked dazed, as she tried to figure out what she had done, but when she realized she'd done nothing, she fell on me, her tiny fists as sharp as stones. We tussled in the dusty yard, pulled each other's hair, kicked and scratched and bit until our parents had to separate us and drive us away from one another, Mami with a switch, Papi with his leather belt. I ran to the bittersweet shade of the oregano bushes and wept until my chest hurt, each sob tearing off a layer of the comfort built from my parents' love, until I was totally alone, defended only by the green, the scent of cooking spices, and the dry, brushed dirt under my feet.

❧ A few mornings later I awoke to Mami's moans. I rolled out of my hammock and crossed to the other side of the curtain. Papi was gone, and Mami lay on her side, a wet rag on her forehead. She was sweaty, her hair stuck to her cheeks and down her neck. She pulled on the rails of the bedstead, as if she were stretching, but her knees were folded up to her belly.

"What's the matter, Mami?" I was scared. She was never sick, but now she was suffering. "What's wrong?"

She opened her eyes and smiled. Her face softened then darkened again, as if seeing me had made her forget her pain, but not for long. "I'm going to have a baby," she moaned.

"Now?"

"Soon as I can," she said with a pained chuckle.

"Does it hurt?"

"Not too much." She winced and rubbed her belly. Tiny bubbles of sweat popped on her upper lip.

"Can you make us breakfast?" She gave me a harsh look between moans, and I felt bad for asking. Just then, Papi walked in, followed by our neighbors, Doña Lola and Doña Zena.

"You're up already!" He said it as if it was unusual for me to be up with the roosters. The women grinned. Doña Lola set a bundle at the foot of the bed, and she and Mami mumbled to each other. Delsa and Norma scuffed in, rubbing their eyes.

"Dawn breakers, eh!" Doña Zena chortled and held out her arms to us. "Come with me, and I'll make you breakfast."

Delsa took one look at her, then at Mami, and her black eyes opened round and wide like those on a doll baby. "What's wrong with Mami?"

"Nothing's wrong," Papi said as he nudged us out in front of him. "Mami's going to have a baby, so Doña Zena will look after you today." As he pushed us out of the house, sniffling and whining, Doña Lola took down the curtain that divided the room in two and rolled our hammocks out of the way.

Delsa wrapped herself around Papi's leg and screeched. Norma ran back into the house and threw herself at Mami. Doña Lola pulled her down off the bed and carried her out dangling from one arm. "Someone is coming to steal your lap, Colorá," she said, as she passed Norma to Doña Zena, who held on to her with an iron grip.

"Negi," Mami whimpered from the bed, "take care of your sisters."

Papi untangled Delsa from his leg and pushed her toward me. He went to the back of the house to light the *fogón*. I grabbed Delsa by one arm while Doña Zena took the other, and we struggled with her and Norma up the road.

"Shut your mouths. You're waking up the neighbors."

They didn't pay any attention to me but continued wailing and kicking against the dirt. Halfway to Doña Zena's house, I gave up trying to control them. I let go of Delsa, and Doña Zena jerked her and Norma along until they half walked, half hopped up the hill.

I didn't understand why we had to leave our house when Mami looked so sick. No one had ever said anything about where babies came from, and I had never connected Mami's swollen belly with my sisters. Until then, that was just the way she looked: black hair, pale skin, big belly, long legs.

Doña Zena dragged Delsa and Norma into her yard, while I straggled behind, fretting about what had just happened, jealous that, even though my lap had been stolen years ago by Delsa and then Norma, another baby was coming to separate me further from my mother, whose rages were not half so frightening as the worry that she would now be so busy with an infant as to totally forget me.

I crested the hill where Doña Zena's house perched, commanding a view of the *barrio*. Mist hung just above the trees, burning off in patches where bright sun dulled the intensity of red hibiscus blossoms, yellow morning glories, the purple centers of passion fruit flowers. Mornings like this inspired much of *jíbaro* poetry, and in my fear over Mami I called up the few verses I'd memorized and repeated them like a prayer as I sat on Doña Zena's steps, my eyes riveted on the slow ribbon of smoke ascending from our *fogón*, my feet buried in lemongrass, dew chilling my toes.

FIGHTING NAKED

Enamorado hasta de un palo de escoba.

❧

He falls in love even with broomsticks.

My parents probably argued before Héctor was born. Mami was not one to hold her tongue when she was treated unfairly. And while Papi was easygoing and cheerful most of the time, his voice had been known to rise every so often, sending my sisters and me scurrying for cover behind the annatto bushes or under the bed. But the year that Héctor was born their fights grew more frequent and sputtered into our lives like water on a hot skillet.

"Where's my yellow shirt?" Papi asked one Sunday morning as he rummaged through the clothes rack he'd put up near the bed.

"I haven't ironed it yet." Mami rocked on her chair, nursing Héctor. "Where are you going?"

"Into town for some things." Papi kept his back to her as he tucked a blue shirt into his pants.

"What things?"

"Plans for the new job." He shook cologne into his hands and slapped it around his face and behind his ears.

"When will you be back?"

Papi sighed loud and deep. "Monín, don't start with me."

"Start what? I asked you a simple question." She levelled her eyes and set her lips into a straight line.

"I don't know when I'll be back. I'll stop in to see Mamá, so I'll probably have dinner there."

"Fine." She got up from her chair and walked out of the house, Héctor attached to her breast.

Papi brushed his leather shoes and stuffed them inside a plaid zippered duffel bag. He put on canvas loafers that had once been white but had yellowed with the dirt of the road. He unhooked his straw hat from the nail by the door and left without kissing us good-bye.

I went looking for Mami behind the house. She sat on a stump under the breadfruit tree, her back to me. Her shoulders bobbed up and down, and she whimpered quietly, every so often wiping her face with the edge of Héctor's baby blanket. I walked to her, tears stinging the rims of my eyes. She turned around with an angry face.

"Leave me alone! Get away from me."

I froze. She seemed so far away, yet I sensed the heat from her body, smelled the rosemary oil she rubbed on her hair. I didn't want to leave her but was afraid to come closer, so I leaned against a mango tree and stared at my toes against the *moriviví* weed. Every so often she looked over her shoulder, and I turned my eyes to the front yard, where Delsa and Norma chased one another, a cloud of dust painting their legs up to their droopy panties.

"Here," Mami stood over me, holding a drowsy Héctor, "put him to bed while I heat you kids some lunch."

Her face was swollen, her lashes clumped into spikes. I slung Héctor over my shoulder, his baby body yielding onto mine. Mami raked her fingers through my hair with a sad smile then walked away, the hem of her dress swinging in rhythm to her rounded hips.

❧ Papi didn't come home for days. Then one night he appeared, kissed us hello, put on his work clothes, and began hammering on the walls. When he'd finished, he washed his hands and face at the barrel near the back door, sat at the table, and waited for Mami to serve him supper. She banged a plateful of rice and beans in front of him, a fork, a glass of water. He didn't look at her; she didn't look at him. While he ate, Mami told us to get ready for bed, and Delsa, Norma, and I scrambled into our hammocks. She nursed Héctor and put him to sleep. Papi's newspaper rustled, but I didn't dare poke my head out.

I drifted into a dream in which I climbed a tall tree whose lower branches disappeared the moment I scaled the higher ones. The ground moved farther and farther away, and the top of the tree stretched into the clouds, which were pink. I woke up sweating, my arms stretched over my head and gripping the rope of my hammock. The *quinqué's* flame threw orange shadows onto the curtain stretched across the room.

Mami and Papi lay in bed talking.

"You haven't given me money for this week's groceries."

The bed creaked as Papi turned away from Mami. "I had to buy materials. And one of the men that works with me had an emergency. I gave him an advance."

"An advance?!"

Mami had a way of making a statement with a question. From my hammock on the other side of the curtain I envisioned her face: eyes round, pupils large, her eyebrows arched to the hairline. Her lips would be half open, as if she'd been interrupted in the middle of an important word. When I saw this expression on her face and heard that tone of voice, I knew that whatever I'd said was so far from the truth, there was no use trying to argue with her. Even if what I said was true, that tone of voice told me she didn't believe me, and I'd better come up with a more convincing story. Papi either couldn't think of another story or was too tired to try, because he didn't say anything. I could have told him that was a mistake.

"You gave him an advance?! An advance??"

Her voice had gone from its "I don't believe you" tone to its "How dare you lie to me" sound.

"Monín," the bed creaked as Papi turned to her. "Can we talk about this in the morning? I need to sleep."

His voice was calm. When Mami was angry, she argued in a loud voice that reached higher pitches the more nervous she became. When Papi argued, he put all his energy into holding himself erect, maintaining a steady calm that was chilling to us children but had the opposite effect on Mami.

"No, we can't talk about this in the morning. You leave before the sun comes up, and you don't show up until all hours, your clothes stinking like that *puta*."

Even when she was very angry, Mami rarely swore or used vulgar language. Papi knew this. It was a clue to how upset she was. He calmly got up and walked to the curtain separating our rooms. I ducked my head back inside my hammock.

"Monín, stop it. You'll wake the children."

"Now you're worried about the children. Why is it that you don't even think about them when it's less convenient. When you're partying with your women and your barroom buddies." The bedsprings creaked violently as she got up. "Do those *hijas de la gran puta* know you have children in this Godforsaken hellhole? Do they know your children go barefoot and hungry while you spend the misery you earn on them?"

"Monín!"

"Don't think just because I'm stuck in this jungle all day long I don't know what's going on. I'm not stupid."

Héctor woke up with a wail. Papi raised the flame on the lamp while Mami reached into Héctor's hanging cradle and lifted him out. Delsa and Norma whimpered from their side of the room. I didn't have to pretend to sleep anymore, so I sat up and watched their silhouettes through the curtain. Mami changed Héctor's diaper with such rough movements, I worried she'd stick a pin into him. Papi stood at the window, looking at where a view would have been if the window were open.

"Look, I don't know who you've been talking to, but I don't want to hear it anymore."

He dressed. Mami lifted Héctor to her shoulder and paced, bouncing him up and down to get him to go to sleep.

"You don't come home until after dark . . . if you come home at all. And weekends, instead of working on this hovel you call a house, you take off with one excuse or another. You have no shame! I'm sick of it."

"Well, I'm sick of it too! Do you think I like hearing you complain all the time? Or that I want to hear about how much you hate it here, and how much better life was in San Juan, and how backward Macún is? I'm sick of it! I'm sick of you!"

He stomped out, probably just to give Mami time to cool

off, which was his way of fighting her. But I thought he was leaving us. "Papi!! Don't go. Please, Papi, stay!" I shrieked. When they heard me, Delsa and Norma joined in, and Héctor, who was almost asleep in spite of my mother's yelling near his ear, screeched.

"See what you've done!" Mami hollered into the dark yard. "Some father you are, running off on your own children!"

She threw Héctor into his cradle and tore Papi's clothes off their hangers by the bed. "Sick of me? Well, I'm sick of you too." She tossed his clothes out the door, grabbed a pitcher of water from the table, and splashed it on them. Then she bolted the door, took Héctor out of his cradle, and sat on her rocking chair, nursing him. Tears streamed down her cheeks into the grooves at the corners of her lips. "You kids shut up and go back to sleep," she yelled. None of us dared get out of our hammocks. We hunkered into them, stifling our sobs. For a long time I listened for Papi. For his voice asking Mami to forgive him, or for his footsteps outside the house. But I fell asleep to the sound of Mami's rocking chair creaking, and her sobs, soft and low like the miaow of a kitten.

The next morning Papi's clothes were scattered in the front yard. They were damp, stained with the muddy tracks of toads and iguanas. As she waited for the coffee water to boil, Mami picked them up and took them to the tub under the avocado tree. That afternoon, when Papi came home, they'd all been washed.

☙ Another day they were arguing, and I heard Mami accuse Papi, as she often did, of seeing another woman behind her back when he said he was going to see *Abuela*.

"For God's sake, Monín. You know I have no interest in Provi. But how can you object to my wanting to see Margie?" Papi asked.

"I know it's not Margie you want to see. It's her mother."

"Monín, please. That's been over for years."

And on they went, Mami accusing Papi and Papi defending

himself. When they'd reached a truce and I had a few moments alone with Papi, I asked him, "Who's Margie?"

He looked at me with a scared expression.

"She's my daughter," he said after a pause. My heart shrank. Having to share my father with Delsa, Norma, and Héctor was bad enough. I waited for him to say more, but he didn't. He sat on a stump and stared at his hands, calloused where the hammer and saw handles rubbed against his skin. He looked so sad, it made me want to cry. I sat next to him.

"Where does she live?"

He seemed to have just remembered I was there. "In Santurce."

"How old is she?"

"Just a year older than you."

An older sister! I'd wondered what it would be like not to be the oldest, the one who set an example for the little ones.

"How come she's never been to see us?"

"Her mother and your mother don't get along."

That much I'd figured out. "You can just bring her sometime. Her mother doesn't have to come."

Papi sighed then chuckled. "That's a good idea," he said and stood up. "I have to get some work done. Can you help me mix concrete?"

I poured the water for him while he stirred cement and sand together. I asked him many questions about Margie, and he answered them in short phrases that didn't tell me much. If we were talking about her and Mami came near, he'd put his hand to his mouth so I'd quiet, and we'd work in silence until she was out of earshot.

At night I tried to imagine what Margie looked like. I envisioned her skin the same carob color as my father's, her eyes as black and her lips as full as his. Her hair kinky like his, not lanky like mine. I imagined her voice to be musical, lilting, the way his was when he read poetry to us.

What times we could have if we were together! She'd be someone I could have fun with, not be responsible for. She'd be able to keep up with me when we ran across the field. She'd climb a tree without being helped. We could play hide-and-seek in the jungled back yard. We'd climb the fence behind the house and steal into Lalao's grapefruit grove to fill our faces with the bittersweet pulp while juice dribbled down our chins and our fingers got sticky. I swayed in my hammock dreaming about Margie, determined to talk my mother into asking Papi to bring her to live with us.

∝ The next day I stood on a stool while Mami pinned the hem on my school uniform.

"Mami, why don't you like Margie's mother?"

"Who?"

"Provi, my sister Margie's mother."

"Negi, I never want to hear you mention that woman's name again, you hear me?"

"But Mami . . ."

"I mean it."

"But Mami . . ."

"Stand still or I'm going to have an accident with these pins."

I stood still as a statue while she finished.

∝ Papi dipped his trowel into the cement mud in the wheelbarrow by his side and slapped the mud onto a foundation block.

"Papi, are you going to bring Margie to see us?"

"I don't know."

He stacked another cinder block and scraped the ooze that came out the sides and bottom.

"She can sleep with me."

"Negi!" Mami sat just inside the door of the house sewing. "Leave your father alone."

"I was just asking a question."

"Get away from there and go play with your sisters. Now!"

Papi looked at Mami from the shadow of his straw hat. He

tipped the brim up and pointed to the pyramid of cinder
blocks by the front gate. "Can you bring me one of those?"

I looked at Mami. She stared at Papi, not at me, her needle
suspended above green fabric.

"Can you try it?" Papi said softly.

It was heavy and slipped from my fingers, almost crushing
my toe.

"*Ave María*, Pablo, don't abuse her. She's just a kid."

"I think she can do it," he shot back at her.

He turned the block so that I could hold it along the sides,
where there was a place to grab onto. The rough edges scraped
against my legs and belly. It was heavy and awkward, but
I managed to carry it over next to the wheelbarrow and
drop it.

"Can I bring another one?" I asked, rubbing my hands
against my teeshirt. They smarted from the weight and the
grooves that the block had dug into my skin.

"No, I can manage." He carried two blocks stacked one atop
the other, set them down carefully, then stood with hands on
hips, his back arched, eyes closed, head thrown back so that
his Adam's apple bulged from his neck.

"I can't bring Margie to see you because she's moved to
Nueva York."

Mami took in a breath. "When?"

He lifted his arms over his head, stretched up, and floated
them slowly to his hips, where they stayed as if he were posing
for a picture. Mami watched him for a while then took her
sewing inside the house.

"You didn't say she was leaving," I whined, and it seemed
that Papi finally realized that all our talk about Margie was not
just my natural curiosity but something more. He turned sad
eyes on me, kneeled, and hugged me. As he grieved on my
shoulder, I wanted nothing more than for Papi to go on losing
people he loved so that he'd always turn to me, so that I alone
could bring him comfort.

* * *

 Margie and "that woman's" disappearance from Puerto Rico didn't mark the end of my parents' fights. They were locked in a litany choked with *should have's*, *ought to's*, and *why didn't you's*. Their arguments accomplished nothing, as far as I could see, except to make everyone miserable. After they fought, Mami was sullen and irritable, and Papi disappeared into himself like a snail into a shell. We children tiptoed around them or else played in the farthest reaches of the yard, our voices dulled lest they incite our parents. To make things more confusing, it was clear that there were moments of tenderness between them. Sometimes I came upon them standing close, arms encircling waists, heads close, as if they shared secrets that transcended the hurt and resentments, the name-calling and deceit.

Almost as soon as Héctor started to gum on mashed-up yucca and boiled sweet plantain, Mami's features softened, her body filled out, and her belly rounded into a soft mound that got in her way whenever she tried to lift one of us into the tub for one of our baths.

I couldn't figure out when or how Papi asked Mami to forgive him and what he did so that she would. But it was clear to me, from their arguments, the conversations I'd overheard between Mami and her female relatives and friends, and from *boleros* on the radio, that Papi, being a man, was always to blame for whatever unhappiness existed in our house.

Men, I was learning, were *sinvergüenzas*, which meant they had no shame and indulged in behavior that never failed to surprise women but caused them much suffering. Chief among the sins of men was the other woman, who was always a *puta*, a whore. My image of these women was fuzzy, since there were none in Macún, where all the females were wives or young girls who would one day be wives. *Putas*, I guessed, lived in luxury in the city on the money that *sinvergüenza* husbands did not bring home to their long-suffering wives and barefoot children. *Putas* wore lots of perfume, jewelry, dresses cut low to show off their breasts, high heels to pump up their calves, and hair spray. All this was paid for with money that should have gone into repairing the roof or replacing the dry palm fronds enclosing the latrine with corrugated steel sheets. I wanted to see a *puta* close up, to understand the power she held over men, to understand the sweet-smelling spell she wove around the husbands, brothers, and sons of the women whose voices cracked with pain, defeat, and simmering anger.

⋖ I started school in the middle of hurricane season, and the world grew suddenly bigger, a vast place of other adults and children whose lives were similar, but whose shadings I couldn't really explore out of respect and *dignidad*. *Dignidad* was something you conferred on other people, and they, in turn, gave back to you. It meant you never swore at people, never showed anger in front of strangers, never stared, never stood too close to people you'd just met, never addressed people by the familiar *tú* until they gave you permission. It meant adults had to be referred to as Don so-and-so, and Doña so-and-so, except for teachers, who you should call Mister or Missis so-and-so. It meant, if you were a child, you did not speak until spoken to, did not look an adult in the eye, did not raise your voice nor enter or leave a room without permission. It meant adults were always right, especially if they were old. It meant men could look at women any way they liked but women could never look at men directly, only in sidelong glances, unless they were *putas*, in which case they could do what they pleased since people would talk about them anyway. It meant you didn't gossip, tattle, or tease. It meant men could say things to women as they walked down the street, but women couldn't say anything to men, not even to tell them to go jump in the harbor and leave them alone.

All these rules entered our household the minute I was allowed to leave home for the long walk to and from school. It wasn't that I hadn't heard them before. Mami and Papi had passed on to me what they knew of *buenos modales*, good manners.

But these rules had little to do with the way we lived at

home. In our family we fought with vigor, adults as well as children, even though we knew we weren't supposed to. We yelled across the room at one another, came in and out of our one room house without saying "excuse me" and "may I come in," or even knocking. Mami and Papi were *tú*, so were our grandparents, aunts, uncles, and cousins. We children spoke whenever we felt like it, interrupted our parents all the time, and argued with them until Mami finally reminded us that we had stepped over the line of what was considered respectful behavior toward parents.

In school I volunteered to wipe down the blackboard, to sharpen pencils, to help distribute lined paper in which we could write our tortured alphabets with the mysterious tilde over the *n* to make *ñ*, the *ü*, the double consonants *ll* and *rr* with their strong sounds. I loved the neat rows of desks lined up one after the other, the pockmarked tops shiny in spots where the surface hadn't blistered, the thrill when I raised my desktop to find a large box underneath in which I kept my primer, sheets of paper, and the pencil stubs I guarded as if they were the finest writing instruments.

I walked home from school full of importance in my green and yellow uniform. It was my most prized possession, the only thing in our house that belonged to me alone, because neither Delsa nor Norma were old enough to go to school.

But school was also where I compared my family to others in the *barrio*. I learned there were children whose fathers were drunks, whose mothers were "bad," whose sisters had run away with travelling salesmen, whose brothers had landed in prison. I met children whose mothers walked the distance from their house to church on their knees in gratitude for prayers answered. Children whose fathers came home every day and played catch in the dusty front yard. Girls whose sisters taught them to embroider flowers on linen handkerchiefs. Boys whose brothers took them by the hand and helped them climb a tree. There were families in the *barrio* with running water inside their houses, electric bulbs shining down from every room, curtains on the windows, and printed linoleum on the floors.

Children fought in school in a way unknown to me at home. Delsa, Norma, and I often tied ourselves into punching, biting, kicking knots that only Mami with her switch was able to untangle. But fighting with other kids was different. When I fought with my sisters, I knew what was at stake, a prized marble, a ripe mango just fallen off the tree, a chance to be the first to color in the Sunday comics from Papi's newspaper. But in school the fights were about something else entirely.

If you looked at someone the wrong way they might beat you up. If you were too eager to answer the teacher's questions you might get beat up. If you rubbed shoulders with the wrong kids you would get beat up. If you mentioned someone's mother at the wrong time or in a certain tone of voice, you would definitely get beat up. Any number of subtle transgressions, from not saying hello when someone greeted you to saying hello to the wrong person, meant a beating. When I explained to Mami why I came home with a torn uniform and bruises, she made it clear that I was forbidden to fight in school. This made no sense to me at all. Not that Mami encouraged our fights at home, but she never said, "Don't fight with your sisters." Her injunctions were always about not punching them too hard. So I had to learn how to avoid the unavoidable, and when I couldn't, I stripped to my underwear in the school yard to defend myself from kids whose mothers didn't mind if their uniforms got dirty.

▶ Papi left one day and didn't return that night. For the next three days he didn't appear. Mami prepared dinner the first night and each night afterward left something for him, but the next morning she'd scrape it all out into the compost, a scowl on her face. We knew better than to ask where Papi was or when he might be coming back. There was no way for her to know, and it was just as well, because knowing would have added fuel to her rage, the brunt of which we children felt in her sullen silences, or increasingly, in her swiftness to spank and hit us with whatever was at hand for reasons that were often as mysterious to us as Papi's whereabouts.

When I got home from school on the fourth day, Mami had bundled our belongings into pillowcases and a tattered suitcase with the handle missing, which she had shut with a tight rope wound into a loop at the top. With Héctor on her hip, she led us up the road, dragging the suitcase with her free hand, while Delsa, Norma, and I struggled with the pillowcases full of clothes.

I didn't know to say goodbye to our house and our *barrio*, nor to wave to the neighbors who looked out curiously as we wound our way to the main road. Delsa, Norma, and I knew not to whine or complain, not to huff too loudly against the strain of the cumbersome pillowcases, not to ask for water or mention food, not to need a bathroom, not to stop to rest or tie our shoelaces or brush the hair from our eyes. We followed Mami in the same bubble of silence in which she walked, her gaze forward, never looking back or sideways at the neighbors who poked one another in the ribs and smirked, who let their eyes fall to the ground and pretended not to see us rather than offer to help us on our way.

It seemed like a very long walk to the highway, and when we got there, we climbed into a *público* car as if this were any other day and we were any family on an excursion into the city. Only when the *público* was well on its way and we had lost sight of the entrance to Barrio Macún did Mami say what we all knew without asking.

"We're moving to the city. Life will be better there."

SOMEONE
IS COMING
TO TAKE
YOUR LAP

Borrón y cuenta nueva.

❧

Erase and start over.

Whenever Mami was fed up with Macún, or with Papi, she ran away to Santurce, a suburb of San Juan, which, by the early fifties, had become as much a metropolis as the capital, though with little of its cachet. It was a commercial center, with distinctly drawn neighborhoods that separated the rich from the poor. Hospitals, schools, private homes, banks, office buildings, restaurants, and movie theaters butted one against the other in a jumble of color and pattern and noise. Softly rounded rectangular buses chugged up and down the streets, trailing a stream of black smoke that made your eyes water.

Mami's mother had been one of fifteen children, and Mami had endless aunts, uncles, and cousins in the *barrios* that stretched like tentacles from the wide avenues and shady plazas. By the time we arrived in Santurce from Macún, with our bundles and expectations, my grandmother, Tata, had left for New York to join her sisters in the Bushwick section of Brooklyn, a place said to be as full of promise as Ponce de León's El Dorado.

Our new home, in La Parada 26, Stop #26, a *barrio* named for an old trolley station, was a one-room wooden house perched high on stilts over sticky black mud that we were forbidden to touch. Most of the houses around us were no better than the ones in Macún, but there was running water into the kitchen and electric light bulbs in the middle of every room. Alongside our house ran a trench that filled with sewage when it rained.

We shared a bathroom with another family. It was a square cement building with a shower at one end and a hole on the floor so the water could drain into the open sewer. During the day, the bathroom was our playhouse, until the men came home from work and reclaimed it, filling the air with the humid scent of Palmolive soap.

I'd been taken out of first grade in the middle of the week during my first semester and, within a day, was in school in Santurce. My new school, made of concrete blocks, was much larger than the one in Macún and had a playground with swings, a slide, and a metal seesaw that was usually too hot to sit on, because the sun fell on it all day long.

"The city is different," Mami told us on our first day. "There are many mischievous people, so you have to be careful where you go and who you talk to." When I walked to school, Mami instructed, I was not to look at or talk to anyone all the way there and back. But there were too many things to see in Santurce. I learned to walk down those rich streets, eyes humbly cast down, with no sense of what lay ten feet in front of me, but with an exquisite awareness of what was on either side.

The way to school took me over muddy sidewalks strewn with garbage, across narrow streets teeming with traffic, people, and stray dogs, and past bars with open doorways and loud jukeboxes that always played *boleros* about liquor and women. A stand offered for sale fruits and vegetables that in Macún I'd been able to pick off the trees. Bright dresses and *guayaberas* in front of a dry-goods store swayed in the breeze like ghosts in daylight. An austere Evangelical church rose next to a *botánica* where one could buy plaster saints, African idols, herbs, candles, potions for finding love and driving away unwanted influences, and protections against the evil eye and ailments of mind or body. In between the buildings, hiding in the shadows of alleys leading to the *barrios*, there were stands for passion-fruit juice and pineapple ices. Carts carried coconut candy, sticks of sugarcane, molasses toffee, and dried papaya slices. And on every corner there were *piraguas* in white paper cones, gleaming pyramids of ice into which the *piragüero* dripped bright-colored syrup.

I was fascinated by the dark doorways of private homes crushed between shops and restaurants. They were barred with ornate wrought iron fences and gates, and inside, women in flowered shifts dusted plastic covered furniture or sat on shaded balconies looking out over the commotion below.

Sometimes, if I walked fast, I caught a glimpse of the Catholic schoolchildren lined up in twos, being led into the chapel by black-clad nuns whose faces were milky white and waxy. The students wore navy blue uniforms with pale blue shirts, navy knee socks, and blue loafers. Their hair was neatly combed, and they looked cleaner than anyone I'd ever seen. I envied them the order of their lives, the precision with which they marched with no prodding and no harsh glances, the mysterious black figures beside them like veiled anchors. I wondered what their lives were like, how many sisters and brothers they had, if they slept in their own beds or had to share, if they ate rice and beans and salted codfish with onions. I knew they were different, or rather, I was different. Already I'd been singled out in school for my wildness, my loud voice, and large gestures better suited to the expansive countryside but out of place in concrete rooms where every sound was magnified and bounced off walls for a long time after I'd finished speaking.

"What a *jíbara*," children jeered when I recited a poem in the dialect of Doña Lola.

"What a *jíbara*," when I didn't know how to use the pencil sharpener screwed to the wall of the schoolroom.

"What a *jíbara*," when Christmas came around and I'd never heard of Santa Claus.

"What a *jíbara* . . . What a *jíbara* . . . What a *jíbara*."

In Santurce I had become what I wasn't in Macún. In Santurce a *jíbara* was something no one wanted to be. I walked to and from school beside myself, watching the *jíbara* girl with eyes cast down, the home-cut hair, the too large gestures and too loud voice, the feet unaccustomed to shoes. I let that girl walk home while I took in the sights of the city, the noise and colors, the music, the pungent smells of restaurants and car exhaust. At night, in the bed I shared with Delsa and Norma, I listened for the *coquí* tree frog to sing me to sleep but instead heard cars backfiring, people fighting, music blaring, and Mami's moans in the dark.

➸ As Christmas neared, the walk to school took on a different tune. The songs floating out of jukeboxes were still about women and liquor, but they had a Christmas twist. A man sang that he would never forgive the ungrateful woman he once loved because she had abandoned him at what was supposed to be the happiest time of year. A woman sang that the man she loved had betrayed her, so she would spend the holidays dreaming of what might have been. And a group of men sang about what a sad Christmas it would be now that their love was away. I felt sorry for the people in those bars.

At home we listened to *aguinaldos*, songs about the birth of Jesus and the joys of spending Christmas surrounded by family and friends. We sang about the Christmas traditions of Puerto Rico, about the *parrandas*, in which people went from house to house singing, eating, drinking, and celebrating, about pig roasts and *ron cañita*, homemade rum, which was plentiful during the holidays.

Even though Papi didn't live with us, he often came to see us and once showed up with strings of red and green electric bulbs, which we tacked around windows and doors.

From the beginning of December, Mami spent most of her time in the kitchen. For weeks the house smelled of crushed onions, fresh oregano, and cilantro. Relatives I'd never met appeared to sit for hours at the kitchen table with Mami and, if he were visiting, Papi, to eat rice with pigeon peas, *pasteles* wrapped in banana leaves, crispy fried green plantains, and boiled yucca. After dinner they drank anisette and I was given the crunchy diamonds that formed in the sugarcane strings inside the bottles. Aunts and uncles came up the alley trailed by girls in white patent-leather shoes and flouncy dresses, their hair rolled into finger curls. The boys hung back, their pomaded hair and scrubbed faces serious, their pressed pants making them look as stiff as paper dolls. Within minutes the girls were playing house with Delsa and Norma, while I chased the boys up and down the alley, getting good and dirty.

My mother's brother, Tío Cucho, came by with a pretty woman named Rita. She was short and dark and wore tight dresses cut low to show the tops of her breasts. Long earrings dangled from her lobes, and bracelets jangled when she moved her hands. She was much smaller than Tío Cucho but made up for it with heels so high she walked on tiptoe. I could tell Mami didn't like Rita by the way she screwed up her nose when Rita walked by or looked away when Rita bent over to rub her leg and her breasts almost tumbled out of her blouse. But Mami was polite and served Rita food and drink as if she didn't mind, laughing at her jokes.

I liked Rita, especially the way she smiled, with bright red lips and large white teeth that reminded me of a billboard for Colgate toothpaste. As they left, Mami took Tío Cucho aside and told him she never wanted him to bring that woman into her house again. Tío Cucho was offended and said if Mami didn't want Rita around, then she wouldn't see him either. But the next weekend he came without her.

According to Mami, Rita was a terrible woman. She lounged in bars and went home with any man who bought her drinks. Mami didn't say this to me. I heard her talking with our next-door neighbor while we were shelling pigeon peas.

"But doesn't she have children?"

"Of course she does. Two boys. And she just leaves them alone to roam the streets like urchins while she's out partying."

"Doesn't your brother care?"

"He's always leaving her, only to come sniffing around her skirts after a few weeks."

"Some women bewitch men."

"Bah! That woman's no witch. She's a slut who'll spread her legs for anything in pants."

Doña Mina looked at Mami and pursed her lips toward me. Mami seemed startled to see me. She took my half-full bowl of shelled peas and emptied them into hers.

"Negi, bring these upstairs. And while you're there, check to see if Héctor is up from his nap."

I took the bowl and strolled away from them, hoping they'd keep talking about Rita, who I hoped was a *puta*, although Mami hadn't used that word. But they both watched after me.

I pretended not to care and bounced up the steps, the peas jiggling back and forth inside the bowl. Their voices fell into whispers then rose again in laughter. I felt so left out and angry, I wanted to stumble and spill the beans, but if I did, Mami would make me pick them up, one at a time, my knees scraping across the splintery floor.

❧ The yard next door was decorated with gold-colored ribbons strung on tall bamboo stems. They waved in the breeze, and flashes of sun winked from within, like stars inside a yellow sky. Someone on the other side of the tall fence raised a bamboo stick with more ribbons attached to it, only these were wet and shimmered brighter than the ones already up. Smoke rose from the front of the yard, along with the delicious smell of oregano and garlic, rosemary, fennel, toasted annatto.

"What are those, Mami?" I asked one morning when the entire yard looked like a sea of yellow, rising and falling in bulbous waves.

"They're pig's guts," she said without looking up from her darning.

"Yecchh!"

She laughed. "They're used to make pork sausages. Our neighbors cook meat in spices and then they stuff them into the pig guts. We had some yesterday, remember?"

"But pig guts are full of . . ."

"They wash the guts out carefully, and they hang them up to dry so that the sun cures them."

It was hard to imagine that the delicious sausages I'd had just the day before were encased in the small intestines of a pig.

"What else was in those sausages?"

"The heart, the liver, chunks of meat, rice, spices, and some blood."

"Blood!"

"To make them solid, so they don't fall apart."

"We eat blood?!"

"What do you think *morcillas* are made of?" she asked with a laugh.

"Don't tell me. I don't want to know."

"Okay." She went back to her sewing.

Morcillas were one of my favorite treat foods. They were black sausages, which were roasted or fried. I especially liked the ones with tiny bits of hot peppers crushed into the meat. "All right, tell me."

"I thought you didn't want to know . . ."

"Is it pig guts?"

"Yes. The outside."

"What's on the inside?"

"Little pieces of meat. Some rice. Spices."

"And blood?"

"Mostly blood. Some people call it blood pudding."

"*Ay Dios mío*, Mami, why do we have to eat that stuff?"

"Because once you kill the animal, it's a sin to waste anything that can be eaten. . . . Besides, it tastes good." She winced.

"Are you okay, Mami?"

"Yes. It's just your baby sister or brother swimming around."

"Can I feel it?"

She took my hand and placed it on her round belly, which rested on her thighs like a giant water balloon. I put my head to it, my hands on either side. A giant wave spread from one end of her belly to the other, and I heard water gurgling as the baby swam around in her private pool.

➥ "Papi, what's a sin?" I was collecting grass for the camels of the Three Magi, who were coming that night with presents for all the children. The only grass to be had in the *barrio* grew in the alley, along the edges of fences that kept chickens and scrawny dogs separated from one another.

"A sin is when you do something that makes God angry."

"Like what?"

"Well, let's see. There's the first commandment, 'Honor thy father and mother.' "

"What's a commandment?"

"It's actually commandments. God wrote ten of them so people would know what to do."

"What do the others say?"

"Thou shalt not take the Lord's name in vain."

"What does that mean?"

"It means you shouldn't mention God except in prayers."

"You can't say '*Ay Dios Mío*'?"

"Not technically."

"But everyone says it."

"Very religious people don't."

"We're not religious, right?"

"We don't go to church, but we believe in God."

"Is it a sin not to go to church?"

"If you're a Catholic."

"Are we Catholic?"

"Yes. But not very good ones."

I finished collecting grass for the camels, while Papi told me more about the commandments. We never got through all ten, because I kept interrupting him for explanations of what murder was, and what adultery meant.

✺ Mami moaned through the night. I worried that if she kept it up, the Three Magi wouldn't come with presents. But in the morning our shoes were filled with nuts and candy, and each one of us had a small gift wrapped in green paper tied with ribbon. Later in the day, Papi played with us outside while, through the open windows, we heard Mami's screams and the midwife's gentle urgings. By the next day we had a new baby sister, whom we named Alicia.

✺ After Alicia was born, Papi came around more often. When he visited, on weekends, and sometimes weekdays after work, he played with us, read the comics aloud, or took us for walks. At first he and Mami didn't talk much. As soon as she saw him come up the alley, she would pick up a basket of mending, or scrub the pots, or reorganize the canned goods on the shelves of the kitchen area. Papi would lift his hat when he came to the door, like the men who sometimes showed up on Sunday mornings selling religious magazines. She'd just ignore him and go on with her work and wouldn't even ask him in. Papi would stand on the threshold and call us to put on our shoes and he'd take us out for a *piragua*, or to come out to the steps and he'd tell us a story. Mami would pretend he wasn't even there. But little by little, he won her over. We'd come back with a half-melted tamarind *piragua* for her. Or he'd bring the newspaper and, instead of taking it with him, he'd leave it for her on the table. Once, I looked up from my place on the steps and she was sitting at the top, elbows on knees, face cupped in her hands, listening to Papi recite a poem he'd written.

One day he came after dinner and she'd saved some food for him. When he stood at the door she told him to come in and sit down. She served him a plateful of rice and beans and fried up a pork chop or two. He ate without looking directly at her if she came close to put down a knife and fork, or to fill his water glass, or to hand him another napkin because the first one was crumpled.

Afterwards they talked out on the steps long after we'd all been sent to bed. It was too far from my bed for me to hear what they said, and they spoke softly. But just listening to their voices made me happy. The rise and fall of their words sounded like a promise, and I strained to hear them over the crack of cars backfiring, dogs barking, and the blaring jukeboxes of bars on the street a few houses from ours. I concentrated on their rhythmic murmurs coming from the steps, and that sound, isolated from all others, soothed and lulled me to sleep.

* * *

❧ We returned to Macún in a rickety truck, our furniture and cooking utensils tied to the sides, our clothes and bedding bundled into cushions. As we bounced along the rutted road, I fidgeted, grazed by low branches from ceiba and *flamboyán* trees, breathing the dust of the highway, the exhaust, and the gritty dirt that flew in all directions and coated my skin, my hair, my teeth. I was taken over by a soft giant that filled my chest and head, its too large heart pounding against my ribs as we lurched up and down the dirt road toward the pebbly hill where our house gleamed in the afternoon sun.

I wanted to jump out of the truck and run, run down the hills dipping into sandy valleys in front of familiar houses bordered with passion fruit and morning glory. To climb the rocky hills at the peak of which our neighbors' porches rose even higher, their balustrades festooned with potted plants, the zinc overhangs sparkling in the midday sun. To climb the grassy mound behind Uncle Cándido's house and grab a pink *poma-rrosa* from the scraggly trees that were forbidden to everyone but family members. To crunch into that succulent fruit that smelled like roses and let the aromatic juice run down my chin and stain my pretty city dress with its bows, buttons, and ribbons. But when I tried to stand up, Mami pulled me down, saying something about my falling out and breaking my neck. I gripped the sides of the truck, fingers digging into metal, the giant in my chest growing larger until it seemed I would explode. The truck creaked to a stop, and I jumped out and ran into our yard, looking from one thing to the next, not knowing if what I was seeing was the same or different from what was there before because it didn't matter; I didn't care. I was home. And I never wanted to leave home again.

❧ I walked the land from post to post, trying to place myself within its borders. Our house stood in the center, its shiny zinc roof splotched with rust at the corners. Next to the house was the kitchen shed, from which a thin curl of smoke wove into the air. Behind the house, under the breadfruit tree, there was a pigsty, now empty, the mud the pigs loved to bathe in dried into dusty ridges. The chicken coop squatted between the pigsty and the mango tree, a branch of which held one end of Mami's laundry line, the other end stretched to the trunk of an acerola bush. Away from the house, near Doña Ana's, the latrine with palm frond walls under a zinc roof was hidden from the road by hibiscus bushes and an avocado tree. The boundary between our land and Doña Ana's was bordered by eggplant bushes, and between us and Doña Lola by annatto, oregano, and yucca.

Behind our house was Lalao's *finca*, which stretched into the next town. Sometimes a herd of cows grazed on this land, or a man on horseback rode the borders, a *sombrero* shading his face, his shirt stained yellow with sweat. We were not allowed to go into Lalao's *finca*, which was surrounded by a well-maintained barbwire fence. Not three feet from our backyard, on the other side of this fence, was a fragrant grove of grapefruit trees. The grapefruits weighed on the branches, huge and round, dark green speckled yellow. In the mornings, I heard them tumble from the trees, and it seemed a waste to let them rot under the branches when we could be enjoying them. But Mami and Papi made it clear that we were never to go into that grove, so I stood at the barbwire fence and stared at the fruits growing and ripening, then falling and rotting on the ground where they formed a pulpy wet mud, which I was sure was sour.

☙ "Look, Negi," Mami said one day. "Take a look at what I found!"

She was gutting a chicken. It looked naked without its feathers, which she'd yanked off in between dips into boiling water. Inside the bloody entrails were globes that quivered as she lifted them out.

"What are they?"

"Eggs that haven't been laid yet. See? No shell."

They looked like soft marbles, pink shooters striated with

red, inside of which an orange/yellow liquid gleamed and threatened to ooze out if the outer membrane broke.

"They're delicious in soup," Mami said, and I believed her, because Mami never lied about food.

That night she served *asopao* with a solid dark ball floating on top of each of our bowls. I bit into the firm center with my front teeth. It tasted like hard-boiled egg yolks mixed with liver. It coated the inside of my mouth with a dry, sticky paste, and the smell of feathers rose from the back of my throat into my nose. I had to scrape my teeth with my tongue several times before the flavor dissipated into the familiar bittersweet oregano and garlic. Mami watched me eat and smiled at me with her eyes. I smiled back. It was delicious, just like she said.

⤜ "If you close your eyes while they're crossed, they'll stay like that!"

Juanita Marín was distraught. She stared at me, her eyes wide. She had long lashes that curled up to her eyebrows, which now formed a single wiggly line from one temple to the other.

I shut my eyes, trying to keep them crossed. She held her breath. I rolled my eyes around my lids and pictured her staring at me in wonder. Then I opened my eyes, still crossed. Two Juanita Maríns gasped and brought up four hands to two mouths with gaps where teeth should have been. I uncrossed my eyes and burst out laughing. Her relief changed to anger, and she bopped me with her fist. That made me laugh harder, and she, in spite of herself, laughed with me.

Juanita was my best friend in Macún. She lived down the road from us, past Doña Lola's house, almost at the funnel end of the *barrio*. Every day we walked home from school together, chatting about what we were going to be when we grew up, and whose father could saw the most wood in the least amount of time. I had an advantage over Juanita. I had lived in Santurce, and I could tell her about things like electric light bulbs and shower nozzles. But Juanita, who had lived in

Macún all her life, could tell me about the secret places in the *barrio* that even our mothers didn't know about. Places like the caves at the narrow end, and the breaks in Lalao's fence, and the shortcuts through the woods that led to the next *barrio* where all sorts of *pocavergüenzas* took place. A *pocavergüenza* was something you should be ashamed of but weren't.

It was in Jurutungo that all the women who seduced all the men in Macún lived. At least, that's the way it seemed to us, because every time we heard our mothers, or our mothers' friends complaining about their husbands' *pocavergüenzas*, they had happened in Jurutungo. It was there that their *sinvergüenza* husbands went when they'd just been paid and wanted to get drunk. It was there that their teenage sons disappeared when they reached a certain age and couldn't be controlled any longer. It was to Jurutungo that women who'd had a bad life retreated with bastard children. Juanita and I never wanted to go there. But we often staked out the secret path, hoping someday to catch someone in the act of sneaking into that ill-reputed *barrio*.

Don Berto, Juanita's grandfather, lived in a shed behind Juanita's house, and every time I saw him he was sitting on its front steps sharpening his machete. His skin was so black and wrinkled that it seemed to absorb light into its crevices, to be let out again in the most glorious smile I'd ever seen on anyone with no teeth. I was fascinated by his pink gums, the tongue spotted with white, the lips almost the same color as the rest of his skin. His gnarly hands stuck out of his shirt like gigantic hairless tarantulas, always moving, always searching for someplace to land. His palms, as pink as his gums, were calloused, and his fingertips were stained with age and soil.

We would sit at his feet listening to his *jíbaro* tales of phantasms, talking animals, and enchanted guava trees. While he spoke, he ran the tip of his machete back and forth, back and forth, over a stone, and we knew that if any of the creatures he

talked about came to life, he would take care of it with one
well-placed *machetazo*.

One morning, while I snapped on my uniform, Mami told
me not to wait for Juanita because she wouldn't be coming to
school.

"Why not?"

"Don Berto died last night, may he rest in peace."

"How do you know?" I was astonished at the way news
travelled in the *barrio*. No neighbors ever appeared at the door
to bring us up-to-date. It was as if whatever happened in the
barrio was conveyed in the breeze to be picked up by whom-
ever was alert enough.

"Never mind how I know! Hurry up and get ready or you'll
be late for school."

I scrambled out, irritated, wondering why parents never answered questions but seemed to have all the answers. In school
many of my classmates' seats were empty, and the teacher explained that Don Berto had died, and the children who were
not there were his grandchildren and great-grandchildren, and
that we must be extra nice to them when they returned because
it was a very sad thing to lose a grandparent. She also said
that she hoped we had all been nice to Don Berto when he was
alive, because now we would never get another chance. I tried
to remember if I'd ever been rude to him, or if I'd ever been in
some small way disrespectful to Don Berto, but, to my relief, I
couldn't come up with anything.

While I was in school, Mami was at the Marín house getting
it ready for the *velorio*. Most of the *barrio's* women had put
in some time dusting, washing the floors and walls, sprinkling
agua florida all over, positioning wreaths, bathing Don Berto
and laying him out in his box. By that night, when we came to
the wake, the house looked festive, decorated with flowers and
candles.

Don Berto was in the middle of the living room, dressed in a
clean white shirt buttoned all the way up. His eyes were
closed, and his hands, which I'd never seen without his machete, were clasped on his chest with a rosary wrapped around

them so that the large cross covered his fingers. A mosquito net hung around the coffin, and every time a new person came to see him, someone would have to lift netting away. Chairs were set up along the walls of the house, and into the yard, and people from the neighborhood, and some I'd never seen before, sat quietly sipping coffee or talking in whispers. When Papi came in, people said hello to him and pulled their chairs closer to Don Berto. Juanita's mother brought a chair up for Papi, and he sat down, took a Bible that had been holding down the mosquito net, opened it, and pulled a rosary from his pocket, which he fingered in silence as the rest of the people bowed their heads and did the same thing.

"Let us pray," Papi said in a dramatic voice, and he began mumbling words that I couldn't understand, and the people repeated the same pattern of sounds, and each time they finished a prayer they'd say, "Amen" and click their rosary beads, but Papi would start over again, and they'd follow, mumbling and clicking their beads. This went on for a long time, so that even though I didn't want to, I fell asleep, and next thing, a rooster was crowing and I woke up next to Delsa.

"Don't put on your uniform because you're not going to school today," Mami said as I came out to the kitchen, rubbing my eyes and scratching myself.

"Why not?"

"You and Juanita are going to lead the procession to the cemetery."

"Why?"

Mami gave me an exasperated look. "Just do as I tell you and don't talk back."

Héctor toddled out, stepped out of his diaper, and aimed his pee in a wide arc toward the chickens pecking at worms near the acerola tree. He grinned toward us happily, and Mami and I had to giggle.

❧ Mami starched and ironed my best dress, which was white with blue flowers on the collar. We walked to the Marín house

right after breakfast. Juanita wore a white dress too, with pale
pink flowers along the hem. The rest of her family was dressed
in black or gray, their hair neatly combed, the boys' heads
shimmering with brilliantine. Juanita and I were given a heavy
wreath to carry. It was held together with wires, two of which
had been twisted into handles at either side. Juanita's mother
wrapped handkerchiefs around the sharp ends so that our
hands wouldn't get scratched.

We walked in the hot dust from Juanita's place to the mouth
of the *barrio*. Black-clad people came out of the houses along
the way to join the procession in back of us, many of them carrying homemade wreaths tied with purple ribbons. At the
highway, traffic was stopped so that the procession could move
into the middle of the road. As we passed, men took off their
hats and bowed their heads and women crossed themselves.

It was a long walk to the cemetery. Behind us, Don Berto's
sons carried the coffin on their shoulders and didn't set it down
all the way there. The world was still, except for the shuffling
footsteps of mourners, the hum of prayers, the click-clack of
rosaries. The wreath we carried weighed on us, pulled on our
skinny arms, strained our shoulders. But it would have been
disrespectful to complain, or to let the ribbon with Don Berto's
name drag on the ground. Every so often Juanita looked at
me with sad eyes. I'd never lost a loved one, so I took on her
grief as if it were mine, tried it on to see if I could feel anything
for the old man who had made me so happy with his tales
and the hypnotizing movement of his machete across the stone.
An echoing hollowness pressed against my ribs and threatened
to escape like air from a balloon. I felt light-headed, empty,
and I held on to the wreath so that it would anchor me to the
ground, so that I could not fly up into the sky, above the trees,
into the clouds where Don Berto's soul waited, machete in
hand. He had become a ghost, a creature that could haunt my
nights and see my every move, like the phantasms he told us
about when we sat at his feet, listening to his stories.

At the cemetery, El Cura said a few words, and then the coffin was lowered, as Juanita's mother and aunts wailed about

what a good man he was and how he didn't deserve to die. They shovelled dirt on top of the box, red moist earth not unlike the dirt I used for making mud people, and I wondered what would happen to him under there, with all that weight on him. I thought about this as we walked back to Macún behind Don Berto's daughters, who were overcome with an attack of *los nervios*, so that their sons ended up half carrying them, half dragging them home.

☞ Papi was to lead the novenas for Don Berto. After dinner he washed and put on a clean white shirt, pulled a rosary and a Bible from his dresser, and started out the door.

"Do you want to come?" he asked me.

"¡*Sí*! I would! ¡*Sí*!"

"Only if you bring a long-sleeve shirt," Mami said. "I don't want you sick from the night air."

We walked on the pebbled road as the sun set behind the mountains. Toads hopped out of our way, their dark brown bodies bottom heavy. The air smelled green, the scents of peppermint, rosemary, and verbena wafting up from the ground like fog.

"Papi, what's a soul?"

"The soul is that part of us that never dies."

"What do you mean?"

"When people die, it's just the body that dies. The soul goes up to the sky."

"I know. Mami told me that already."

He laughed. "Okay, so what more do you want to know?"

"What does the soul do?"

"It goes to live with Papa Dios in Paradise."

"When people are alive . . . what does the soul do?"

He stopped and stared at the tip of his work shoes. "Let's see, what does it do?" He massaged his forehead as if that would make the answer come out quicker. "Well, it is the soul of a person that writes poetry."

"How?"

He pinched his lower lip with his thumb and index finger, and pulled it back and forth in small tugs. He dropped his hand and took mine in his then began walking again.

"The soul lives inside a person when he's alive. It's the part of a person that feels. A poet's soul feels more than regular people's souls. And that's what makes him write poetry."

Clouds had formed above the mountains in streaks, like clumps of dough that had been stretched too thin.

"What does the soul look like?"

He let out a breath. "Well, it looks like the person."

"So my soul looks like me and your soul looks like you?"

"Right!" He sounded relieved.

"And it lives inside our bodies?"

"Yes, that's right."

"Does it ever come out?"

"When we die . . ."

"But when we're alive . . . does it ever come out?"

"No, I don't think so." The doubt in his voice let me know that I knew something he didn't, because my soul travelled all the time, and it appeared that his never did. Now I knew what happened to me when I walked beside myself. It was my soul wandering.

The sun dipped behind the mountains, leaving flecks of orange, pink, and turquoise. In the foreground, the landscape had become flat, without shadow, distanceless.

"Papi, what happens to the body when it's buried?"

"It decomposes," he said. "It becomes dust."

We were joined by a group of mourners on their way to the Marín house. They wished us all a good evening, and the rest of the way we walked in dreadful silence.

Papi settled into his place in front of the house, next to an altar with a picture of Don Berto holding his machete. I wondered if his soul had already gone to live with Papa Dios, or if he was floating around watching to see if his daughters and sons were paying him the proper respect now that his body was rotting under the ground. I tried to send my soul up, to meet him halfway between heaven and earth, but I couldn't get out, held by the fear that if he saw my soul he might try to take it with him.

❧ "Someone is coming to take your lap, freckles," Doña Lola cuddled Alicia. We sat in her kitchen, sipping coffee from blue enamel tin cups. Mami had told me to take the baby when I brought a bag of pigeon peas to Doña Lola, who would give us coffee in return. She grew it in the crags that rose behind her kitchen, up the hill from the latrine. I had helped her pick the red, swollen fruit, and she had roasted them in a giant frying pan on her *fogón* then laid the blackened beans out to cool before storing them in an odd assortment of cans and jars.

"Papi said by the time the new baby is born we will have electricity."

"Ah, yes," Doña Lola sighed, "electricity. Pretty soon they'll bring water, too, and then they'll pave the road and bring cars, buses maybe. Ah, yes."

"Buses, Doña Lola?"

"Trucks and buses. And then the *Americanos* will come looking for *artesanías*." She spit into the yard and chuckled as if remembering a private joke. "Those *Americanos* are really something. . . ."

"Do you know any?"

"Oh, I've known a few. Yes. A few. You know, it's an *Americano* that owns the *finca* back there."

"Lalao's *finca*?"

"Bah! *A otro perro con ese hueso.* That *finca* doesn't belong to Lalao. That man doesn't own the hole to lay his corpse in."

"But everyone says . . ."

"*Del dicho al hecho hay un gran trecho.*"

"What does that mean?"

"It means there's a long way between what people say and what is. That *finca* belongs to Rockefela."

"Who's he?"

"An *Americano* from the *Nueva Yores*. He's going to build a hotel back there." The *finca* stretched across the road to the

horizon, the tall grass broken now and then by groves of
lemon, orange, and grapefruit trees, herds of cattle, and, in the
distance, a line of coconut palms.

"What will they do with all those cows?"

Doña Lola guffawed. "You're worried about the cows?
What about us?"

"Well, we don't live on the *finca* . . ."

"Do you think they will let us stay here if they build a
hotel?"

"Why not?"

"*Yo conozco al buey que faja y a la víbora que pica.*" She
swallowed the last drop of coffee and got up from her stool
brusquely, startling Alicia, who reached her arms out to me
and clung to my neck the minute she was close enough.

I loved Doña Lola's *refranes*, the sayings she came up with in
conversation that were sometimes as mysterious as the things
Papi kept in his special dresser. "I know the bull that charges
and the serpent that stings" could only mean that she dis-
trusted Americans, and that this mistrust had come from
experience.

But in the time I'd lived in Macún I'd never seen an American, nor had I ever heard mention of a Rockefela, nor plans
for a hotel in what everyone called Lalao's *finca*.

When I came home, Alicia on my hip, a can of freshly
roasted coffee in my hand, Mami was peeling *ñame* and *yautía*
tubers for that night's supper.

"Mami, is it true that they're going to build a hotel on
Lalao's *finca*?"

"That will be the day!"

"Doña Lola said they'll make us all move."

"They've been talking about bringing electricity here since
before you were born. And the rumor about a hotel in Lalao's
finca is older than the hopes of the poor. Your granddaughters
will be *señorita* before anything like that happens around
here."

I was relieved we wouldn't have to move and helped Mami
peel the sweet potatoes.

"Where are *los Nueva Yores*?" I asked later as I tore the fish bones out of the soaking salted codfish.

"That's where Tata lives." Tata was my mother's mother, who had left Puerto Rico while I was still a toddler. Every so often Mami received a letter from her with a money order, or a package with the clothes my cousins in the United States had outgrown. "It's really called *Nueva Yor*, but it's so big and spread out people sometimes call it *los Nueva Yores*."

"Have you ever been there?"

"No, I haven't. . . . Maybe someday . . . ," she mused as she set a pot of water to boil on the fire. "Maybe."

❱ "¡*Ay! Ay Dios Mío Santo, ayúdame. ¡Ay!*" Mami was having another baby. I was in charge of the younger kids, having been told to stay in the yard and out of the house until Doña Ana, our next-door neighbor, came to get us. Even from the far corner of the yard we heard Mami screaming, and Doña Lola and the midwife urging her. Every so often one of them came out and grabbed hot water from a big caldron in the *fogón* or poured a cup of coffee from the pot on the embers. They'd go back in and shut the door behind them, not allowing us even a peek into our mother's pain.

At dusk Doña Ana and her daughter Gloria came to get us, and we walked through the path that connected our yards, Héctor on my hip, Delsa carrying Alicia, Norma dragging a change of clothes for us bundled into a pillowcase, just in case we had to spend the night.

Mami's screams got louder and more shrill as we walked away from the house, as if she could feel us leaving. Norma whimpered; Héctor's eyes darted back and forth, and a solemn expression was on his usually smiling face. Alicia happily sucked her thumb and pointed at everything we passed, chirping, "What's that? What's that?" Delsa tried to comfort everyone, or perhaps just herself. "Don't worry," she repeated over and over. "It's just Mami having a baby, that's all. It's just a baby. Mami will be all right." But none of us were comforted

that easily, although by now we had learned not to make a
fuss.

We ate Doña Ana's rice and beans with stringy fried chicken
and waited in the yard, huddled together. I told stories learned
from Don Berto or made up some of my own, none so scary
as to chase away sleep. The next morning we were herded
back to our own yard, into our house, where Mami was
propped up on pillows nursing our new baby sister, and Papi,
in the kitchen, installed a kerosene cookstove.

‣ "Everybody, take off your clothes!" It was the middle of the
afternoon, the first week in May. The air had cooled in a matter of seconds. A whisper of rain was beginning through a
sunny sky, distant black clouds not close enough to throw the
valley into darkness. Mami ran from the window, her face
glowing, to the basket of house clothes and slipped out of her
flowered dress into a faded shift.

"Quickly! Keep your panties on, girls, just take off your
shirts. Hurry!" She helped us undress one by one while we
laughed and asked her why. She didn't answer just giggled and
took our clothes and stacked them on her rocking chair. She
carried Edna, who was a few days old, to the threshold, and let
a few sprinkles of rain dot her forehead, and rubbed them
over the baby's face and shoulders before returning her to her
cradle.

"Come. Follow me." She ran and stood in the middle of the
yard smiling. The black clouds raced across the valley, but
where she was standing, it was still bright. Light rain fell like
dew on her, moistening her dress against her shoulders, her
rounded belly, her hips. She raised her head to the sky and let
the rain fall on her face, and she pushed the drops into her
hair, down her neck, into the crevice between her breasts. We
clustered on the threshold.

"What's she doing?" Delsa whispered.

"She's taking a bath," Norma answered, her yellow eyes
enormous.

"What are you waiting for?" Mami sang to us from the yard.

"But it's raining, Mami," Delsa said, sticking her hand out as if to prove her point.

"Yes," Mami said. "It's the first rain in May. It's good luck to get wet by the first May rain."

She took Delsa's hand, and Héctor's; he was holding on to the door frame as if glued there. She waltzed them to the yard then danced them around in circles. The rest of us stepped out gingerly, watching the black clouds crest the mountain and drop into the valley. Rain fell in thick drops now, exploding craters in the dry earth, banging against the zinc walls.

We held hands because it seemed the right thing to do, circled around as the ground became mud and the rain fell harder, cascading down our faces, into our mouths. We circled and sang a school yard rhyme:

> *¡Que llueva, que llueva!*
> *La Virgen en la cueva,*
> *los pajaritos cantan,*
> *la Virgen se levanta.*
> *¡Que llueva, que llueva!*
>
> Let it rain, let it rain!
> The Virgin in the cave.
> Birds sing,
> The Virgin rises.
> Let it rain, let it rain!

Mami let go our hands and ran under the roof overhang, where water fell in a thick stream. She gave us each a turn at being massaged by the torrent, which banged against our skinny bodies and bounced off in silver fans onto the ground. She rubbed the water into our scalps, behind our ears, under our arms, then sent us to chase one another in the slippery mud. We squished our toes and fingers into it, rubbed it on our arms, our bellies, behind our knees, then let the rain wash it off in long streams of red and orange that dribbled back into the soft earth. We squealed and laughed and sang silly rhymes, until the first bolt of lighting broke open the clouds, and thunder sent us all scampering inside, shivering, to be dried off by a laughing Mami, her eyes bright, her face flushed.

For the rest of the month, the rains came, heavy, angry downpours called *vaguadas* that soaked into the ground, turning our yard into a slippery, muddy swamp. Thunder and lightning seemed to strike just over our heads, the sound magnified by the metal roof and walls. The low-slung clouds threw the valley into twilight, and we had to keep the *quinqués* lit all day so we could find our way in the shuttered house.

Papi couldn't leave for work if the rains started early, and he passed the time reading magazines he retrieved from his special dresser. If the rains began after he'd left for work, however, we wouldn't see him for days. Mami didn't seem as bothered by his absence and fed us soups, or creamy rice with milk, or hot *sancochos* made up of whatever leftovers she could fit into the pot. When she wasn't feeding us, she sewed, if she had fabric, or polished the bedstead and Papi's dresser, or mended whatever was worn, ripped, or needed patching.

We slept long hours, the rain drumming against the walls, the angry rolls of thunder galloping over our zinc roof. We collected rain in barrels that filled up, topped off, overspilled, and still the *vaguadas* came like a once-welcome guest that couldn't stay away, eroding the ground into deep furrows that the summer sun burned into long, dry scars, deep wounds that never healed.

THE AMERICAN
INVASION OF
MACÚN

Lo que no mata, engorda.

❧

What doesn't kill you, makes you fat.

Pollito, chicken
Gallina, hen
Lápiz, pencil
y Pluma, pen.
Ventana, window
Puerta, door
Maestra, teacher
y Piso, floor.

Miss Jiménez stood in front of the class as we sang and, with her ruler, pointed at the chicks scratching the dirt outside the classroom, at the hen leading them, at the pencil on Juanita's desk, at the pen on her own desk, at the window that looked out into the playground, at the door leading to the yard, at herself, and at the shiny tile floor. We sang along, pointing as she did with our sharpened pencils, rubber end out.

"*¡Muy bien!*" She pulled down the map rolled into a tube at the front of the room. In English she told us, "Now gwee estody about de Jun-ited Estates gee-o-graphee."

It was the daily English class. Miss Jiménez, the second- and third-grade teacher, was new to the school in Macún. She looked like a grown-up doll, with high rounded cheekbones, a freckled *café con leche* complexion, black lashes, black curly hair pulled into a bun at the nape of her neck, and the prettiest legs in the whole *barrio*. Doña Ana said Miss Jiménez had the most beautiful legs she'd ever seen, and the next day, while Miss Jiménez wrote the multiplication table on the blackboard, I stared at them.

She wore skirts to just below the knees, but from there down, her legs were shaped like chicken drumsticks, rounded and full at the top, narrow at the bottom. She had long straight hair on her legs, which everyone said made them even prettier, and small feet encased in plain brown shoes with a low square heel. That night I wished on a star that someday my scrawny legs would fill out into that lovely shape and that the hair on them would be as long and straight and black.

Miss Jiménez came to Macún at the same time as the community center. She told us that starting the following week, we were all to go to the *centro comunal* before school to get breakfast, provided by the Estado Libre Asociado, or Free Associated State, which was the official name for Puerto Rico in the Estados Unidos, or in English, the Jun-ited Estates of America. Our parents, Miss Jiménez told us, should come to a meeting that Saturday, where experts from San Juan and the Jun-ited Estates would teach our mothers all about proper nutrition and hygiene, so that we would grow up as tall and strong as Dick, Jane, and Sally, the *Americanitos* in our primers.

"And Mami," I said as I sipped my afternoon *café con leche*, "Miss Jiménez said the experts will give us free food and toothbrushes and things . . . and we can get breakfast every day except Sunday . . ."

"Calm down," she told me. "We'll go, don't worry."

On Saturday morning the yard in front of the *centro comunal* filled with parents and their children. You could tell the experts from San Juan from the ones that came from the Jun-ited Estates because the *Americanos* wore ties with their white shirts and tugged at their collars and wiped their foreheads with crumpled handkerchiefs. They hadn't planned for children, and the men from San Juan convinced a few older girls to watch the little ones outside so that the meeting could proceed with the least amount of disruption. Small children refused to leave their mothers' sides and screeched the minute one of the white-shirted men came near them. Some women sat on the folding chairs at the rear of the room nursing, a cloth draped over their baby's face so that the experts would not be upset at the sight of a bare breast. There were no fathers. Most of them worked seven days a week, and anyway, children and food were woman's work.

"Negi, take the kids outside and keep them busy until this is over."

"But Mami . . ."

"Do as I say."

She pressed her way to a chair in the middle of the room and sat facing the experts. I hoisted Edna on my shoulder and grabbed Alicia's hand. Delsa pushed Norma out in front of her. They ran into the yard and within minutes had blended into a group of children their age. Héctor found a boy to chase him around a tree, and Alicia crawled to a sand puddle where she and other toddlers smeared one another with the fine red dirt. I sat at the door, Edna on my lap, and tried to keep one eye on my sisters and brother and another on what went on inside.

The experts had colorful charts on portable easels. They introduced each other to the group, thanked the Estado Libre Asociado for the privilege of being there, and then took turns speaking. The first expert opened a large suitcase. Inside there was a huge set of teeth with pink gums.

"*Ay Dios Santo, qué cosa tan fea,*" said a woman as she crossed herself. The mothers laughed and mumbled among themselves that yes, it was ugly. The expert stretched his lips into a smile and pulled a large toothbrush from under the table. He used ornate Spanish words that we assumed were scientific talk for teeth, gums, and tongue. With his giant brush, he polished each tooth on the model, pointing out the proper path of the bristles on the teeth.

"If I have to spend that much time on my teeth," a woman whispered loud enough for everyone to hear, "I won't get anything done around the house." The room buzzed with giggles, and the expert again spread his lips, took a breath, and continued his demonstration.

"At the conclusion of the meeting," he said, "you will each receive a toothbrush and a tube of paste for every member of your family."

"*¿Hasta pa' los mellaos?*" a woman in the back of the room asked, and everyone laughed.

"If they have no teeth, it's too late for them, isn't it," the expert said through his own clenched teeth. The mothers shrieked with laughter, and the expert sat down so that an *Americano* with red hair and thick glasses could tell us about food.

He wiped his forehead and upper lip as he pulled up the cloth covering one of the easels to reveal a colorful chart of the major food groups.

"*La buena* nutrition is *muy importante para los niños.*" In heavily accented, hard to understand Castilian Spanish he described the necessity of eating portions of each of the foods on his chart every day. There were carrots and broccoli, iceberg lettuce, apples, pears, and peaches. The bread was sliced into a perfect square, unlike the long loaves Papi brought home from a bakery in San Juan, or the round *pan de manteca* Mami bought at Vitín's store. There was no rice on the chart, no beans, no salted codfish. There were big white eggs, not at all like the small round ones our hens gave us. There was a tall glass of milk, but no coffee. There were wedges of yellow cheese, but no balls of cheese like the white *queso del país* wrapped in banana leaves sold in bakeries all over Puerto Rico. There were bananas but no plantains, potatoes but no *batatas*, cereal flakes but no oatmeal, bacon but no sausages.

"But, *señor*," said Doña Lola from the back of the room, "none of the fruits or vegetables on your chart grow in Puerto Rico."

"Then you must substitute our recommendations with your native foods."

"Is an apple the same as a mango?" asked Cirila, whose yard was shaded by mango trees.

"*Sí*," said the expert, "a mango can be substituted for an apple."

"What about breadfruit?"

"I'm not sure . . ." The *Americano* looked at an expert from San Juan who stood up, pulled the front of his *guayabera* down over his ample stomach, and spoke in a voice as deep and resonant as a radio announcer's.

"Breadfruit," he said, "would be equivalent to potatoes."

"Even the ones with seeds?" asked Doña Lola, who roasted them on the coals of her *fogón*.

"Well, I believe so," he said, "but it is best not to make substitutions for the recommended foods. That would throw the whole thing off."

He sat down and stared at the ceiling, his hands crossed under his belly as if he had to hold it up. The mothers asked each other where they could get carrots and broccoli, iceberg lettuce, apples, peaches, or pears.

"At the conclusion of the meeting," the *Americano* said, "you will all receive a sack full of groceries with samples from the major food groups." He flipped the chart closed and moved his chair near the window, amid the hum of women asking one another what he'd just said.

The next expert uncovered another easel on which there was a picture of a big black bug. A child screamed, and a woman got the hiccups.

"This," the expert said scratching the top of his head, "is the magnified image of a head louse."

Following him, another *Americano* who spoke good Spanish discussed intestinal parasites. He told all the mothers to boil their water several times and to wash their hands frequently.

"Children love to put their hands in their mouths," he said, making it sound like fun, "but each time they do, they run the risk of infection." He flipped the chart to show an enlargement of a dirty hand, the tips of the fingernails encrusted with dirt.

"Ugh! That's disgusting!" whispered Mami to the woman next to her. I curled my fingers inside my palms.

"When children play outside," the expert continued, "their hands pick up dirt, and with it, hundreds of microscopic parasites that enter their bodies through their mouths to live and thrive in their intestinal tract."

He flipped the chart again. A long flat snake curled from the corner at the top of the chart to the opposite corner at the bottom. Mami shivered and rubbed her arms to keep the goose bumps down.

"This," the *Americano* said, "is a tapeworm, and it is not uncommon in this part of the world."

Mami had joked many times that the reason I was so skinny was that I had a *solitaria*, a tapeworm, in my belly. But I don't think she ever knew what a tapeworm looked like, nor did I. I imagined something like the earthworms that crawled out of the ground when it rained, but never anything so ugly as the snake on the chart, its flat body like a deck of cards strung together.

"Tapeworms," the expert continued, "can reach lengths of nine feet." I rubbed my belly, trying to imagine how long nine feet was and whether I had that much room in me. Just thinking about it made my insides itchy.

When they finished their speeches, the experts had all the mothers line up and come to the side of the room, where each was given samples according to the number of people in their household. Mami got two sacks of groceries, so Delsa had to carry Edna all the way home while I dragged one of the bags full of cans, jars, and bright cartons.

At home Mami gave each of us a toothbrush and told us we were to clean our teeth every morning and every evening. She set a tube of paste and a cup by the door, next to Papi's shaving things. Then she emptied the bags.

"I don't understand why they didn't just give us a sack of rice and a bag of beans. It would keep this family fed for a month."

She took out a five-pound tin of peanut butter, two boxes of cornflakes, cans of fruit cocktail, peaches in heavy syrup, beets, and tuna fish, jars of grape jelly and pickles and put everything on a high shelf.

"We'll save this," she said, "so that we can eat like *Americanos cuando el hambre apriete.*" She kept them there for a long time but took them down one by one so that, as she promised, we ate like Americans when hunger cramped our bellies.

*   *   *

✑ One morning I woke up with something wiggling inside my panties. When I looked, there was a long worm inside. I screamed, and Mami came running. I pointed to my bottom, and she pulled down my panties and saw. She sat me in a basin of warm water with salt, because she thought that might draw more worms out. I squatted, my bottom half in, half out, expecting that a *solitaria* would crawl out of my body and swim around and when it realized it had come out, try to bite me down there and crawl back in. I kept looking into the basin, but nothing happened, and after a long time, Mami let me get up. That night she gave us only a thin broth for supper.

"Tonight you all get a *purgante*," she said.

"But why," Delsa whined. "I'm not the one with worms."

"If one of you has worms, you all have worms," Mami said, and we knew better than to argue with her logic. "Now go wash up, and come get your medicine."

The *purgante* was her own concoction, a mixture of cod-liver oil and mugwort, milk of magnesia, and green papaya juice, sweetened to disguise the fishy, bitter, chalky taste. It worked on our bellies overnight, and in the morning, Delsa, Norma, Héctor, and I woke up with cramps and took turns at the latrine, joining the end of the line almost as soon as we'd finished. Mami fed us broths, and in the evening, a bland, watery boiled rice that at least stuck to our bellies and calmed the roiling inside.

✑ "Today," Miss Jiménez said, "you will be vaccinated by the school nurse."

There had never been a school nurse at Macún Elementary School, but lately a woman dressed in white, with a tall, stiff cap atop her short cropped hair, had set up an infirmary in a corner of the lunchroom. Forms had been sent home, and Mami had told me and Delsa that we would be receiving polio vaccines.

"What's polio?" I asked, imagining another parasite in my belly.

"It's a very bad disease that makes you crippled," she said.

"Is it like meningitis?" Delsa asked. A brother of one of her friends had that disease; his arms and hands were twisted into his body, his legs splayed out at the knees, so that he walked as if he were about to kneel.

"No," Mami said, "it's worse. If you get polio, you die, or you spend the rest of your life in a wheelchair or inside an iron lung."

"An iron lung!?!?" It was impossible. There could not be such a thing.

"It's not like a real lung, silly," Mami laughed. "It's a machine that breathes for you."

"¡Ay Dios Mío!" Polio was worse than *solitaria*.

"But how can it do that?" Delsa's eyes opened and shut as if she were testing to see whether she was asleep or awake.

"I don't know how it works," Mami said. "Ask your father."

Delsa and I puzzled over how you could have an iron lung, and that night, when Papi came home from work, we made him draw one for us and show us how a machine could do what people couldn't. He drew a long tube and at one end made a stick figure face.

"It looks like a can," Delsa said, and Papi laughed.

"Yes," he said, "it does. Just like a can."

☙ Miss Jiménez sent us out to see the nurse two at a time, in alphabetical order. By the time she got to the *S*'s, I was shaky, because every one of the children who had gone before me had come back crying, pressing a wad of cotton against their arm. Ignacio Sepúlveda walked next to me, and even though he was as scared as I was, he pretended he wasn't.

"What crybabies!" he said. "I've had shots before and they don't hurt that much."

"When?"

"Last year. They gave us shots for tuberculosis." We were

nearing the lunchroom, and Ignacio slowed down, tugged on my arm, and whispered, "It's all because of politics."

"What are you talking about? Politics isn't a disease like polio. It's something men talk about at the bus stop." I'd heard Papi tell Mami when he was late that he'd missed the bus because he'd been discussing politics.

Ignacio kept his voice to a whisper, as if he were telling me something no one else knew. "My Papá says the government's doing all this stuff for us because it's an election year."

"What does that have to do with it?"

"They give kids shots and free breakfast, stuff like that, so that our dads will vote for them. "

"So?"

"Don't you know anything?"

"I know a lot of things."

"You don't know anything about politics."

"Do so."

"Do not."

"Do so."

"Who's the governor of Puerto Rico, then?"

"Oh, you could have asked something really hard! . . . Everyone knows it's Don Luis Muñoz Marín."

"Yeah, well, who's *el presidente* of the Jun-ited Estates?"

"Ay-sen-hou-err."

"I bet you don't know his first name."

I knew then I had him. I scanned Papi's newspaper daily, and I had seen pictures of *el presidente* on the golf course, and of his wife's funny hairdo.

"His first name is Eekeh," I said, puffed with knowledge. "And his wife's name is Mami."

"Well, he's an imperialist, just like all the other *gringos*!" Ignacio said, and I was speechless because Mami and Papi never let us say things like that about grown-ups, even if they were true.

When we came into the lunchroom, Ignacio presented his arm to the nurse as if instead of a shot he were getting a medal.

He winced as the nurse stuck the needle into him and blinked a few times to push back tears. But he didn't cry, and I didn't either, though I wanted to. There was no way I'd have Ignacio Sepúlveda calling me a crybaby.

   ⤳ "Papi, what's an imperialist?"

He stopped the hammer in midstrike and looked at me. "Where did you hear that word?"

"Ignacio Sepúlveda said Eekeh Aysenhouerr is an imperialist. He said all *gringos* are."

Papi looked around as if someone were hiding behind a bush and listening in. "I don't want you repeating those words to anybody . . ."

"I know that Papi. . . . I just want to know what it means. Are *gringos* the same as *Americanos*?"

"You should never call an *Americano* a *gringo*. It's a very bad insult."

"But why?"

"It just is." It wasn't like Papi not to give a real answer to my questions. "Besides, *el presidente*'s name is pronounced Ayk, not Eekeh." He went back to his hammering.

I handed him a nail from the can at his feet. "How come it's a bad insult?"

He stopped banging the wall and looked at me. I stared back, and he put his hammer down, took off his hat, brushed his hand across his forehead, wiped it on his pants, sat on the stoop, and leaned his elbows back, stretching his legs out in front of him. This was the response I expected. Now I would hear all about *gringos* and imperialists.

"Puerto Rico was a colony of Spain after Columbus landed here," he began, like a schoolteacher.

"I know that."

"Don't interrupt."

"Sorry."

"In 1898, *los Estados Unidos* invaded Puerto Rico, and we became their colony. A lot of Puerto Ricans don't think that's right. They call *Americanos* imperialists, which means they want to change our country and our culture to be like theirs."

"Is that why they teach us English in school, so we can speak like them?"

"Yes."

"Well, I'm not going to learn English so I don't become American."

He chuckled. "Being American is not just a language, *Negrita*, it's a lot of other things."

"Like what?"

He scratched his head. "Like the food you eat . . . the music you listen to . . . the things you believe in."

"Do they believe in God?"

"Some of them do."

"Do they believe in phantasms and witches?"

"Yes, some Americans believe in that."

"Mami doesn't believe any of that stuff."

"I know. I don't either."

"Why not?"

"I just . . . I believe in things I can see."

"Why do people call *Americanos gringos*?"

"We call them *gringos*, they call us spiks."

"What does that mean?"

"Well," he sat up, leaned his elbows on his knees and looked at the ground, as if he were embarrassed. "There are many Puerto Ricans in New York, and when someone asks them a question they say, 'I don spik inglish' instead of 'I don't speak English.' They make fun of our accent."

"*Americanos* talk funny when they speak Spanish."

"Yes, they do. The ones who don't take the trouble to learn it well." He pushed his hat back, and the sun burned into his already brown face, making him squint. "That's part of being an imperialist. They expect us to do things their way, even in our country."

"That's not fair."

"No, it isn't." He stood up and picked up his hammer. "Well, I'd better get back to work, *Negrita*. Do you want to help?"

"Okay." I followed him, holding the can of nails up so he wouldn't have to bend over to pick them up. "Papi?"

"Yes."

"If we eat all that American food they give us at the *centro comunal*, will we become *Americanos*?"

He banged a nail hard into the wall then turned to me, and, with a broad smile on his face said, "Only if you like it better than our Puerto Rican food."

▶ The yard in front of the *centro comunal* teemed with children. Mrs. García, the school lunch matron, opened the door and stepped out, a bell in her hand. We quieted before she rang it. She beamed.

"Good." There was whispering and shoving as we crowded the door to be the first in for breakfast. Mrs. García lifted the bell in warning. We settled down again.

"Now," she said in her gruff voice, "line up by age, youngest first."

The smaller children, who had been pushed to the back of the crowd by bigger ones, scurried to the front. I took my place halfway between the younger and the older ones, who scowled at us and jammed the line forward with rough shoves.

"Stop pushing!" Mrs. García yelled. "There's enough for everyone."

She opened the double doors and we rushed ahead in a wave, goaded from behind by boys who crushed against us with their chests and knees.

The *centro comunal* had been decorated with posters. Dick and Jane, Sally and Spot, Mother and Father, the Mailman, the Milkman, and the Policeman smiled their way through tableau after tableau, their clean, healthy, primary-colored world flat and shadowless.

"Wow!" Juanita Marín whispered, her lips shaped into a perfect O.

People who looked like Mother and Father held up tubes of Colgate toothpaste or bars of Palmolive soap. A giant chart of the four basic food groups was tacked up between the back windows. In a corner, the Puerto Rican seal, flanked by our flag and the Stars and Stripes, looked like a lamb on a platter. Above it, Ike and Don Luis Muñoz Marín faced each other smiling.

"What's that smell?" I said to Juanita as we shuffled closer to the counter lined with steaming pots.

"It's the food, silly," she giggled.

It was a sweet-salty smell, bland but strong, warm but not comforting, lacking herbs and spices.

"It's disgusting!"

"I think it smells good." She pouted and took a tray, a pale green paper napkin, and a spoon.

The server picked a blue enamel tin plate from a stack behind her and scooped out a bright yellow blob from the pot in front of her. She dumped a ladleful on Juanita's plate and slid it onto the tray.

"You'd like some eggs too, wouldn't you?" she asked me with a smile.

"Those are eggs?"

"Of course they're eggs!" she laughed. "What else could they be?" She heaped a mound of it in the middle of my plate, where it quivered, its watery edges green where they met the blue.

"They don't look like eggs."

Ignacio Sepúlveda poked his tray into my ribs. "You're holding up the line!"

"They're *huevos Americanos*," said the next server, whose job it was to spear two brown sausages with a fork and slip them onto the plate. "They're powdered, so all we do is add water and fry them." She arranged my sausages to flank the eggs. "And here are some *salchichas Americanas*, so you can put some meat on those bones." She laughed, and I gave her a dirty look. That only made her laugh harder.

The next server slapped margarine on two bread squares, which he laid like a pyramid over the eggs. Next, a girl not much older than the kids behind us poured canned juice into a bottom-heavy glass, which she put on our trays so carelessly it splashed out and made watery orange puddles that ran to the corners of our trays.

We sat on long benches attached to plastic tables, Juanita and I across from one another.

"This is great!" she chirruped in her reedy voice, lips wet with anticipation. Her black eyes took in the colors of our American breakfast: maroon tray, blue plate, yellow eggs, brown sausages, milky white bread with a thin beige crust, the hueless shimmer of margarine, orange juice, pastel green paper napkin, silvery spoon. "Wow!" she oohed again.

I rearranged the food so that none of it touched and dipped my spoon into the gelatinous hill, which was firmer than I expected. It was warm and gave off that peculiar odor I'd smelled coming in. It tasted like the cardboard covers of our primers, salty, dry, fibrous, but not as satisfyingly chewy. If these were once eggs, it had been a long time since they'd been inside a hen. I nicked the tip of the sausage with the spoon and tongued it around before crushing it between my teeth. Its grease-bathed pepperiness had a strong bitter aftertaste like anise, but not sweet. The bread formed moist balls inside my mouth, no matter how much I chewed it. The juice might have had oranges in it once, but only a faint citrus smell remained.

I was glad the food wasn't tasty and played it around the blue plate, creating yellow mountains through which shimmering rivers of grease flowed, their edges green, the rolled up balls of white bread perfect stones along strips of brown earth studded with tiny black flecks, ants perhaps, or, better yet, microscopic people.

* * *

Are ju slippin? Are ju slippin?
Bruder John, Bruder John.
Mornin bel sar rin ging.
Mornin bel sar rin ging.
Deen deen don. Deen deen don.

Miss Jiménez liked to teach us English through song, and we learned all our songs phonetically, having no idea of what the words meant. She tried to teach us "America the Beautiful" but had to give up when we stumbled on "for spacious skies" (4 espé chosk ¡Ay!) and "amber waves of grain" (am burr gueys oh gren).

At the same time she taught us the Puerto Rican national anthem, which said Borinquén was the daughter of the ocean and the sun. I liked thinking of our island as a woman whose body was a garden of flowers, whose feet were caressed by waves, a land whose sky was never cloudy. I especially liked the part when Christopher Columbus lands on her shores and sighs: "¡Ay! This is the beautiful land I've been searching for!"

But my favorite patriotic song was "*En mi viejo San Juan*," in which a poet says good-bye to Old San Juan and calls Puerto Rico a "sea goddess, queen of the coconut groves."

"Papi . . ." He was on his knees, smoothing the cement floor of the new kitchen he was attaching to the house.

"*Sí.* . . ." He put his trowel down and squeezed his waist as he stretched his back. I squatted against the wall near him.

"Where was Noel Estrada going when he was saying good-bye to Old San Juan?"

Papi reached over and turned the radio down. "I think he was sailing from San Juan Harbor to New York."

"It's such a sad song, don't you think?"

"At the end he says he'll come back someday."

"Did he?"

"The last verse says he's old and hasn't been able to return."

"That makes it even sadder."

"Why?"

"Because he says he's coming back to be happy. Doesn't that sound like he wasn't happy in New York?"

"Yes, I guess it does."

"Maybe he didn't want to go."

"Maybe." He picked up his trowel, slid a thin layer of cement on it, and levelled it on the floor, smoothing and stretching it in arcs that formed half circles, like grey rainbows.

❧ "Look how pretty this is!"

Mami held a yellow blouse with a ruffled collar against her bosom, patted the neckline into shape, and stretched it across her shoulders to check the fit. It was a wonderful color against her skin, making the freckles on her nose look like gold specks.

"I'll put it away for now. It's a little small." She was pregnant again, and her belly pressed against the fabric of her dress and strained the seams that zigzagged down the sides, where bits of flesh showed pale and soft between the stitches. She folded the blouse and pulled a dress out of the box. Delsa and I both grabbed for it, but Mami yanked it out of reach and crossed her arms, crushing it against her.

"Stop that! Let me see what size it is." She held it up. It was perfect for me. It had red dots on white puffy sleeves, a white bodice, a white skirt with a stripe of red dots at the hem, and two dotted heart-shaped pockets.

"Negi, I think this one is for you."

I grabbed it and ran to the other end of the room, where Norma was already trying on pink shorts with a matching tee shirt. I stuck my tongue out at Delsa, who sent daggers with her eyes, but only until Mami pulled out a sky-blue dress with ruffles and lace on the collar. Perfect for Delsa.

Tata, Mami's mother, had sent us a box from New York full of clothes that Mami's cousins no longer wore. Clothes that were almost new, with no stains or tears or mended seams. Héctor, the boy in our family, was the only one to get new pants and shirts, because none of Mami's New York relatives had boys his age. But for us girls there were shiny patent-leather shoes with the heels hardly worn, saddle shoes that had already been broken in, a red sweater with a bow at the neck and only one button missing, pleated skirts with matching blouses, high heels for Mami, a few nightgowns, and a pair of pajamas that I claimed, because I loved the cowboys and Indians chasing each other across my body, down my arms and legs.

"Our cousins must be rich to give up these things!" Norma said as she tried on a girl's cotton slip with embroidered flowers across the chest.

"Things like these are not that expensive in New York," Mami said. "Anyone can afford them."

She sat on the edge of the bed and unfolded a letter that had been taped to the inside of the box. A crisp ten dollar bill fell out. Héctor and Alicia dove for it and wrestled one another to be the first to get it. While they fought, Delsa calmly picked it up and handed it to Mami.

"What does the letter say, Mami?" I asked.

"It says she hopes we like the presents." She looked up at me, her eyes shiny. "Maybe you could write Tata a letter and tell her we love them."

"Sure!" I liked writing letters. Especially if they were going far away. I had often written things for Mami, like addresses on envelopes she sent to Tata in New York, or notes for my teachers, which I wrote and she signed.

That night I wrote Tata a letter. It took me a long time, because we were just learning cursive in school, and I had to look up the shapes of some letters on the back of the book Miss Jiménez had given us for penmanship practice. I found it difficult to form the capital *E* of my first name, with its top and bottom curlicues and uneven-size bulges that faced in what seemed like the wrong direction no matter how many times I wrote it. So I signed it Negi, which I considered to be my real name. When I finished the letter, Mami read it out loud.

" 'Dear Tata, We liked the presents you sent us. The dress

with the polka dots fits me and Delsa looks pretty in the blue dress. Mami is saving the yellow blouse for after the baby. We love you and thank you for the things you sent. Love, Negi.' ... You made a mistake. ..."

"What?"

"You didn't start with a salutation."

"Yes I did. See? Dear Tata."

"I know, but you also have to write, 'I hope when you receive this letter you are feeling well. We are all well here, thank God.' You can abbreviate '*A Dios Gracias*' by writing 'A.D.G.' if you want to."

"Why does it have to start that way?"

"All letters start that way."

"But why?"

"I don't know!" she said, exasperated. "That's how I learned it. And every letter I get starts that way. If you don't have a salutation at the beginning, it's not a real letter. ... Besides, it's rude not to wish the reader good health, and God has to be thanked first thing. ... You'd better write it again."

"I don't want to write it again."

"You have to." She set it down on the table. "Finish it and I can take it to the post office tomorrow." She walked away.

"I'm not doing this stupid letter over," I mumbled.

"What was that?" She'd whirled in her tracks and was at me before I could blink my eyes, her left hand gripping my arm.

"Nothing! I didn't say anything."

Mami stood over me, crushing my arm, right hand at her side, the fingers trembling. I wanted to grab her fingers, to bite into them, to make them hurt, those fingers that sometimes soothed but so many times splayed against my skin in smacks, or, fisted, knuckled my head in *cocotazos* that echoed inside my brain. She slammed me against the chair. The rungs dug into my bony back.

"Finish it." I could almost touch the heat she gave off, the faint sweaty smell of her anger. Hot, quiet tears dribbled down my cheeks in a steady flow, like the faucet at the public fountain. The drone inside my head was louder, my ears felt warm, red, too big for my head. Mami stood there watching, as I picked up the pencil, carefully tore a sheet from my notebook, and, in labored script, wrote, "Dear Tata, I hope when you receive this letter . . ."

    ☙ *My bonee lie sober de o chan,*
     My bonee lie sober de sí,
     My bonee lie sober de o chan,
     O breen back my bonee 2 mí, 2 mí . . .

"What's that smell?" The breakfasts at the *centro comunal* had fallen into a pattern of *huevos Americanos* alternating with hot oatmeal, which at least tasted like oatmeal, except it was not as smooth, sweet, and cinnamony as the oatmeal Mami made.

"They must be giving us something new today," said Juanita Marín.

The steaming pots were gone. Instead, there was a giant urn in the middle of the table and a five-pound tin of peanut butter. One of the servers scooped a dollop of peanut butter into the bottom-heavy glasses, and another filled them with warm milk from the urn.

"Here's a spoon so you can stir it," she said as she put the glasses on our trays.

I carried my tray to the usual table Juanita and I shared. Even she, who loved the breakfasts, had a suspicious expression on her face. We faced each other, looked down at the glass full of milk with the brown blob on the bottom, looked at each other again, then at the milk.

"Are you going to taste it?" I asked her.

"Sure," she said, unconvinced. "Are you?"

"Sure." I stirred the milk, and beige pellets floated up from the bottom, like sand encased in a shimmery oil that skimmed the top and bubbled around the whirlpool I made with my spoon. Juanita stirred hers too. I took a sip from the spoon but couldn't really taste much except the milk. Juanita spooned a dribble into her mouth. She smiled.

"Yum!" But it wasn't her usual happy "Yum!" It was more of an "I'm going to pretend to like this in case it's good" kind of "Yum!"

I wrapped my hands around the glass, lifted it to my lips, and drank. A consoling warmth compensated for the milky smell, and the gritty, salty-sweet taste. The peanut butter, which was supposed to dissolve in the milk, broke off into clumps, like soft pebbles.

I gagged, and the glass fell out of my hand, spilled over my uniform, and crashed to the tile floor where it broke into large chunks that gleamed in the pebbly milk. I threw up what little I'd swallowed, and children around me jumped and receded into a tittery circle of faces with milky mustaches. Mrs. García pushed through the crowd and pulled me away from the mess, while one of the servers dragged a dirty mop across it.

"*Now* look what you've done!" she said, as if this were something I did every day of the week to annoy her.

"I couldn't help it!" I cried. "That milk tastes sour!"

"How can it taste sour?" she yelled as she wiped me down with a rag. "It's powdered milk. We made it fresh this morning. It can't get sour."

I remembered a word Mami used for food that made her gag. "It's . . . *repugnante!*"

"I suppose you'd find it less repugnant to go hungry every morning!"

"I've never gone hungry!" I screamed. "My Mami and Papi can feed us without your disgusting *gringo* imperialist food!"

The children gasped. Even Ignacio Sepúlveda. Mrs. García's mouth dropped open and stayed that way. From the back, a loud whisper broke the silence: "Close it, or you'll trap flies!" My face burned, but I couldn't stifle a giggle. Mrs. García closed her mouth and forgot about me for a moment.

"Who said that?" Everyone looked innocent, eyes cast down, lips fighting laughter. She grabbed me by the arm and dragged me to the door. "Get out! And tell your mother I need to speak to her."

Before she could push me, I pulled my arm from her grip and ran, not sure where I should go because the last thing I wanted to do was go home and tell Mami I'd been disrespectful to an adult. I dragged my feet down the dirt road, leaving my body behind, burying it in dust, while I floated in the tree-tops and watched myself from above, an insignificant creature that looked like a praying mantis in a green and yellow uniform. By the time I got home, I had decided to lie to Mami. If I told her the truth, she was sure to hit me, and I couldn't bear that humiliation on top of the other. When I came into the yard, my sisters and brother surrounded me, their curiosity comforting, as they pulled on my dirty clothes with remarks that I smelled bad.

"What happened to you?" Mami asked, all eyes. And all of a sudden I felt very sick. "I threw up in the lunchroom," I said, before falling into a faint that lasted so long that by the time I woke up from it, she had taken off my soiled uniform and washed me down with *alcoholado*.

For days I lay sick in bed, throwing up, racked by chills and sweats that left the bedcovers soaked and sent Delsa to sleep with Norma and Héctor, swearing that I was peeing on her. If Mrs. García ever talked to her, Mami never said anything. After what seemed like weeks, I went back to school, by which time the elections had been won, the breakfasts ceased, and my classmates had found someone else to tease.

WHY WOMEN REMAIN *JAMONA*

La verdad, aunque severa, es amiga verdadera.

❧

Truth, although severe, is a true friend.

One Sunday Mami starched and ironed my white piqué dress, packed a few changes of clothes in a small bag, and told me I was to spend a few days with Papi's mother.

"Your *abuela* is old, so you be a good helper," Mami told me as she braided my hair.

"How long will I be there?"

"About a week. Papi will take you, and he'll pick you up next Sunday. Don't look so worried. You'll have fun!"

Papi dressed in his best clothes, and while the day was still cool, we set out for Santurce. The *público* made many stops on the way, to pick up and drop off passengers, most of them, like us, dressed for a journey. When we reached Bayamón, the closest city to Macún, we had to change *públicos*. We were early, so we walked to the *plaza del mercado*. It was a square cement building with stalls along the walls and in the middle, forming a labyrinth of aisles dead-ending into kiosks with live chickens in wire cages, shelves of canned food, counters stacked high with *ñames* and *yautías*, coffee beans and breadfruit. Colored lights swung from the rafters where pigeons and warblers perched, forcing vendors to put up awnings against bird droppings.

"Are you hungry?" Papi asked, and I nodded, searching for the food stalls I smelled but could not see. We turned at the corner where a tall stack of rabbit hutches butted against a stack of dove cages.

"I smell *alcapurrias*," I said as Papi led me past a long table on which a tall gray woman arranged plaster heads of Jesus crowned with thorns, blood dripping into his upturned eyes, in an expression similar to the one Norma took on when she was annoyed. The woman set a Jesus down, her fingers caressing the thorns, and watched us, her long, mournful face horselike, her large eyes almond shaped, the corners pointing down as if weighed by many tears. The space around her felt cold, and I changed sides with Papi as we passed her on our way to the far end of the market, which was light and noisy with birds chirping overhead and a few well-placed speakers through which blared my favorite *chachachá*, "Black Eyes, Cinnamon Skin."

"What can I get you?" the counterman asked as he wiped in front of us with a rag that spread a thin film of grease on the Formica surface.

"Let me have a couple of those *alcapurrias* and two Coca-Colas," Papi said. "You do want a Coca-Cola, don't you?" he asked, and I nodded my head as I whirled on the stool, which rattled as it spun me faster and faster. Colors blended into one another in streaks of red, yellow, brown, and orange. Music came in and out of my ears, a syncopated half song that was familiar and foreign at the same time.

"You'd better stop that, or you'll hurt yourself."

I tried to brake the stool by sticking my leg out and hooking my foot on the one next to it. That threw me off balance and I fell, spinning to the ground. Papi was next to me in a flash.

"Are you okay?" he asked, but I felt heavy and light at the same time. My legs were wobbly, and when I looked around, there were two of everything. Two Papis and two of the gray woman next to him like shadows.

"She's all right," he said to her and drew me back to the stool. I was floating in a fog of colors and smells and warbling birds and voices singing, "I like you, and you, and you, and no one else but you, and you, and you."

"Jesus doesn't love children who don't behave," the gray woman said. Her voice crackled like a worn record. "And he will punish them."

"Just ignore her," the counterman said. "She's crazy." He set a hot *alcapurria* and a frosty Coca-Cola in front of me. "Leave my customers alone," he shouted at her and waved the greasy rag the way Don Berto used to wave his sharp *machete*.

"That's what happens to women when they stay *jamonas*," he said with a snort, and Papi laughed with him. The gray woman retreated to her bleeding heads.

"Papi, what's a *jamona*?" I asked as we left the market, our bellies full.

"It's a woman who has never married."

"I thought that was a *señorita*."

"It's the same thing. But when someone says a woman is *jamona* it means she's too old to get married. It's an insult."

"How come?"

"Because it means no one wants her. Maybe she's too ugly to get married. . . . Or she has waited too long. . . . She ends up alone for the rest of her life. Like that woman in the *mercado*."

"She was ugly, that's for sure."

"That's probably why she stayed *jamona*."

"I hope that never happens to me."

"No, that won't happen to you. . . . There's our *público*. Let's run for it."

We dodged across the street holding hands, avoiding cars, people, and stray dogs sunning themselves on the sidewalk.

"What do they call a man who never marries?" I asked as we settled ourselves in the front of the *público*.

"Lucky," the driver said, and the rest of the passengers laughed, which made me mad, because it felt as if he were insulting me in the worst possible way.

▶ "*¡Ay Santo Dios, bendícemela!*" Abuela hugged me and crossed herself. "She's so big!"

Her hands were large-knuckled, wrinkled; her palms the color and texture of an avocado pit. She rubbed my hair back and held my chin in her strong fingers.

"She looks just like you, Pablito," she told Papi, which made both of us feel good. "Look at the line of her hair. The same shape as yours. . . . A large forehead," she said as she led us into her house, "is a sign of intelligence."

"She's the best student in her class," Papi said, which wasn't entirely true. Juanita Marín was much smarter. "And you should hear her recite poetry!"

"Just like you, Pablito. You were always memorizing poems."

Abuela's house was two stories high and made of cement, with a front garden on which grew medicinal herbs and flowers. She and my grandfather, Don Higinio, lived on the ground floor, and her son Bartolo and his family lived upstairs. Abuela's Miami windows were draped with white crocheted curtains, as was the glass-topped table, the sofa, the doors to all the rooms, and all the beds and dressers. The tablecloth was bordered with yellow and brown pineapples. Red crocheted roses on bright green petals hemmed the doilies on the side tables.

Abuela fed us *sancocho*, a vegetable stew thickened with mashed tubers, with cornmeal dumplings floating on top. Papi and I sat at the table, while she drifted in and out of the kitchen bringing us food, water, a chunk of bread, and finally, a steaming cup of sweetened *café con leche*. As soon as we'd finished eating, Papi stood up from the table and stretched.

"I'd better get going, Mamá. It's a long way to Macún."

"But we just came, Papi. It doesn't take so long to get home. . . ."

"I have to see some people on the way," he snapped, his back to me. He unhooked his hat from the nail by the door, knelt in front of me, and pushed the hair off my forehead. His eyes had a peculiar expression, as if he were begging. He kissed and hugged me, and in his arms there was a plea. I was confused by the rage that thudded into my stomach like a fist. I was certain that he was not going home to Mami and my sisters and brothers and that somehow I had been used.

I didn't return his embrace. I stood stiff and solid, swallowing the bitter lump that had formed in my throat, and swore to myself I wouldn't cry, wouldn't beg him not to go, wouldn't even miss him when he left. I pulled out of his arms.

"Now, you be a good girl and do as Abuela tells you," he said, trying to sound stern. "I'll come get you next week."

I sat on the sofa, stuck my legs out in front of me, and studied the scabs on my shins, the brown scars of countless wounds and scrapes. "*Sí.*"

I felt his eyes on me and knew he knew I knew. He kissed Abuela's forehead. "Bless me, Mamá," he said in a near murmur. She touched his shoulder and mumbled softly, "May the Good Lord keep you on your journey, Son, and may He watch over you." She crossed the air in front of him and, without looking back, he left. She watched him go, her head shaking from side to side as if she felt sorry for him.

"Come, let me show you where you'll sleep," she said as she led me to the back of the house.

I followed Abuela into the room next to hers, where she had laid out fresh sheets and a pillow. The bed was large, covered with a crocheted spread on which two peacocks stood beak to beak. The drape covering the blinds also had peacocks on it, only they faced forward, their plumage spread into a thousand blue-green eyes that seemed to watch us.

"Change into something comfortable," she told me and showed me where to put my belongings. "I have some things to do in the kitchen."

When she was done, she sat on her rocking chair facing the door, took up a basket of crochet, and began working. She worked quietly. The needle flashed as her fingers flew in, around, and out. I could find nothing to do, so I sat on the sofa and watched, not daring to speak for fear I'd break her concentration. After a long time, she put the work in her basket, covered it with a cloth, and stood up from her chair, knees creaking.

"I'm going to say my prayers," she said. "If you get hungry, have some crackers from the tin." She disappeared into her room.

I sat on the stoop and watched the street beyond the garden fence. People came and went, dressed in their Sunday clothes, some looking as if they were going somewhere, others wrinkled and worn, as if they'd already been away and couldn't wait to get home. Every so often a car or truck rumbled up the hill, chased by scrawny dogs whose barks sounded hoarse and exhausted. Next door was a shack not much better than ours in Macún. My Aunt Generosa lived there with my cousins, most of whom were older than I was. I had met Titi Generosa when we lived in Santurce and liked the sound of her loud, coarse voice and the way she moved her hands when she spoke, as if she were kneading words.

As evening fell, the street slowed, and all life and sound came from inside, as if it were time for secrets. But nothing could remain private in the echoing treble of cement walls and ceilings. People talked, or fought, or sang *boleros* while they showered, and every sound was amplified in the cul-de-sac where Abuela's house sat. Spoons clanked against pots, and the street filled with the steamy smells of garlic, hot oil, and spices. Radios blared frenzied *merengues* from one house, while from another, an Evangelist exhorted his listeners to abandon their sinful lives and seek salvation in the arms of Jehovah, *Aleluya,* Amen!

I wondered where Papi had gone, who he had to see on a Sunday afternoon in San Juan. I remembered Margie and her mother and imagined them in New York, wearing beautiful clothes and eating bright yellow eggs. I mulled over Mami's words that men were always up to one *pocavergüenza* or another. That, Mami claimed in one of her bean-shucking discussions with Doña Lola, was men's nature. And Doña Lola had nodded and then shook her head so that I wasn't sure if she was agreeing with Mami or not.

I wondered if it were true, as Mami claimed when she and Papi fought, that he saw other women behind her back. And if he did, was it because he didn't love us? My eyes watered, my mouth filled with a salty taste, but if I cried, Abuela would hear me and think I didn't want to be with her. From the stoop, I could hear the rhythmic clicks of her rosary beads and the soft hum of her voice reciting prayers whose music was familiar to me, but whose words I'd never learned. And I wished that I knew how to pray, because then I could speak to God and maybe He or one of His saints could explain things to me. But I didn't know any prayers, because Mami didn't believe in churches or holy people, and Papi, even though he read the Bible and could lead novenas for the dead, never talked to us about God.

I determined not to cry, because if she asked me, I didn't want to tell Abuela why. But the pressure was too much, and as the tears came, I looked around for something with which to hurt myself so that when Abuela asked, I could show her a reason for the tears. I put my hand in the doorjamb and slammed the door shut.

The pain burned across my knuckles, through my fingers, and a scream, louder than I had intended, brought Abuela to my side. She hugged me, walked me to the sink, where she poured cool water over my hand, dried it with the soft hem of her dress, rubbed Vick's VapoRub on the pain, and held me against her bosom. She half carried me to her chair, pulled me onto her lap, and rocked me back and forth, back and forth, humming a lullaby I'd never heard.

∽ Later Abuela wrapped my hand in a white rag and tucked me into bed. She shuttered the house and, after making sure I was settled, went into her bedroom, where I heard her moving about, the springs of her bed creaking as she sat on it and got up again, sat, got up, until it seemed as if she were rocking herself to sleep.

My hand throbbed. I shushed the pain by rubbing the inside of my arm and told myself that next time I shouldn't slam the door so hard. The chinks on the window slats changed color, from russet to an intensely dark blue that deepened into impenetrable darkness, until it didn't matter if my eyes were open or closed. I dropped into a solid sleep unbroken by the distant sounds of cars and barking dogs, or the careful unlatching of the door when my grandfather came back in the middle of the night, fed himself from whatever was left in the kitchen, went into his own room, slept, and woke up and left before the sun rose. It was days before I realized he lived in the small room near the front door, the only room in the house unadorned by Abuela's crochet.

⮞ Abuelo slept in a narrow metal cot with a thin mattress wrapped in white sheets. There was a small table and a chair in his room, and on the wall a picture of Jesus wearing the same exasperated expression as the statues in the *mercado*, his wounded hands palm up as if he were saying, "Not again!" A coconut palm frond knotted into a cross was nailed above the picture.

By comparison, Abuela's room was opulent, with its double bed, thick mattress, four bedposts from which to tie the mosquito netting, pillows, and a small crocheted rug. Her dresser held a brush and comb, an altar to the Virgin and Child, a rosary, a Bible, candles, a missal, a small bottle filled with holy water, a picture of Papa Pío the Pope, and cards on which were printed prayers to saints with names like San Francisco, Santa Ana, Santa Bárbara, and San José. Papi had told me that Abuela didn't know how to read, and I wondered what words looked like to her. Did she recognize any of them? Or were they just a pattern, like crochet stitches?

After the first night, she closed the doors and windows right after supper but didn't make me go to bed. I stayed up reading the day-old newspaper Abuelo left behind or traced the flower patterns on paper napkins with a ballpoint pen.

One rainy afternoon Abuela pulled out her needlework basket. "Would you like to learn?" she asked timidly, as if she'd been working up the courage to ask.

"*Sí*, I would!" I had looked closely at the elaborate motifs of her tablecloths and doilies and had tried to draw them on lined notebook paper or on flattened grocery bags. I had sat mesmerized in the almost holy silence in which she worked, as she wove the needle in and out of stitches, forming pictures with thread.

She found a needle with a large hook and had me sit on the stoop, between her legs, so that she could look over my head and adjust my fingers as she helped me guide the thread in and out of the loops. She taught me how to count stitches, how to make chains that became rows, how to join rounds, when to fill in, and when to build space around stitches. After a while, I learned why the silence in which she worked seemed so magical. To crochet well, I had to focus on the work, had to count and keep track of when and where I increased or decreased stitches, and keep a picture in my head of what the finished cloth should look like, all the while estimating how much cotton thread it would take, and making sure when I ran out of one spool, that the other was joined in as seamlessly as possible. Sounds dwindled into dull, distant murmurs, backgrounds receded into a blur, and sensations waned as I slid under the hypnotic rhythm of a hook pulling up thread, the finished work growing into my palm until its very weight forced me to stretch it out on my lap and look, and admire, and be amazed at what my hands had made.

⚝ Abuelo was a quiet man who walked with his head down, as if he had lost something long ago and was still trying to find it. He had sparse white hair and eyes the color of turquoise. When he spoke, it was in a low rasp, in the *jíbaro* dialect, his lips in an apologetic half smile. His hands were rough, the nails yellowed and chipped, the fingertips scarred. He left the house before dawn, pushing before him a cart he had fashioned from pieces of plywood and bicycle parts. At the produce market he stacked a pyramid of oranges on the top and kept two more sackfuls in the cabinet underneath.

He spent his days at the corner of Calle San Cristóbal in Old San Juan, peeling oranges with his pocket knife and scooping out a triangular hole through which tourists could suck the sweet juice. Each orange brought him five cents. He slipped the nickels into his right-hand pocket, to jingle as he walked home at the end of the day, the pocket sagging against his thigh.

Evenings when I heard the rattle of his cart I ran out to open the garden gate for him, and each time, he searched the lower cabinet to see if he had any oranges left. There was always one in the farthest corner, and once he'd secured his cart against the side of the house, he sat on the stoop and peeled it for me in one long ribbon that curled and whirled and circled on itself orange, white, orange.

⮑ Sunday morning before breakfast Abuela handed me my piqué dress, washed and ironed.

"We're going to Mass," she said, pulling out a small white *mantilla*, which I was to wear during the service.

"Can we have breakfast first, Abuela. I'm hungry."

"No. We have to fast before church. Don't ask why. It's too complicated to explain."

I dressed and combed my hair, and she helped me pin the *mantilla* to the top of my head.

"All the way there and back," she said, "you should have nothing but good thoughts, because we're going to the house of God."

I'd never been to church and had never stopped to classify my thoughts into good ones and bad ones. But when she said that, I knew what she meant and also knew bad thoughts would be the only things on my mind all the way there and back.

I tried to look as holy as possible, but the white *mantilla* tickled my neck and the sides of my face. I wished I didn't have to wear it, and that was a bad thought, since all the women and girls walking in front of us wore theirs without any complaints.

I love my mother, my father, all my sisters and brothers, my *abuela* and *abuelo*, all my cousins, the governor of Puerto

Rico, Doña Lola, my teacher. A boy went by too fast and
bumped into me, so I bumped him back, and that was bad, because Jesus said we should turn the other cheek, which
seemed stupid, and there went another bad thought.

I counted all the squares on the sidewalk up to the steps of
the church, then I counted the steps, twenty-seven. No bad
thoughts.

The church was cool, dark, and sweet smelling. Abuela
dipped her fingers into a bowl at the entrance and crossed herself. I dipped my fingers, and there was nothing but water. I
tasted it, and she gave me a horrified look and crossed herself.
She took my hand and walked me down the aisle lined with
pews. When we came to the front, she half knelt, looking up to
the altar, and crossed herself again before sliding in to take
her seat. I did the same thing.

We were early. Music came from somewhere behind us.
When I turned around to see, Abuela leaned down and whispered, "Face forward. You should never look behind you in
church." I was about to ask why, but Abuela put her fingers to
her lips and shushed me as everyone stood up. I couldn't see
anything except the back of the man in front of me. He wore a
wrinkled brown suit that stretched into folds around his waist
because he was so fat. That must have been a bad thought.

The church's windows were of colored glass, each window a
scene with Jesus and his cross. The two I could see without
turning my head were beautiful, even though Jesus looked like
He was in a lot of pain. The priest said something, and everyone knelt. The altar had an enormous Jesus on his cross at the
center, the disciples at his feet. Tall candles burned in steps
from the rear of the altar to the front, where the priest, dressed
in purple and yellow robes, moved his hands up and down
and recited poetry that everyone in the church repeated after
him. Two boys wearing white lace tunics helped him, and I
was jealous, because their job seemed very important. Envy, I
knew, was a bad thought.

I counted the times people stood up, knelt down, stood up.
That didn't seem right. I shouldn't be in church counting

things. I should feel holy, blessed. But I got an itch in the space between my little toe and the sole of my foot. I scraped my shoe against the kneeling bench on the floor. The itch got worse. We knelt again, so I leaned back and took the shoe off to scratch my foot. But I had to get up, because the person next to me wanted to get through. And other people in the same pew got up and squeezed past me, kicking my shoe toward the aisle in the process. Abuela leaned down. "I'm going to take communion. You wait right here."

As soon as she was gone, I slid over to the end of the pew and looked up the aisle. No shoe. I felt for it with my foot all along under the pew but couldn't find it. It was wrong to look back in church, so it seemed that it would be worse to look down. But I didn't want Abuela to come back and find me with one shoe missing.

The people who went up to the altar knelt in front of the priest so he could put something into their mouths. As soon as Abuela knelt, I dove under the pew and looked for my shoe. It was under the pew behind us so I crawled under ours, over the kneeling bench, and stretched to get the shoe. I crawled up just as Abuela came down the aisle. I knelt piously, my hands in prayer, and stared in front of me, trying to look like I was having nothing but the very best thoughts. Abuela went into the pew in front of me, looked over, seemed confused, got out, then knelt next to me. "How foolish. I thought we were one pew up," she whispered.

When everyone had come back, I realized the man with the wrinkled brown suit was two pews up, and I looked up at Jesus on his cross and prayed, "Please, Jesus, don't let her find out I moved during the service." Which I knew was a bad thought.

❧ I packed my clothes and put the doily I had made for Mami into a corner of my small bag. Abuela made fish head soup with plantain dumplings, and we ate some for lunch.

"Don't take your dress off," she said. "When he comes to pick you up, Pablito might be in a hurry to get back."

But Papi didn't come. Sunday stretched long and hot, through *siesta* time. Abuela made coffee in the late afternoon, and we sat at the table with a stack of soda crackers.

"He'll probably come for dinner," she said. But the blue haze of evening shrouded the street, stifled sounds, and sent everyone indoors to their secrets, and Papi didn't come. Abuela went in to say her prayers. "He must have been held up. Why don't you change into something comfortable."

I took off my white piqué dress, which was no longer clean and starched. I thought, The minute I change clothes he's going to show up. But he didn't, and when Abuela came out from her prayers, we sat by the door, working our needles in, around, up, and out, silently making patterns with thread that might have told a story had either one of us known how to transform our feelings into shape.

Instead, she worked an altar cloth she'd promised Father David, and I added red flowers to the doily I'd made for Mami. And neither one of us said what we both knew. That Papi wasn't coming. That perhaps the person he had to see the Sunday before needed him again, and he went there, and maybe that person needed him so much that he had forgotten about us, just like he sometimes forgot about Mami chasing after babies in Macún. We worked our crochet until it was too dark to see, until after Abuelo had brought his cart into the yard and tied it up against the fence, until he'd peeled an orange in one long ribbon, until we'd closed up the house and gone into our separate rooms and had wrapped ourselves in the white cotton sheets edged with crocheted scallops.

And I thought about how many nights Mami had left food warming on the ashes of the *fogón*, how often she'd sat on her rocking chair, nursing a baby, telling us to be still, that Papi would be coming any minute, but in the morning he wasn't there and hadn't been. I thought about how she washed and pressed his clothes until they were new-looking and fresh, how he didn't have to ask where anything was because nothing he ever wore stayed dirty longer than it took Mami to scrub it against the metal ripples of the washboard, to let it dry in the sun so that it smelled like air. I wondered if Mami felt the way I was feeling at this moment on those nights when she slept on their bed alone, the springs creaking as she wrestled with some nightmare, or whether the soft moans I heard coming from their side of the room were stifled sobs, like the ones that now pressed against my throat, so that I had to bury my face in the pillow and cry until my head hurt.

  Every night, right after dinner, Abuela slipped into her room, put on a faded green nightgown embroidered with small yellow flowers, and undid her hair. Two twisted ropes of hair fell past her knees, one over each shoulder. She combed first one side, then the other, loosening the ropes into strands of white, gray, and a few black hairs, her fingers weaving in and out of them until each side looked like a serene waterfall against a pale forest.

"Our Father, who art in heaven . . . ," I repeated after Abuela.

"Hallowed be thy name . . ."

"What does that mean?"

She raked her fingers through her hair, fluffing it, untangling the knots. "It means His name is holy."

"Hallowed be thy name . . ."

"Thy kingdom come . . ." Abuela fed me the prayer in short phrases that echoed the rhythm I'd heard when Papi led novenas and when she clicked her beads at night before bed. It was like learning a song. If I left something out, the rhythm didn't work.

"Give us this day our daily bread. . . ." I imagined a long loaf of *pan de agua*, the kind the baker made with a coconut frond down the center of its crunchy crust.

"And forgive us our trespasses . . ."

"What does that mean?"

"We're asking God to forgive any sins we might commit by mistake."

"Forgive us our trespasses . . ."

"And lead us not into temptation . . ." She didn't wait for me to ask: "That means we're asking God to keep us from sinning."

When I'd repeated the prayer several times and could recite most of it without stumbling, she taught me how to cross myself.

"Cross your thumb over your pointing finger, like this. . . . No, not with that hand. . . . You must always use your right hand," she said, holding it out to make sure I knew the difference.

"Why?"

"Because the left hand is the hand of the Devil."

I wondered if that meant the Devil had two left hands but didn't dare ask because just saying the word *Devil* made Abuela drop her voice into a near whisper, as if the Devil were in the next room.

"Then you go straight down to your heart. . . . Then across . . . No, this side first." I'd seen women cross themselves so many times, it had never occurred to me there was a right way and a wrong way to do it. "Then you kiss the cross on your fingers." I did as she showed me. "You must always cross yourself before and after saying the Lord's Prayer. Let me see if you can say the whole thing."

I tried to look grave, eyes down, face expressionless, the way people in *velorios* looked when Papi led them in prayer. I lowered my voice to a near mumble, quieted my lips until they barely moved, and let the rhythm guide the words out and up to the sky where Abuela said Papa Dios, my other Father, lived.

❧ "¡*Hola, Negrita*!" Mami wore a printed dress she called a muumuu, which stretched across her pregnant belly like a round plot of exotic flowers. I couldn't get enough of her to hug, so I clung to her hand as she huffed up the three steps into Abuela's house. "How are you, Doña Margara?" she asked cheerily, as if she knew the answer.

"Oh, I'm fine, *m'hija*, just fine," Abuela said, pulling out a chair for Mami to sit in. "How about some lemonade?"

"Wonderful!" Mami's cheeks were flushed, partly from the hot walk down the street, partly because she'd colored them. Her hair was twisted up and held with pins that she kept pushing in so they wouldn't fall out.

"I hope you don't mind that I came to bring Negi home. I've missed her." Now that she was sitting, I could hug her around the neck, kiss her soft, powdered face, smell the fruity perfume she put on for special occasions.

"I missed you too, Mami." I whispered, and she pulled me close and kissed the top of my head.

Abuela brought in a pitcher of lemonade and three glasses. "I thought Pablito was coming on Sunday. We waited all afternoon. . . ."

Mami's face flashed into the hard expression I'd come to expect when she talked about Papi. "You know how he is," she said to his mother.

Abuela nodded and poured us lemonade. "Who's watching the children?"

"My neighbor's daughter."

"Who?" I asked. Mami turned to me as if she'd just remembered who I was.

"Gloria." She sipped her drink. "Guess what? We have electricity!"

"Really?"

"Yes! We only use the *quinqués* if the lights go out." She turned to Abuela. "Which is every time the wind blows hard." They laughed.

I leaned against Mami and sipped my drink, listening to them talk about people whose names were familiar, but whom I hadn't met—Flor, Concha, Chía, Cándida, Lalo. They talked about whose daughter had run off with whose son, who'd had babies, who had died, the price of groceries, the hot weather, the rickety buses between San Juan and Santurce. They talked as if they were good friends, and I wondered how that could be since they seldom saw each other. They came back to the subject of Macún, how things seemed to be better now that we had electricity and running water was weeks away.

"Of course," Mami said, "with Pablo gone all the time it's hard to know . . ." Her face darkened again. She looked down at the floor, rubbed circles on her belly. The silence around her was total, not rich and full like Abuela's when she crocheted, but empty and sad and lonesome.

"Negi," Abuela said, "go take a shower and get ready so that your mother doesn't have to wait for you." I didn't want to leave Mami, but Abuela's eyes were stern, and with her head, she signaled in the direction of the bathroom.

I set my glass down and went. Although I leaned against the bathroom door, trying to hear what they said, I only caught snatches: "always been that way . . . ," "upsets the kids . . . ," "think of yourself . . ," "alone with children . . . ," "make it work . . . ," "don't know how. . . ." And, in a louder voice, "Negi, why don't we hear water running?"

I opened the faucets and let cool water wash over me, wishing it could melt away the fear that made the thumps of my heart louder than usual. When I came out, my hair dripping, the tips of my fingers wrinkled, Mami and Abuela still sat across from each other. Abuela's face was sad, and she looked older, as if years, rather than minutes, had passed since I last saw her. Mami's rouge was streaked, and her eyes were swollen. She pretended to smile, and I pretended not to see it as I went by wrapped in a towel, stepping lightly, as if the floor would break under my weight.

I dressed to their murmurs in the other room, their voices soft but strained, and I wondered if men ever talked like this, if their sorrows ever spilled into these secret cadences. I combed my hair, put on my socks, buckled my leather shoes. And still they talked, and I couldn't understand a word they said. But their pain bounced off the walls and crawled under my skin, where it settled like prickly bristles.

It seemed to me then that remaining *jamona* could not possibly hurt this much. That a woman alone, even if ugly, could not suffer as much as my beautiful mother did. I hated Papi. I sat on the bed in his mother's house and wished he'd die, but as soon as the thought flashed, I slapped my face for thinking such a thing. I packed my bag and stepped into the room where Mami and Abuela sat. When they looked up at me, it seemed as if we were all thinking the same thing. I would just as soon remain *jamona* than shed that many tears over a man.

MAMI GETS
A JOB

Con el agua al cuello y la marea subiendo

❧

With water to the chin and the tide rising

The sky fell to the tops of the mountains. The air hung heavy, moist. Birds left the *barrio*, and insects disappeared into hidden cracks and crevices, taking their songs. A cowboy rounded up the cattle in Lalao's *finca*, and on her side of the fence, Doña Ana led her cow to the shack behind her house. The radio said Hurricane Santa Clara was the biggest threat to Puerto Rico since San Felipe had destroyed the island in 1918.

"Papi, why do they name hurricanes after saints?" I asked as I helped him carry a sheet of plywood he was going to nail against the windows of our house.

"I don't know," he answered. The hurricane warning must have been serious if Papi couldn't stop to talk about it.

Mami bundled our clothes, pushed her rocking chair, the table and stools, her sewing machine, and the pots and pans into a corner, tied everything to the socles, pressed it all against the strongest wall of the house, and covered it with a sheet, as if that would keep everything from being blown away.

"Negi, take the kids to Doña Ana's. We'll be there in a while."

I rounded up Delsa, Norma, Héctor, Alicia, and Edna. For once I didn't have to chase them all over the place, didn't have to threaten, yell, or pull their ears for ignoring me. They lined up solemn as soldiers, Alicia and Héctor hanging on to Norma's hand, Edna on Delsa's hip. The baby was asleep in his hanging cradle, but Mami took him out, bundled him in flannel sheets, and handed him to me.

"Take Raymond. Make sure no drafts get to him."

The baby was thirty days old, and we had to be careful about infections, foul breezes, and the evil eye. Mami had strung a nugget of coral and an onyx bead on a safety pin and attached it to Raymond's baby shirt at birth. It was the same charm she had used on all of us, kept in a little box among her thimbles and needles between babies, to be brought out and pinned to the tiny cotton shirts, supposedly for the first forty days and forty nights of our lives. She claimed she didn't believe "any of that stuff," but each time, the charm stayed on long after it was supposed to.

We trudged single file along the path connecting our yard with Doña Ana's. Her sons had nailed plywood sheets to the windows and along the front of her house, so that the only way in was the back door leading to the latrine, barn, and pigsty. These structures had also been reinforced with plywood, and debarked tree limbs buttressed every wall. As we passed from the barn, we heard the muffled and frightened moo of the cow, the frantic squealing of pigs, and the rustle and cackle of hens and roosters.

Inside the house, every crack and chink had been plugged with rags to keep the wind out. Mattresses were stacked, bunches of green bananas hung from the rafters, the gash where the machete had cut dripped white sticky ooze onto the floor. The room was shadowy, lit with *quinqués* and fat candles, steamy with the fragrance of garlic and onions. Several old hens had been sacrificed and everyone contributed something to the communal meal that would be cooked on our kerosene stove, spiced with Doña Lola's fresh oregano, and shared by the four families who would pass the hurricane in Doña Ana's one-room cement house.

Papi and Mami brought in bundles of food, clothes, blankets, and baby diapers. Papi put his battery-operated radio on a shelf and kept it tuned the whole time the hurricane blew, even though all we heard was static. Although Doña Ana's house was no bigger than ours, its sturdy concrete walls and roof made it safe and cozy. The warmth of the thirty or so people inside, the familiar aroma of spices and good cooking, and the hushed play of children was extraordinarily comforting, the way wakes were, or weddings or baptisms.

The men set up a domino table and took turns playing, the losers giving up their chairs to the ones waiting their turn. The women cut up chickens, peeled plantains, cubed potatoes, made *sofrito*, washed dishes, brewed coffee, and tended babies. The *muchachas* huddled in a giggly group between the plantains and the mattresses, while the *muchachos* crouched against the wall opposite, pretending to play cards. We kids played among ourselves or circulated among the various groups, observing the domino game, snatching boiled chicken hearts or livers, carrying mysterious messages from the older boys to the older girls.

Every so often a thump quieted everyone, and arguments erupted about which tree had fallen in which direction. The cows and pigs couldn't be heard above the roar of the wind, the thunder, the crashing zinc sheets from less sturdy roofs, and the flying outhouses lifted in one piece by the wind and swept from one end of the *barrio* to the other.

After we had our *asopao* with plantain dumplings, we curled against one another on the mattresses and slept, lulled by the crackling radio inside and the steady gusts of the hurricane outside.

We heard the ominous quiet of the hurricane's eye as it passed over us. Papi and Dima, Doña Ana's son, pried the door open a crack. It was raining lightly, gray misty drops like steam. The men stepped outside one at a time, looked around, up to the sky, down to the soaked ground that turned into muddy pools wherever their feet had sunk. The women clustered at the door, forming a wall through which we children couldn't pass, although we managed to catch a glimpse by pressing against their hips and thighs, crouching under their skirts, between their legs, against their round calves striated with varicose veins and dark, curly hair.

Mist hung over the yard littered with branches, odd pieces of lumber, a tin washtub that seemed to have been crushed by a giant, and the carcass of a cow, with a rope around her neck still tied to a post. Doña Ana's barn still stood, and the animals inside whimpered softly, as if their normal voices would make the wind start up again. The men walked the edges of the yard in a semicircle, their hands outstretched like the stiff figures I liked to cut from folded newspapers.

A sliver of sun broke through like a spotlight and travelled slowly across the yard, forming a giant rainbow. The women pointed and held up the smaller children to see, while those of us big enough to stand by ourselves crowded the door in awe of that magic spectacle: the figures of our fathers and brothers moving cautiously in a world with no edges, no end, and that bright slice of sun travelling across it, not once touching them.

ℝ "We had eleven avocado trees and nine mango trees," Mami was saying. "Now there's only the two avocados and three mangos left."

"My entire coffee patch washed right off the hill." Doña Lola spit into the yard. "And you can see what it did to my medicinal herbs. . . . Even the weeds are gone."

Doña Lola's house, nestled at the side of the mountain, had been spared, but the adjoining kitchen had disappeared, except for the three stones of her *fogón*. Our outside kitchen, too, had flown away, as had our latrine. The whole *barrio* had been stripped of anything too flimsy, too old, or too weak to withstand the winds and rain that had pelted the island for hours, flooding towns and washing downhill entire communities built along the craggy slopes. No one in Macún died, but many lost their belongings, poultry, pigs, milk cows, vegetable gardens, kiosks for selling fried codfish fritters, and shops where rusty old cars received one more chance at the road.

"Pablo said the government will help rebuild . . ."

"¡Sí, cuando las gallinas meen!" Doña Lola laughed, and Mami chuckled, her eyes twinkling at me to see if I understood what Doña Lola meant by "when hens learn to pee." I'd been around enough hens to know they never would.

Papi and Uncle Cándido repaired our house, replaced parts of the roof, extended the house to incorporate a kitchen and a site for a bathroom, anticipating the day when water would be piped down the hill to our end of the *barrio*. They rebuilt the latrine with shiny zinc walls and added a new, more comfortable seat. Mami propped up her pigeon pea and annatto bushes, which had been flattened by the storm, and soon they bloomed again, their leaves as new and fresh as babies.

🠧 For months after the hurricane all people talked about was money. Money for the cement and cinder blocks that rose out of the ground in solid, grey walls and flat square roofs. Money for another cow, or a car, or zinc for the new outhouse. Money to install water pipes, or to repair the electric wires that had gone down in the storm and hung like limp, useless, dried-up worms.

Even children talked about money. We scoured the side of the road for discarded bottles to exchange for pennies when the glass man came around. Boys no older than I nailed together boxes out of wood scraps, painted them in bright colors, and set off for San Juan or Río Piedras, where men paid ten cents for a shoeshine. Papi made *maví*, bark beer, and took two gallons with him to the construction sites where he worked, to sell by the cup to his friends and passersby. Even Doña Lola, who seemed as self-sufficient as anyone could be in Macún, cooked huge vats of rice and beans to sell in the refillable aluminum canisters called *fiambreras* that men took to work when their jobs were not near places to eat. Mami talked about sewing school uniforms and actually made a few. But she soon realized that the amount of work she put into them was more than she was paid for and abandoned the idea while she thought of something else.

🠧 "Negi, help me over here."

Mami stood in the middle of the room, her dress bunched on her hips, hands holding fast a long-line brassiere that didn't want to contain her. "See if you can catch the hooks into the eyes, all the way up."

The cotton brassiere stretched down to her hipbones, where it met the girdle into which she had already squeezed. There were three columns of eyes for the hooks spaced evenly from top to bottom. Even when I tugged on both ends of the fabric, I had trouble getting one hook into an outermost eye.

"It's too small. I can't get them to meet."

"I'll hold my breath." She took in air, blew it out, and stretched her spine up. I worked fast, hooking her up all the way before she had to breathe again in big, hungry gulps.

"Wow! It's been a while since I wore this thing," she said, pulling her dress up. "Zip me up?"

"Where are you going?"

"There's a new factory opening in Toa Baja. Maybe they need people who can sew."

"Who's going to take care of us?"

"Gloria will be here in a little while. You can help her with the kids. I've already made dinner."

"Will you work every day?"

"If they hire me."

"So you won't be around all the time."

"We need the money, Negi."

Mami twisted and sprayed her hair, powdered her face, patted rouge on already pink cheeks, and spread lipstick over already red lips. Her feet, which were usually bare, looked unnatural in high heels. Her waist was so pinched in, it seemed as if part of her body were missing. Her powdered and painted features were not readable; the lines she'd drawn on her eyebrows and around her eyes and the colors that enhanced what always seemed perfect were a violation of the face that sometimes laughed and sometimes cried and often contorted with rage. I wanted to find a rag and wipe that stuff off her face, the way she wiped off the dirt and grime that collected on mine. She turned to me with a large red smile.

"What do you think?"

I was ashamed to look, afraid to speak what I saw.

"Well?" She put her hands on her hips, that familiar gesture of exasperation that always made her seem larger, and I saw the unnatural diamond shape formed by her elbows and narrowed waist. I couldn't help the tears that broke my face into a million bits, which made her kneel and hold me. I wrapped my arms around her, but what I felt was not Mami but the harsh bones of her undergarments. I buried my face in the soft space between her neck and shoulder and sought there the fragrance of oregano and rosemary, but all I could come up with was Cashmere Bouquet and the faint flowery dust of Maybelline.

❧ She woke early, sometimes even before Papi, cooked the beans and rice for our supper, ironed our school uniforms and her work clothes, and bathed, powdered, and stuffed herself into her tortuous undergarments. In whispers, she gave me instructions for the day, told me when she'd be back, warned me to help Gloria with the children, promised to sew the buttons on Héctor's shirt when she came home that night.

Papi was not around as much once Mami began work, and our mornings took on a rhythm that left him out the days he was home, each one of us engaged in our own morning rituals of waking, dressing, eating breakfast, and walking the two miles to school. My classes began the earliest, at 7:30, and I left home while the air was still sweet and the ground moist, our neighbors' houses looming like ghosts in light fog or receding behind greyness when it rained.

My Uncle Cándido's house was halfway to school. He complained to Mami that I never looked up when I went by, never greeted anyone, never looked anywhere but down at the ground.

"If you keep walking like that," he said, "you'll develop a hunchback."

But that threat wasn't enough to keep me from wrapping my arms around myself. Books pressed against my chest, I strode head down, looking closely at the way the ground swelled and dipped, listening to the crunch of my hard school shoes on the pebbled stretches and their swish on the sandy patches. And when I didn't look at the ground, I was blind and would sometimes get to school and not know how. On those mornings my eyes closed in on me and showed me pictures inside my head, while my legs moved on their own up the hills, down the ruts, through the weeds, across gullies, between the aisles of my schoolmates' desks and to my own, alphabetically in the rear of the classroom. I'd sit down, open my notebook, write the date at the top of the page, and look up to Miss Jiménez and her cheery "*Buenos días, clase.*" I would then realize I'd come all the way to school with no memory of the journey, my mind a blank slate on which I would write that day's lessons.

❧ With Mami at work, I took advantage of Gloria's vigilance with the younger kids to make my own getaway into the *montes*, up trees, behind sheds and outhouses, and once, on a dare, into Lalao's *finca*, where I filled the skirt of my dress with the coveted grapefruits.

"Where did these come from?" Mami asked when she came home from work.

"I found them," I said.

"No, she didn't. She sneaked into Lalao's *finca* with Tato and Pepito." Delsa smirked, and Mami's eyes disappeared behind a frown.

"Haven't I told you not to go in there?"

"They were on the ground, just on the other side of the fence. . . ."

She looked at the grapefruits, green speckled with yellow and tiny black dots. Their citrus fragrance filled the room like smoke.

"Don't go in there again," she said, picking one up, "or I'll really let you have it."

She peeled one in long strips and sucked on the sweet juice hungrily. I sought Delsa's eyes and saw fear, not of Mami but of me, because Delsa knew that while Mami was at work the next day, I'd get her for tattling.

❧ One morning Mami cooked our dinner, left everything ready for Gloria, dressed, and got us off to school one at a time. When I came home, she was still there, her work clothes stretched on the bed, rumpled and forgotten.

"Where's Gloria?" I asked.

"She escaped," Mami said, which meant that Gloria had eloped. No girl ever ran away by herself, although boys disappeared for weeks the minute they thought of themselves as men.

"Is she coming back?"

"I don't know. No one knows the man she ran off with."

Mami couldn't go to work for a couple of weeks, and we had to live with her bad temper and complaints. "I'm not the kind of person to sit around doing nothing," she said to Doña Ana, and I wondered how she could think of her housework as nothing when she spent hours doing it.

* "So how do you like the factory?" Doña Lola asked Mami as we shucked pigeon peas in her new kitchen.

"It's good work," Mami answered, pride in her voice. "I started as a thread cutter, and now I'm a sewing machine operator."

"¡*Qué bueno*!"

Doña Lola's son Tato ran into the kitchen. "Is there anything to eat?"

"Rice and beans in the pot."

Tato rattled lids and dropped a spoon on the new cement floor. Doña Lola stood up with a jerk. "Let me serve you," and under her breath, "Men are so useless."

Tato looked at me from beneath his long lashes. Doña Lola handed him a tin plate mountained with white rice and red beans. He sat in the corner, spooning it in as if he hadn't eaten in a week.

He was a year older than I, skinny, brown as a chocolate bar, his hair orange, his hazel eyes full of mischief and laughter. He was the dirtiest boy I'd ever seen, not because he didn't wash, but because he couldn't stay clean no matter how many times Doña Lola dunked him in the tin tub in back of the house.

Tato was not afraid of anything. He caught bright green lizards, pinched their jaws at the side, and forced them to bite his earlobes, to which they clung like festive, squirming decorations. He trapped snakes and draped them around his neck, where they writhed in sumptuous silvery waves that seemed to tickle. He speared iguanas and roasted them on open fires, claiming that their meat was tastier than chicken. He was an expert slingshot maker, and it was he who taught me to choose the forked branches that we stripped of bark, dried in the sun, and carved until we could tie split inner tube strips and a rubber square that held the lethal stones we shot with uncanny accuracy.

I was as good as he with both slingshots and painstakingly constructed bows and arrows, with which I could drop birds in flight. We had an uneasy, competitive friendship, made more special by the fact that Mami didn't approve.

"You're almost *señorita*. You shouldn't be running wild with boys," she'd tell me. But I didn't have anything in common with the girls my age. Juanita Marín had found more kindred friendships at her end of the *barrio*, and Doña Zena's daughters, who were about my age, were kept on a tight leash because of their parents' religiosity, which didn't allow for outside influences. My sisters close to my age were not as interesting as the neighborhood boys who ran and climbed and didn't mind getting dirty.

Tato put his dish and spoon in the dishwater. "Let's go play outside." His small, dirty face betrayed no hint of what we were really going to do.

"Can I Mami?"

She cracked the tip off a pod, pulled the string, snapped the casing open, slid her thumb inside the slithery shell, and added the peas to the mound in the bowl between her knees. She looked at me with a warning. "Don't go too far. We're going home soon."

I thought maybe she had read our minds, and for a minute I was afraid to go with him.

"Come on!" Tato called from the yard.

I backed out of the kitchen, but Mami and Doña Lola had gone back to their shucking. We ran around the yard a couple of times to throw them off then sneaked into the oregano bushes that grew thick and fragrant behind the outhouse.

"You first," he said.

"No way! You first."

He pulled down his shorts and just as quickly pulled them up. "Your turn," he said.

"I didn't see anything!"

"Yes you did!"

"I didn't. And I'm not going to show you mine until I do!"

Although I'd seen both Héctor's and Raymond's penises when I changed their diapers, I'd never seen one outside the family. Tato had no sisters, so I was pretty sure he'd never seen a girl's private parts. I, of course, had seen several of those, too.

"Well, I'm not pulling my pants down again!" Tato said walking away.

"Fine. I don't have to see your silly old little chicken, I've seen my brothers', and I bet they're nicer than yours."

"Those are baby *pollitos*. I'm already big. Mine has hair on it!"

"Oh, sure!"

"It does. And it gets so big, it can already go into a woman."

"You're disgusting!"

"I can get it into a woman and wiggle it around and around, like this." He wriggled his finger in arches that circumscribed a space much larger than his hand, at the same time wiggling his hips in figure eights.

"You're sick!" I ran into Doña Lola's yard just as Mami came out.

"I was coming to find you," she said, looking behind me. Tato watched us from the path into the bushes. "Grab that bag. We're going home."

Doña Lola handed me a sackful of pigeon peas.

"Tato, go and feed those pigs! They've been squealing all afternoon." He ran off, and Mami led the way up the road to our house.

"What were you two doing in back of the outhouse?" she asked casually.

"Just playing." I hoped she hadn't heard us talking. She didn't say any more, and I took the shortcut home, through the yucca plants, past the barren mango tree at the edge of Lalao's *finca*.

➤ Another day Tato and I were behind the latrine.

"I can see it better if you squat," Tato said, crouching in front of me to get a better look at the smooth slit between my legs.

"Forget it!" I pulled up my panties.

"But it's not fair. You saw mine real good!"

"*Sí*. And you lied. There's no hair on it at all."

"You didn't look close enough."

"There was nothing to see. It's just as shrivelled and small as my baby brother's."

"You have to rub it to make it big."

"No way am I touching your dirty little *pollito*!"

"It'll grow big and long, you'll see!"

"No way!"

"I'll touch you if you touch me."

"I don't want you to touch me!"

"It feels good." He rubbed his crotch as if he had an itch. He thrust his hips out toward me. "Oooh, it's so good. . . . Mmmm!" He closed his eyes and smacked his lips like he was eating the sweetest candy.

I stared at him writhing, his tongue flicking in and out of his mouth, foamy spit at the corners, his eyes rolling in his head, his hands moving faster and faster. "Men are such pigs!" The words flashed into my head like the headline on a newspaper, only I heard it too, in the voices of Mami and Doña Lola, Gloria and Doña Ana, Abuela, *bolero* singers, radio soap opera actresses, and my own shrill scream into Tato's face.

"¡*Cochino*!" Pig! His eyes popped open, and his mouth dropped into a grimace that became a lewd, ugly, humiliating smile. He tried to grab between my legs, and, enraged, I drew back my foot and kicked as hard as I could so that it seemed that I lifted him on my shin before he crumpled to the ground, hands between his legs, no longer rubbing but holding fast to what I was afraid had come loose.

Mami and Doña Lola came running. Between sobs, Tato told them I had kicked him for no reason at all, and Mami dragged me home, her fingers pinching my bony arm.

I screamed, trying to explain what Tato had tried to do. But Mami wouldn't listen. I pulled loose and ran, and she chased me into our yard and through the house. On the way out the kitchen door, she grabbed a frying pan and thwacked my head. She tied my wrists together in one of her strong hands, and beat me, again and again, raising welts on my arms, my back, the back of my head, my forehead, behind my ear. My sisters and brothers came out from wherever they'd been playing, even Raymond who had just learned to walk, and they watched as Mami lifted the pan over her head and let it fall on the ball I had become, hanging from her hand like an unripe fruit on an unbending tree.

"Don't you ever, ever do that again," she growled, and I wasn't sure if she meant kicking a boy between his legs or letting him see my private parts. Because it seemed to me she knew what Tato and I did behind the latrine while she and Doña Lola talked about their lives. She knew, and she was waiting for me to do something worse than what I could imagine so that she could do something far worse than what I would expect. I let my body go limp to take her abuse, and part of me left my body and stood beside my sisters and brothers, their eyes round, tear filled, frightened, their fingers interlaced into each other's, their skinny bodies jerking with every hit I took.

* * *

❧ Gloria came back to live in a neat wood house in the middle of a coconut grove behind her mother's property. Her *marido* was from a nearby *barrio* and worked for the electric company.

"Maybe now," Mami joked, "we'll get light back in Macún."

As soon as Gloria returned, Mami unfolded her work clothes, washed her hair, and polished her shoes. But instead of Gloria coming to our house every morning, we now went to her shady house under the palms.

One day she handed me a small paper bag, tightly packed with something soft. "Throw this into the latrine, would you please?"

"What is it?"

"Nothing that concerns you."

"Then why should I throw it out?"

"Are you this mouthy all the time or just with me?"

"All the time."

"I figured. Take the thing out and I'll tell you about it when you come back."

I was tempted to open the bag and look inside, but she kept her eye on me as she changed Raymond's diaper. When I looked down the hole of the latrine I noticed a couple of little bags like the one I held floating on the dark smelly waste at the bottom.

"Okay, I threw it out." She put Raymond and Edna down for their afternoon *siesta*. The air was light, breezy, aromatic of guavas, which grew in tall bushes along the side of her house. "What was inside the bag?"

"A Kotex."

"What's that?"

She poured water into a bowl and salted it generously. "How old are you?"

"Ten."

She grabbed two green plantains from a high shelf and brought them to the table. "And Doña Monín hasn't told you about being a *señorita*?"

"She told me I should stop playing with boys because I'm

almost *señorita*, and that I should keep my legs closed when I sit."

Gloria laughed so hard she almost dropped the knife she found near the *fogón*.

"What's so funny?" I was embarrassed and pleased. Clearly there was a lot more to this *señorita* business, and Gloria knew what it was. I laughed with her, sensing she was about to tell me something my mother was supposed to but hadn't.

"Do you know where babies come from?"

"Everybody knows that!"

"Do you know how they're made?"

I'd seen roosters chase hens, catch up, climb on top of them, and dig sharp beaks into the hen's head as she cackled and screeched and he flapped his wings. I'd seen male dogs chase females, the male climb on top of the female, ride her while she tried to shake him off, and dig his narrow pink penis into her backside. I'd seen bulls ride cows, horses hump mares, pigs rolling in mud, their bodies connected under the female's tail. And I'd seen eggs laid, bloody puppies wet and shimmery, calves encased in a blue bubble, slippery wet ponies thin and vulnerable, and hundreds of pink piglets suckling engorged teats. But until Gloria asked, I'd never put it together that in order for me and my four sisters and two brothers to be born, Papi had to do to Mami what roosters did to hens, bulls did to cows, horses did to mares. I shuddered.

"Yes, I know how babies are made."

Gloria slit a plantain from tip to tip, peeled the casing back, and cut diagonal slices which she dipped in the salted water.

"Before you can make babies, you have to be a *señorita*, which means you bleed once a month." Gloria then explained what a period was, how long it lasted, what a woman had to do so her clothes wouldn't get soiled. "Very soon you will be a *señorita*," she said, "and then you have to keep your legs crossed, just like your Mami says, all the time." She laughed at her own joke, which didn't seem so funny to me. "Ay, you're so solemn! I must have scared you. Don't worry, it's nothing. Just a nuisance you learn to live with. Every woman does."

But I wasn't worried about my period, which couldn't possibly be worse than the worms I'd found in my panties. I imagined Mami and Papi, in bed, stuck together in the middle. I remembered Tato's words that he could stick his penis in a woman, and I realized that's what Papi did to Mami after we'd all gone to sleep and the springs on their bed creaked in rhythms that always ended in a long, low moan, like a moo, or a hoarse whimper.

ʃ Mami was one of the first mothers in Macún to have a job outside the house. For extra money women in the *barrio* took in laundry or ironing or cooked for men with no wives. But Mami left our house every morning, primped and perfumed, for a job in a factory in Toa Baja.

The *barrio* looked at us with new eyes. Gone was the bland acceptance of people minding their own business, replaced by a visible, angry resentment that became gossip, and taunts and name-calling in the school yard.

I got the message that my mother was breaking a taboo I'd never heard about. The women in the neighborhood turned their backs on her when they saw her coming, or, when they talked to her, they scanned the horizon, as if looking at her would infect them with whatever had made her go out and get a job. Only a few of the neighbors stood by Mami—Doña Ana, whose daughter watched us, Doña Zena, whose Christian beliefs didn't allow for envy, and Doña Lola, who valued everyone equally. Even Tío Cándido's wife, Meri, made us feel as if Mami was a bad woman for leaving us alone.

I was confused by the effect my mother's absence caused in other people.

"Why, Mami? Why is everyone so mean just because you have a job?" I pleaded one day after a schoolmate said Mami was not getting her money from a factory but from men in the city.

"They're jealous," she said. "They can't imagine a better life for themselves, and they're not willing to let anyone else have it either. Just ignore them."

But I couldn't close my ears to their insults, couldn't avert my eyes quickly enough to miss their hate-filled looks. I was abandoned by children who until then had been friends. The neighbors on the long walk to and from home were no longer friendly; they no longer offered me a drink of water on a hot afternoon or a dry porch when it rained.

Papi seemed to have the same opinion about Mami's job as the neighbors. He looked at her with a puzzled expression, and several times I heard her defend herself: "If it weren't for the money I bring in, we'd still be living like savages." He'd withdraw to his hammers and nails, to the mysterious books in his dresser, to the newspapers and magazines he brought home rolled up in his wooden toolbox.

I had worried that not having Mami around would make our lives harder, but at first it made things easier. Mami was happy with her work, proud of what she did, eager to share with us the adventures of her day in the factory, where she stitched cotton brassieres she said had to be for American women because they were too small to fit anyone we knew.

But her days were long, filled in the morning with the chores of making both breakfast and dinner, getting seven children ready for school or a day with Gloria, preparing for work, going there and back, returning to a basketful of mending, a house that needed sweeping, a floor that needed mopping, sheets that had to be washed and dried in one day because we didn't have two sets for each bed. As she settled into her routine, Mami decided she needed help, and she turned to me.

"You are the oldest, and I expect you to be responsible for your sisters and brothers, and to do more around the house."

"But isn't Gloria going to take care of us?"

"I can't count on anyone from outside the family. Besides, you're old enough to be more responsible."

And with those words Mami sealed a pact she had designed, written, and signed for me.

 "Delsa, you'd better get in here and do the dishes before Mami gets home."

Delsa looked up from the numbers she wrote in her composition book. Rows and rows of numbers, over and over again, in neat columns, in her small, tight script. "It's not my turn." She went back to her homework.

"Whose turn is it then?"

"Yours. I did it yesterday."

The sink was full. Plates, cups, spoons, pot lids, the heavy aluminum rice pot, the frying pan, all half submerged in gray water with a greasy scum floating on the top. "Norma!"

"What!"

"Come here. I'm going to teach you to wash dishes."

"I'm watching Raymond."

"Well, let Héctor watch him."

"I don't want to."

"If these dishes aren't washed by the time Mami comes home . . ."

"You do them, then."

I didn't want to either. I didn't want to do any of the things Mami asked of me: feed the kids an after-school snack; make sure they did their homework; get Raymond and Edna from Gloria's; change the water on the beans and put them on the stove to cook over low heat; sweep the floor; make the beds; mound the dirty clothes in the basket; feed the chickens and the pigs. Delsa and Norma were supposed to help, but most of the time they refused, especially when I tried to get them to do the unpleasant tasks like changing Raymond's diaper or scrubbing the rice pot. Almost every day just before Mami came home I scrambled around to do all the things she'd asked me to take care of that morning. And almost every day I received either a lecture or *cocotazos* for not doing everything.

"You're almost *señorita*. You should know to do this without being told."

"I just can't . . ."

"You're lazy, that's your problem. You think everything will be handed to you."

"No I don't," I whimpered, my hands protecting my head from the inevitable blows.

"Don't you talk back!" And she pushed me away as if I were contagious. "The least you can do is set an example for your sisters and brothers."

I looked at Delsa, who at nine could already make perfect rice, and at Norma, who swept and mopped with precision, and at Héctor, who dutifully changed out of his uniform into play clothes every day without being told. "What makes them so good and me so bad?" I asked myself. But there were no answers in Delsa's solemn eyes, or in Norma's haughty beauty, or in Héctor's eagerness to please. Every night Mami told me how I had failed in my duty as a female, as a sister, as the eldest. And every day I proved her right by neglecting my chores, by letting one of the kids get hurt, by burning the beans, by not commanding the respect from my sisters and brothers that I was owed as the oldest.

‚ I wished I could trade places with my cousin Jenny. She was an only child who ran her parents with tantrums and demands that, had they come from me, would have got me a swift slap or a *cocotazo* from Mami's sharp knuckles. Jenny was so spoiled that even Papi, who never criticized anybody, complained that Jenny had no manners and no respect for her elders. She was so bad that we were not allowed to play with her.

Jenny was a year younger than I was, but I'd heard Mami tell Doña Lola that Jenny was already *señorita*. Her body had developed into a petite figure like her mother's, with round hips and pointy bumps on her chest. While it had been a long time since I'd seen her sitting on her mother's lap sucking her breast, I assumed that becoming *señorita* had rid her of that habit. But it hadn't changed very much else about her. She still boasted about the clothes and shoes, dolls, games, and jewelry that her parents bought for her. She slept in her own bed, in a room decorated with dolls that had never been played with,

with a closet full of pretty dresses and shiny patent-leather shoes.

Envy, Doña Lola had once said, eats at you from the inside and turns your eyes green when you look at the person of whom you're jealous. If so, my eyes must have turned the color of the lizards that lived inside banana leaves every time I passed Jenny's house. I hated the fact that even though she was a brat, she got whatever she wanted. She had no chores around the house, no sisters or brothers with whom to share her clothes and toys, no limits as to where she could go, whom she could go with, or how long she could stay out. She didn't have to do her homework, didn't have to do anything she didn't want to, and her parents, the quiet, patient Tío Cándido and the tinny-voiced Meri, wouldn't say a thing, wouldn't beat her or yell at her or call her humiliating names. I was so jealous of Jenny that I couldn't stand to be with her. Mami and Papi had forbidden that we fight anyone for any reason, yet every time I came near Jenny, I wanted to beat her up, to wipe the smirk off her face, to quiet her boasting once and for all so that she would see what it was like to hurt.

→ "Jenny got a bicycle!" Delsa's eyes shimmered, her little hands fluttering in front of her as they drew a picture in the air of a girls' bike. "And she's giving everyone a ride."

I dropped the mop in the middle of the floor and ran after her. Up the road, past Doña Zena's house, Jenny straddled her two-wheeler. She wore shorts and sneakers, and a tight white shirt that displayed the bumps on her chest.

Children clustered around Jenny while she showed off the shiny fenders, the thick tires, the handlebars with multicolored streamers.

"Who else wants a ride?" she asked, enjoying the attention, the voices clamoring her name. I was choking with rage. I gathered my sisters and brothers, who clustered possessively around Jenny.

"Come on, let's go. We have to get home."

"Aw, come on, Negi," Jenny cried. "They want a ride on my new bike."

"I don't care. Mami doesn't want us playing all the way up here."

"I'll ride the bike down closer to your house. Then you can all get a turn."

"Forget it."

"But why, Negi?" Héctor whined.

"Just forget it, okay?"

Jenny followed us on her bike as I shoved the kids in front of me toward the house. "You're not their mother. You can't tell them what to do!" she cried.

"Yeah!" Delsa yelled. "You're not Mami. You can't order us around," and my sisters and brothers backed away from me, pushing against each other to be next to Jenny's bike.

"You're always so bossy," Norma yelled. "You think you're a grown-up or something."

I wanted to cry that no, I didn't think I was a grown-up, and it wasn't fair that they all got to ride on the bike and I didn't. I wanted to remind them that Mami didn't want us playing with Jenny, but it would be wrong to say that in front of her. I grabbed Raymond by the hand and pulled him toward me.

"Fine, if you want to ride on that stupid bike, then go ahead. But when Mami gets home . . ."

"I want to ride on the bike too," Raymond wailed beside me, wriggling his hand out of mine. "I want a ride!"

And he ran to Jenny, who scooped him up and tried to balance him on the handlebars.

"Jenny, he's too little to do that."

"He's all right. . . . You sit on the seat," she said to him, "and I'll ride standing up."

"Stop it, Jenny. He'll fall off. Raymond, get off that bike."

"Leave us alone. I know what I'm doing." She stood up on the pedals and pushed off slowly. Raymond giggled. "See, he's having a good time."

"Well, if you don't care," I yelled back, "then I don't care either. Go ahead and ride the stupid bike!" I glared at Delsa

and Norma, who, as the next oldest, should have known better. "You two are in trouble. . . . You're supposed to obey me
when Mami's not around. She left me in charge."

They laughed and chased after Jenny, who was riding the
bike faster, with Raymond gripping the seat underneath him.
My face was hot, and tears tickled my eyes, but I wasn't about
to let them see me cry. I turned toward home, dejected and
abandoned by my sisters and brothers who wouldn't stand by
me against this spoiled brat.

As I reached our yard I heard a scream. Raymond, Jenny,
and the bike had fallen over. "Serves them right," I thought
and continued into the yard. But the screams were loud and
frightened, more than I would have expected from a simple
fall. They were screams of terror, of pain. I ran, and as I did, it
seemed that the whole *barrio* was converging in a circle
around the bicycle, around Raymond whose toes were caught
in the chain, his foot twisted on itself, mangled into a mess of
blood, grease, and dirt.

Doña Zena and Doña Ana shooed us away. I gathered my
sisters and brothers, like a hen her chicks, and stood by the
side of the road as someone pulled the bicycle apart and took
Raymond's foot out. His shrieks cut into me, and I wanted to
run to him, but the adults surrounded him and wouldn't let
anyone through. Someone wrapped his foot, and someone else
took him to the emergency room in Bayamón. Mami was
found at her job and brought there, and Papi too, somehow. I
was left to care for my sisters and brothers. We ate the rice and
beans that Gloria made for us, and in silence we bathed and
dressed for bed, crawled under the mosquito netting, tucked
ourselves in, and listened, listened for Papi to come home, or
Mami to come home, or Raymond to come bouncing in with
his goofy grin. But they didn't, and he didn't, and I fell asleep
dreading what Mami would do to me when she found out that
I had walked away and let Raymond get hurt.

But Mami didn't do a thing. Somehow Raymond's accident
became Jenny's fault. Mami, Meri, Tío Cándido, and Papi
talked, and every neighbor who had seen what happened

talked, and it was agreed that Jenny was to blame. Even though no one said so, it had been my responsibility to watch the kids, especially Raymond, who was the youngest. But no one yelled at me or called me names or beat me because I hadn't watched my sisters and brothers. Jenny was accountable. I was furious that she was getting all the attention for something that was my fault.

∾ Mami had to quit her job to care for Raymond. For many months she ran from one doctor to another because Raymond's foot wouldn't heal. The doctors told her that so much bicycle grease had got into the wound that they couldn't be sure if they'd cleaned it all out. Raymond, Mami told Papi, would be plagued by all sorts of problems with his foot for the rest of his life, and she went on to list diseases the doctors had told her he was likely to develop. Diseases that all ended with *-itis*.

But the more frantic Mami became in her search for the right treatment for Raymond, the more distant Papi became, as if we were all wounded in some way that he couldn't help. There were more fights, more arguments, more yelling in the night, more long absences. Until it seemed as if anything would be better than living with these people who hated each other.

∾ One day as I walked back from school, it started to rain. I stood under an oak tree for a while, but the rain didn't let up. I put my books under my shirt, took off my shoes, and ran from tree to tree.

At the entrance to Barrio Macún, Mami and my six sisters and brothers clustered at the *público* stop with bundles all around them. Mami was annoyed.

"What took you so long? I almost left you behind."

"Where are we going?"

"We're moving to Santurce."

"But I have a math test tomorrow!"

"Well, then, you're lucky, aren't you?"

The kids were quiet. They must have been as scared as I was, but none of us dared say anything.

We waited a long time for a *público* that could take all of us, our bundles, and our suitcases.

"Are you moving?" the *público* driver asked with a laugh, and Mami glared at him. He didn't say anything more after that.

It took us three hours to get to the city. The rain was heavy, and traffic into Santurce was backed up for miles because of floods. Mami sat up in front with Edna and Raymond, while Delsa, Norma, Héctor, Alicia, and I sat in the back. We didn't dare speak or move because Mami kept looking at us with a dark expression on her face. She passed us a chunk of bread and cheese, and the *público* driver gave her a dirty look. I guessed he didn't like people eating in his car.

When the *público* let us off, all we could see was the pale yellow light of electric bulbs reflected on water, and tall stacks with a red neon sign flashing CORONA BREWERY. As heavy rain drops plunked on either side of us, Mami told us to be careful, because we were walking on a bridge. It was slippery and narrow, with nothing to hold on to along the sides. If we took one false step, we would fall into black, smelly water.

I raised my head to the rain, to wash my face and clear the nasty stench that lodged in my nostrils, as if my insides were rotting. But the foul air was thick and oppressive, clinging to us as if anything new, clean, and fresh had to be contaminated by this noxious atmosphere or it wouldn't survive.

We arrived at Doña Andrea's house, and her husband helped us get our things in. She showed Mami into a back room with two beds, and we fell into them, so tired we didn't even have dinner or look to see where we were.

EL MANGLE

De Guatemala a guata-peor

❧

From Guatemala to guate-worse

The *barrio* floated on a black lagoon. Sewage drifted by in a surprising variety of shapes, sizes, and colors. It was easy to tell what people in El Mangle ate because pieces of food stuck to the turds that glided past. I watched out the window, wondering who each load belonged to, whether what came out from their insides gave a clue to what they looked like.

"Negi, what are you doing up so early?" Mami whispered.

"I have to go to the bathroom," I whispered back. My bladder was so full that I'd had to keep my legs crossed all the while I'd looked out the window. Seeing all that water hadn't helped.

She groaned. "The bathroom is over here." She led me through a curtain into the front room. There was a hammock stretched across one end and a couch lumpy with a sleeping body. We walked into another room, and Mami turned on an overhead bulb. The brightness made my eyes water, so that I could barely see the circle cut in the wood floor.

"It's just like a latrine," Mami said. "You squat and do your business. But be careful to keep your legs far apart so that you don't fall in. Would you like me to go first and show you how it's done?"

I nodded. Mami squatted, her back to me. She looked over her shoulder.

"Be very careful when you aim, so that you don't pee all over the floor."

She got up and pulled up her panties.

"Now you."

I stood over the hole and spread my legs as far as I could. Below, water flowed to the left, faster than it did by the bedroom window. I felt dizzy. Cold air came up between my legs, and I jumped back and bumped into Mami.

"What's the matter?"

"I . . . I felt something."

"There's nothing there. Don't be such a *jíbara*."

She shoved me gently towards the hole. "Are you going to pee or not?"

My bladder was bursting. "The hole is too big."

Tears burned the back of my eyes, but if I cried she'd get mad at me.

"We can't change the size of the hole."

"Don't they have an *escupidera*, like we do at home?"

"No." She held my shoulders. "I'll hold on to you until you get used to it."

"Okay." I stood over the hole again, trying not to look down. A tickle of cold air sent goose bumps up the small of my back. I pulled my panties down to my knees and had to step away from the hole because they got in my way when I tried to squat.

"Now what?"

"I can't squat with my panties on. The hole's too wide."

"Take them off," she said, pulling them down for me.

Someone down there can look up through the hole and see my private parts, I thought. There is someone down there. A dead person is in that water waiting for me to squat so that it can claw me in and drown me in turds and pee. There are eyes looking up from that black pool, seeing parts of me that even I can't see.

"Just hold on to me," Mami whispered. "Don't be scared."

I squatted slowly, holding on to Mami's hands so that if the dead reached up for me, she could pull me back. I looked down to aim and saw something waving in the water. I couldn't stand it anymore. I screamed, jumped back again, and crashed against Mami.

"What's the matter!"

Doña Andrea stood at the door, her hair in curlers.

"She's afraid of the bathroom," Mami said, holding on to me.

"Do you think something's going to float up and take you?"

She laughed. Mami laughed. I leaned against the wall, unable to stop crying. I wished Doña Andrea would leave. But she and Mami stood there laughing like it was the funniest thing in the world. My face burned.

"Stop laughing at me!" I screamed. I punched Mami in the belly, and she gasped. She clasped my hands in hers and held me against the wall.

"Stop that," she growled. Her hands were firm around my wrists, hurting me. I squirmed, trying to get away.

"Ah, she's got a temper," Doña Andrea snorted.

I wished she'd shut up. Mami pushed me toward the hole.

"Now get over there and do what you have to do before I get mad."

I'd embarrassed her in front of Doña Andrea, but I didn't care. They shouldn't have laughed. The water under the hole ran blacker and swifter, and there was no way I was going to squat. No way.

"Fine," Mami said, letting go of me. "If you refuse to use the bathroom, then you'll just have to hold it in the rest of the day, because there's no other place to do it."

No I didn't. I didn't have to hold it in. I didn't.

She walked to the door. Doña Andrea nodded her approval. Mami looked back at me, not sure if she should leave. She seemed to be at the other end of the world, with Doña Andrea behind her, small as a cockroach, holding the door open. Mami took one step out, but before she could leave, hot urine trickled down my legs into a pool on the floor.

☙ Doña Andrea poured cornflakes into blue plastic bowls. At home, we never had cereal in the middle of the day, but she was taking care of us while Mami went looking for work, and she didn't know the rules.

"You know, if you hit your mother, when you die they won't be able to bury you."

The air was sucked out of me. Delsa's eyes opened wide, and her mouth fell open.

"Why? Why can't they?" I croaked.

"Because," she sprinkled a spoonful of sugar into the bowl, "if you hit your mother, when you die, your arm sticks out in front of you, like this, and it stays like that, so you can't fit in your coffin."

"Can't they push it down?"

"No. If they try, it springs right up."

"Maybe they can tie it down, with a rope or something."

She gave me a funny look. Delsa and Norma giggled.

"These are things God does to bad little children. You can't do anything about them." She slammed a bowl of cornflakes in front of me.

"She's wrong. All they have to do is tie the arm down," I whispered to Delsa and Norma. "And if that doesn't work, they build a coffin that's tall and wide enough so that the arm fits."

"Stop with the whispering and giggling," Doña Andrea snapped.

She poured canned milk over the cereal. I hated the flavor of canned milk, but Mami had told us that when somebody gives you something to eat, you eat it, even if you throw it up later.

Doña Andrea was short and round and had a wart on her cheek. Her hair was stringy, and she was missing a few teeth. Raymond was afraid of her, and Héctor said she looked like a witch. I had to spank them both for being disrespectful.

Her house floated at the end of a narrow pier with one other house. Between them a rowboat floated in the black water, held by a rope knotted around a rusty hook. Doña Andrea made us stay inside all day because there was no place to play outside.

"I don't want one of you falling into the lagoon," she said, and I shuddered at the thought of touching that dirty water.

Being cooped up inside all day was boring. In Macún, we could run and climb trees and jump from rock mountains. But in El Mangle, we couldn't do anything. There wasn't even schoolwork because Mami wouldn't sign us up for school until she found a job.

Mami wanted to rent the house next to Doña Andrea. Then we would have our own kitchen, our own rooms, and she would bring our furniture from Macún.

"Mami, when is Papi coming to see us?" I asked one day as she sat on the steps of our future house, rubbing her feet.

"I don't know," she said in a sharp voice and looked away.

It occurred to me then that she hadn't told him where we were.

Papi wouldn't live in such a place because he couldn't stand strong smells. They made his mouth water, which made him spit. So at home in Macún our latrine was far from the house.

But in El Mangle, we couldn't get away from the stench. The air smelled like the brewery, and the water like human waste. Food didn't taste good. The smell lived inside us, and even though Mami used a lot of garlic and oregano when she cooked, it didn't help. I could still taste shit when I ate.

❧ The school was made of stone. Mami said the floors were marble, which was why they were so shiny. The uniform was an ugly mustard shirt with a chocolate-colored skirt and brown shoes. Unlike every other teacher I'd ever had, my new teacher, Sra. Leona, insisted on Spanish and refused to answer when we said "Mrs."

"It is a bastardization of our language," she said, "which in Puerto Rico is Spanish."

I didn't like her. She was always angry, and she was mean. Once she hit a boy with a ruler because he laughed when she dropped a map. He wasn't the only one to laugh, but she picked on him.

When I came to school in the middle of the year, my class was studying fractions. In Macún, we hadn't got to fractions, so I was lost and had a hard time following what Sra. Leona wrote on the board. I read the pages in my math book that other kids had read weeks earlier, but nothing made any sense. Mami couldn't help me. She said she had never studied fractions when she was in school.

Sra. Leona wrote some fractions on the board and called on the boy behind me to solve the first one. She didn't just expect you to solve it, you were supposed to explain how to do it as you went along. I was cold and sweaty at the same time. The boy mentioned integers. I didn't know what they were. He wrote a bunch of numbers on the board, and Sra. Leona smiled at him as he returned to his seat.

"Esmeralda, come up and solve the next one."

I knew she was going to call on me. I just knew it. The problem was $2/3 + 4/6 =$.

I walked as slowly as I could to the blackboard, looking hard at the numbers. I tried to solve the problem in my head, so that by the time I got to the blackboard, it would be figured out and I wouldn't make a fool of myself. $2/3$. That means if there are supposed to be three bananas you have only two of the three. Okay. Four-sixths means if there are supposed to be six guavas you have only four. All right. Wait a second. How many bananas? Two. Right. And four guavas. What does that make? I don't think the fruit trick works with this.

The chalk was dry and powdery. Sra. Leona stared at me through thick glasses that made her eyes bulge. Two parts of three plus four parts of six. Can it be six parts of nine? I don't think so because six parts of nine is smaller than two parts of three. That wasn't working, so I tried a new tactic. If you cut an orange into three pieces the slices are bigger than if you cut it into nine pieces. If you cut it into six pieces the slices are bigger than if you cut it in nine but smaller than if you cut it in three. So what does that make?

"Esmeralda, do you need help?"

Someone behind me giggled. Sra. Leona shushed him.

"No, Sra. Leona, I'm just thinking."

"Think a little faster, would you please? We don't have all day."

Six oranges. No, one orange, six pieces. Three bananas. Four guavas. No, two bananas.

"Didn't you learn fractions in that school for *jíbaros* you came from?"

The kids laughed. Sra. Leona smiled. Her teeth were small. I was so cold, my knees shook.

"We were just beginning . . ."

"I see. Those country schools are always so far behind. That's why we have so many ignorant *jíbaros* . . ."

"I'm not ignorant." She grabbed the chalk from my hand and wrote some numbers on the board. I stepped toward my seat.

"No, young lady. You stand right there and watch, so you can learn."

My classmates laughed. Someone threw a spitball. In the back of the room three boys sang a *jíbaro* song about coming from the mountains to the city. Sra. Leona turned around and stared at them through her thick glasses and they quieted down, but the minute she turned her back they started again, in a softer voice.

She talked about converting this to that and adding this, and integers, but I didn't hear her. I left my body standing in front of her, suffering spitballs and whispered insults. I sent the part of me that could fly outside the window to the *flamboyán* tree in the yard.

The orange flowers covered me as I sat in their midst. They smelled bitter, like the white sticky ooze that dribbled out from cut stems. From the tree I watched Sra. Leona writing on the board, and me standing nearby, head lowered, eyes focused on the shiny floor. She finished the equation with a great flourish of taps and scratches on the blackboard and looked at me, a triumphant look on her face.

"And that's how you do it, all right?"

I came back inside. "All right."

"You can return to your seat now," she said, and I walked back as fast as I could, my shoes making a flat sound on the cold marble.

❧ The walk home from school was long. No one walked with me. I didn't want anyone to know where I lived. I walked past a bar, a grocery store, a doctor's office, past a *botánica*, its window plastered with pictures of a blonde Virgin Mary, a bloody Jesus Christ, and a tree with a thick trunk and branches stretching out from it like an umbrella. "The Tree of Life" it was called.

Cement houses with wrought iron porch railings and flowery gardens were clustered behind the businesses. From inside one of the houses, a dog barked as I approached and passed. Inside another, birds chirped a song unlike anything I'd ever heard from birds in the trees of Macún. I wished we lived in one of those houses, with their large rooms and lamps instead of bare bulbs hanging from the ceiling.

Girls from my school walked in groups ahead of me, and one by one they went into these nice homes where mothers, dressed in simple skirts and blouses, with hair neatly combed, no paint on their faces, waited by the door and closed it lovingly after their daughters. Once one of them smiled at me, and I was so grateful I wanted to run into her arms and be swallowed by the ruffles on her blouse. Another gave me a dirty look, as if I had no right to walk on her neat street.

At my door, no one was waiting. Mami was working. Doña Andrea gave me a cup of milk with coffee and a chunk of bread with butter, and then I had to watch my sisters and brothers until Mami came home.

Even though we could walk to school on our own, we were still not allowed to play outside the house. I did my schoolwork and helped my sisters with theirs. I waited for Mami. I drew pictures of butterflies and flowers, trees on grassy hills, hummingbirds kissing hibiscus blossoms, all the things that didn't exist in El Mangle. I pasted my pictures on the wall near the cot Delsa and I shared. She liked looking at them too.

☙ Mami talked to Doña Andrea. She smiled and nodded her head and smiled again. When Doña Andrea handed her a pot full of chickpeas with pig's feet, Mami didn't want to accept it.

"Come on," Doña Andrea said, "I cooked them for you. You don't have the time to make them after work."

"All right, but only if you let me make you some *arroz con dulce* one of these days."

"Don't worry about it. Enjoy it." And she pressed the pot into Mami's hands.

Chickpeas with pig's feet and white rice was one of my favorite dishes. Mami put pumpkin in the chickpeas, and I munched into it, expecting it to be hard and chewy but discovered that it melted in my mouth. I gnawed on the meat around the pig's feet and sucked the bones until the salty, slippery membrane slid out and swished around my tongue. As we ate, we threw the bones out the window, plink, into the water.

At dusk I could see the remains of other people's suppers floating by the window, chicken and pork chop bones, lettuce leaves, breadcrumbs, sometimes noodles. On Fridays people ate fish or vegetables with no meat because of God.

&ewsp; When we first came to El Mangle, I wouldn't drink, and I didn't take a bath because I thought the water came from the lagoon. But one day Mami took me by the hand.

"Come," she said. "See this pipe connected to our faucet? Watch. It stretches all the way down and turns here, under the pier. It never touches the water." We walked to where our pier joined the dock with many other piers and curved bridges attached to it. Each pier had one or two houses at the end, their pilings thick and tall above the black water. "Do you still see the pipes?" They were sturdily attached by metal collars to the splintery boards of the dock. "Now we follow them down this way." We followed the dock toward the shore, where the pipes, now joined by many others, disappeared under the cement sidewalks leading to San Juan. After that, I didn't mind the water.

"At least," Mami said, "we don't have to walk for miles with pails full of water on our heads."

❧ Some evenings, Mami let me sit on Don Pedro's boat, which was tied to a piling between our house and Doña Andrea's. At first I was afraid of falling in the lagoon, but Don Pedro showed me that the boat was safe, as long as I didn't move around in it too much. I pushed it along the dock until it floated behind the houses and there was nothing in front of me but black water, and in the distance, mountains. Smoke curled up from the shore on the other side of the lagoon. Gulls circled, dove down, then flew up again. The sun floated over the mountains, stained the blue sky red-orange, and flattened the lagoon until it looked like a mirror for the stars. The mountains became shadows as the sun dove behind them, and the lagoon shimmered silver and white. It was so still and quiet that I could hear the water swish against the sides of the boat and the pilings that held up El Mangle. I remembered all the times Papi and I sat on our steps, watching the sun go down. My throat felt tight and my eyes stung with tears. If I came back looking like I'd been crying, Mami would worry, and if I told her why, she'd be angry. It was better just to swallow the tightness in my throat and rub the hurt away. That way no one would ever know.

❧ One day, Mami said I had been asked to do something very, very special. Not everyone could do it, and she wanted to know if I wanted to.

"What is it?"

Mami sat across from me. "Doña Cony had something sad happen. Her baby, her youngest son, died yesterday."

"Oh."

"Isn't that sad?"

"Yes. It's very sad. She must be really sad."

"She is. Especially because when the baby died, his eyes didn't close."

"How come?"

"No one knows. But he can't be buried like that."

"Why not?"

"He just can't."

"What difference does it make, if he's dead?"

Mami gave me a look. "He won't go to Heaven."

"Oh."

She took a deep breath. "So Doña Cony asked me if you could close the baby's eyes."

"No way!"

"It will only take a minute. You'll wear your white piqué dress, and I'll take you out for ice cream after."

Something told me Mami had already said I would do it.

"Do I have to touch it?"

"Of course, but not for long. It only takes a minute."

"What if when I touch it, it grabs me?"

"He's dead. He can't move."

"But in all the stories the dead walk around and do things . . ."

"That's grown-up dead. This little baby couldn't even walk yet. He's going to be an angel. But only if someone closes his eyes."

"Why?"

"Because his soul is trapped in his body. Once you close his eyes, it can fly up to Heaven."

"Why do I have to do it?"

"Because the *curandera* saw you and picked you out from among many little girls for this honor. You should be proud you were chosen."

"What *curandera*? When did she see me? Who is she?"

"Negi, if you don't want to do it, I'll tell her, and then she'll have to find someone else. But if you want to do it, we have to be there in a few minutes."

It sounded scary, but I'd never seen a dead baby. I hoped to see its soul trapped inside its head.

Mami pulled out my white piqué dress. I was only allowed to wear it to visit relatives. She tied a white ribbon around my waist and held it with a safety pin so it wouldn't slip.

"I look like I'm going to make communion."

Mami chuckled. We never went to church. Maybe the Virgin Mary was not protecting me, like she did Catholic children.

Maybe when I went to close the baby's eyes, the Devil would take both of us down into the black waters. Or maybe God Himself would strike me dead on the spot.

"Shouldn't we go to church first? Maybe a priest should bless me or something, you know, to make me holy."

"Turn around and let me fix this bow."

She never listened. I asked her questions, and she pretended I hadn't. It made me mad.

"Let's go."

My sisters and brothers were with Doña Andrea. She came out of her house and made me turn around so she could look at me.

"Oh, you look so nice," she said, "so innocent."

We walked along the dock connecting our house to the main pier from which many other piers and bridges stretched to houses in the water.

Mami pulled me along faster than I could walk. We'd never been this way. The *barrio* was bigger than I thought. An old man sat on the threshold of his house and waved at us. A woman hung laundry on a line stretched between her house and the next one. She leaned way out of her window, until it looked like she would fall in the water. When she saw us, she grinned and went inside.

My patent-leather shoes slipped on the rotting wood of the pier.

"Can you walk a little slower, Mami?"

She waited for me to catch my breath. She curled a loose strand of hair behind my ribboned braids.

"You look so pretty in white," she said and hugged me.

She was soft, warm. Her arm heavy around my shoulders, she pointed to a house at the end of a long walkway stretching out from a pier.

"That's where we're going."

The house was painted the same bright green as the lizards that hide in plantain leaves. A limp black bow hung by the open door.

Mami tugged on my dress here and there, pulled down her

skirt, and grabbed my hand tight. She was as scared as I was. I took a deep breath.

"Okay," I said, "I'm ready."

My shoes tapped against the wood, as if I were dancing. It was disrespectful to make so much noise when death was so near. I wished I could float over the wood so I wouldn't make so much noise. It was hard to do when I was scared. It took a lot of concentration. But by the time we reached the house, I was floating.

The baby's coffin lay on a table draped in white cloth. Shirred white lace hung on the walls behind him and in a canopy above the coffin.

Two women met us at the door. They held long white rosaries with enormous silver crosses. One of them was dressed in mourning, the other in white, turbaned, her brown skin ashimmer. She had sparse eyebrows over protruding eyes; one eye was brown, the other green.

"Ah," she said, "here is our little angel."

She put both hands on my shoulders and kneeled so we could be the same height.

"My name is Nicasia. The lady behind me is the baby's mother. Do you know her?"

Doña Cony looked familiar. I nodded at Nicasia's green eye. She looked behind me at my mother.

"Thank you for letting your daughter do this. The Good Shepherd will repay your kindness."

She stared at me. I didn't know which of her eyes to look into.

"Are you a little scared?" she asked.

I nodded.

"It is good to be afraid of what you don't understand." She closed her eyes.

Her fingers pressed into my shoulders, her nails dug into my skin. I wanted to turn around, to find Mami, but I couldn't move my head. I could only look into the knot on Nicasia's turban.

"Dear Lord, bless this child. Bless her and protect her."

Doña Cony joined the prayer. "¡*Aleluya*! Let Him be adored!" Behind me, Mami breathed hard.

"Dear Virgin, Protectress of Little Children, bless this child."

"Yes, *Virgencita*, protect all the children."

"Dear Lord, bless and protect this woman who has brought us her child to perform this sacred duty."

"Bless her, Lord. And her whole family."

Nicasia's eyes were filmy, the lids half covering her pupils. She looked up and scanned the space behind me, where the baby's coffin was. She hummed and nodded her head, as though agreeing with somebody, but there was no one there. Just the dead baby. She stared at me again, and her face melted. I couldn't take my eyes off hers. They were so big I could see myself. She let her head fall to her bosom, took a deep breath, and shook all over.

"You have a powerful spirit protecting you. It's always there watching. It takes care of you so that nothing bad can happen. You need not be afraid."

My knees rattled. I wanted to float away, or to fly outside the window, but I couldn't. Nicasia held me down with her strong fingers.

"It's your guardian angel." She opened her eyes wide. "Do you know what a guardian angel is?"

I nodded. She smiled. Her two front teeth were trimmed with gold.

"Very good. Are you ready?"

I nodded again. My voice was scared.

Nicasia pressed against my shoulders harder as she stood up from kneeling. Her bones cracked and rattled, as though there were no one inside the long white dress. She led me to the table. There was a white carnation with a small white rosary wrapped around it. Nicasia gave it to me.

"Hold this in your left hand." She wrapped the dangling ends of the rosary around my wrist.

The coffin was covered with a mosquito net. Doña Cony removed it, and Nicasia turned me toward the baby. I didn't want to look at it, but I did. It was a small baby, dressed in white christening clothes with ruffles and ribbons and lace. It was smiling. Its eyes were grey with almost no whites. There was nothing inside them.

Nicasia took my right hand and dipped it into a bowl of water.

"This is holy water," she said.

I pulled my hand away. I was afraid the holy water would burn my fingers. But Nicasia stuck my hand back in and held it there. The holy water felt cool and soft.

Nicasia held my hand above the baby's face and tucked my thumb, ring, and little fingers into my palm.

"Just hold your fingers like this and listen to the prayer. When I tap you on the shoulder with the rosary, you put your fingers on the baby's lids and hold them down until I tap you again."

I nodded. The sun splashed in the door and hit my legs but didn't warm the rest of me. Mami stood behind me, breathing quietly. I tried to follow her breath, my eyes closed so that I wouldn't have to look at the baby's empty face.

Nicasia mumbled words I didn't understand. Doña Cony clicked her rosary and whispered "Amen" every once in a while. Nicasia tapped me on the shoulder lightly. I opened my eyes and let my fingers rest on the baby's lids and held them there as Nicasia continued her foreign prayer. The baby's skin was cold. His eyes felt like egg yolks. If I pressed hard, they would pop.

Nicasia tapped me on the shoulder and I took my hand away. She looked inside, and Doña Cony and Mami stepped closer to the coffin. The baby's eyes were shut. The lids were wet from the holy water, which made the baby look as if he'd been crying. I scraped my fingers against the piqué of my dress. It felt rough and dry, but I couldn't get rid of the feeling that death was stuck to me.

Mami hugged me, and Nicasia hugged me, and Doña Cony hugged me. I was cold and moved toward the door, where a rectangle of sunshine called me.

"I want to go home," I said to Mami. My throat hurt.

"Okay, okay. In a minute." She and Nicasia talked quietly. Doña Cony pulled the mosquito net over the baby.

"I want to go home." My head was heavy with muttering voices. My tongue was large and thirsty.

"Just a minute!" Nicasia handed Mami a small bottle. Mami thanked her and backed toward me, still talking.

"Please, Mami."

She frowned. The air was stiff. Outside, a breeze rippled water against the pilings. A seagull landed on the dock and stepped toward the door.

"Get out of there," it told me.

Doña Cony hugged Mami and shook her hand as if checking to see if it was still attached. I backed out of the house and down the steps. The seagull flew to the end of the walkway, to the pier that led to my house.

"Stay right there," Mami warned. "Wait for me."

The sunlight was yellow. Sweat soaked my scalp and dripped down my forehead, into my ears. It tickled, but the voices went away. My head felt light, my tongue its normal size. The seagull stepped along the pier, looked at me, then flew toward the mountains. Mami came out of Doña Cony's house.

"It's very rude to leave without saying good-bye," she said, shoving me ahead of her.

We walked quickly down the pier. The old man no longer sat in front of his house. The woman who hung out laundry was now sweeping the dust from her house out the door. When we reached the bridge by our house, I ran as fast as I could and took the steps in one leap.

I ripped the white ribbons out of my hair and threw them out the window. I clawed at the dress, trying to get it off as fast as I could. Mami yelled because I was not careful and the dress tore. But I wanted to get out of it. I stepped out of my panties, socks, and patent-leather shoes and ran into the shower. The cold water gave me shivery goose bumps. I rubbed castile soap into my hair, under my arms, between my toes. But most of all, I scrubbed the two fingers that had touched the baby. No matter how much soap I put on them, they felt cold and oily, and I didn't know if I'd ever get the feeling of death off them.

❧ I'd never hated going to school before. But I couldn't stand Sra. Leona, and even though this was the nicest school I'd ever seen, I didn't want to go there.

Sra. Leona didn't like me either. She called on me when she thought I didn't know the answer. It irritated her that most of the time I did. I read ahead in my books, so she couldn't catch me, so she could ask all she wanted. I refused to give her the chance to make fun of me.

My favorite classes were geography and social studies. I had a different teacher for them. Her name was Srta. Juárez. She was surprised when I drew a map of the continents with the countries, the major rivers, and the mountain ranges all in the right places.

When he lived with us, Papi sometimes helped me with homework, and when he saw how good I was with maps, he said I would grow up to be a cartographer. When I had told Miss Jiménez, my teacher in Macún, she had said I was more of a topographer, because cartographers' maps were flat, while mine had the bumps and dips of mountain ranges and valleys.

"Today," Sra. Leona said, "we will write a composition using the words you were assigned."

She wrote the words on the blackboard. Someone asked if we were supposed to use all ten words, and she laughed and said that would be impossible.

"Use as many as you can, but not less than five."

It was a stupid assignment. I hated her.

I wrote the words at the top of the page. Sra. Leona walked up and down the aisles between our seats, and stopped and hovered over me.

"Esmeralda, try to form those letters better. I always have trouble reading your handwriting."

The point on my pencil broke. She looked at me through her thick glasses, and I wished I were bigger and could punch her.

"Go sharpen your pencil."

She treated me like I had a disease. If I died and never came back to school, she'd probably be happy. But not for long. I'd come back to haunt her. I'd fill her inkwell with glue. I'd put hot peppers in her face cream. I'd curl a snake under her pillow.

I sat down to write the stupid composition using her ten stupid words. I would use all of them, just because she thought I couldn't. *Incandescent* and *Caramelize* must go together somehow. *Bannister* and *Delimitation. Boundary.* "A cartographer draws the Delimitation of Boundaries in maps." There, I'd even given her a word bigger than the assigned ones. What else could I say about cartographers? I had to think.

The door of the classroom was open. Across the hall, someone recited a poem I knew by heart.

"Esmeralda, is there something in the hall you'd like to share with us?"

Kids laughed. Sra. Leona hated it when my mind went elsewhere than her classroom.

"I was just thinking, Sra. Leona."

She curled her lip.

"Well. This is no time for daydreaming. You're supposed to be writing, not thinking."

I couldn't help it. I laughed. The idea that you were not supposed to think in school seemed funny. The kids behind me gasped. Sra. Leona's face turned red.

"What's so funny?" she growled.

I was laughing so hard that I had to hug my belly. Tears streamed down my cheeks. Slowly, as if a tide were rising around us, the rest of the class laughed while Sra. Leona stood at the front of the room with a dumb look on her face. She grabbed the long pointer from the blackboard and banged it on the desk.

"Quiet. Quiet, I say."

The pointer cracked in two. The bottom half flew off the

desk and out the door into the hall. Kids in the back banged their desks and roared. Sra. Leona held half the pointer in her hand, her eyes bulging behind her glasses, her face red, and her lips pulled back over yellow teeth. She screamed.

"Shut up, *Carajo*!"

We'd never heard a teacher swear. We all shut up at the same time and stared at her. She looked as surprised as we were. In the back of the room a kid giggled, then another, and another. There were footsteps in the hall and Sra. Leona turned to the door with a panicked expression. She shushed us. We were trying to control our giggles, but it was impossible. She was almost at the door when my father appeared.

I jumped from my seat and ran into his arms, sobbing and laughing. He pulled me to the stone steps leading to the outside. Sra. Leona closed the classroom door behind us. Papi wiped the tears from my face with his handkerchief. He held me against his side and rubbed my head.

"It's all right," he whispered. "Don't cry. It's all right."

We sat on the steps and I told him how mean Sra. Leona had been. How awful the place we lived in was. How scared I was when I closed the baby's eyes. It felt good to tell Papi these things. We sat there until the lunch bell rang. Kids filed out of classrooms and looked at us. Some of them pointed and laughed.

"Wait here," he said. He went into the classroom and I heard him talking to Sra. Leona. He laughed. She laughed. He backed out of the room carrying my books. He waved to her and thanked her. He took my hand and led me down the steps. She came out of the room as we were going out the door. Papi didn't see her, but I did. She gave me a dirty look and pre-tended to spit in my direction. Then she turned her back and walked away, her heels clicking on the hard polished floor.

LETTERS FROM
NEW YORK

Escapé del trueno y di con el relámpago.

❧

I ran from thunder and hit lightning.

I will not forgive you again.
I've closed my heart.
It is useless to cry.
It is useless to call.
I will never forgive you.

The jukebox blared the lover's troubles. His voice cracked a little when he sang that his heart was closed. But no matter how final he meant it to sound, eventually he would forgive his woman, and they would go on living, loving, and fighting. Just like Mami and Papi.

Once he found us living afloat the black lagoon, Papi wooed Mami back, and we moved to one of Santurce's busiest avenues. The building had once been a private house, but the new owner had divided it in half to make a two-room apartment in the back and a bar facing the street. He had placed a jukebox in one corner of the front room and a tall formica counter along the side wall. A pool table, lit from above by a single yellow bulb, seemed to float over the sticky tile floor between the music and the liquor.

"You are never to go into the bar," Mami told us on our first day, "and don't ever talk to anyone going in or out of there. When you go to school, follow the route we've walked, and don't stop anywhere in between."

My new school was a few blocks down the congested avenue, through a gate into a cracked cement yard ringed with hurricane fencing. I walked to and from school alone, unable to befriend the sassy girls with budding figures or the boys who leaned against fences and lampposts to hiss and leer.

"If a boy says something to you," Mami warned, "just ignore him. He'll find someone else to bother." But boys paid no attention to my scrawny legs and flat torso. If they took notice of me at all, it was to comment on how fast I walked.

"What are you running away from?" they'd call out as I whizzed past, books tight against my chest, eyes focused on the spot in front of my feet.

At home we grouped into a tight knot, two adults and seven children inside two rooms. The wall dividing our side of the house from the bar was made from shiny sheets of fake wood panelling, but the rest of the walls were rough, splintery boards painted pale green. The front room was just big enough for a table and two chairs, and Héctor and Raymond's fold-out cot. The girls' beds were along the walls of the back room. Mami and Papi's bed was against the panelled wall, a curtain separating it from our side of the room.

Our nights were punctuated by the deafening percussion of drunken ballads, clashing billiards, clinking glasses, and nightly brawls.

"I can't sleep, Mami," one of us would complain, and Mami would find cotton to stuff our ears.

"Try this," she said, knowing it wouldn't help. Nothing helped. Over the din, we heard men laughing, yelling obscenities.

"You are not to repeat those bad words, or you'll get a mouth full of hot peppers," she'd scold.

Sometimes a woman's voice broke through, and then the men shouted louder, glass shattered violently, and the songs on the jukebox went from *boleros* about betrayal to *guarachas* and *merengues* about the good life.

"Those are not good women. Decent women don't go into such places," Mami explained, a scared look on her face.

We slept with windows and doors bolted. At night, the bar's customers, in search of a bathroom, found their way to the rear of the building, where they peed against our walls or retched under the tree. Mornings, on our way to school, we hopped over curdled puddles of vomit and fetid urine stains on the dirt.

"At least," Mami said, "we have electricity and running water. We didn't have that in Macún."

❧ Raymond's foot was still raw and blistered from his accident almost a year earlier. Sometimes, with no warning, he'd develop a high fever, and pus formed in angry bubbles along the scars left by many operations. Mami would rush him to a clinic, where the wound was once again scraped and dressed in bandages. After many such visits the doctors finally told her that it might be best if Raymond's foot were amputated.

"Are they crazy?" Mami complained to Papi that night. "They can't figure out how to cure him, so they just give up."

"They know what they're doing, Monín."

"Whose side are you on, anyway?" She scooped Raymond onto her lap, with effort because he was already five years old, tall and gangly. "Just because everyone has given up on him doesn't mean I'm going to." She cradled him and rocked him back and forth until even I could feel her warmth, her yielding softness. "Don't worry," she muttered into his hair, "I won't let them cut off your foot." Raymond reached up with his skinny arms and grabbed her by the neck tightly, as if that alone would keep the thing from happening. "I'll find a specialist . . . someone who knows what he's doing . . . not like those charlatans in white coats that call themselves doctors." Her voice was soft but angry, as if it were the doctors' fault Raymond's foot got snared on a bicycle chain. I folded inside myself, wishing I could go back to the dusty road in front of our house and grab Raymond off the bike before Jenny rode away with him.

❧ "There's a letter from Tata!" Mami sang, waving a thick envelope. She ripped it open. "With a note for you, Negi."

My grandmother in New York didn't write very often, but when she did, I sent her one of my best school compositions, or a drawing, or a joke copied from the newspaper. She rarely responded directly but sent hugs and kisses in Mami's letters.

The lined airmail paper was so thin I took it into the shade because the midday sun shone right through it. She had folded it tightly, as if she didn't want anyone else to open it. "Dear Negi," she wrote in a broad, graceful script. "Thank you for the story you wrote for school. It was very good, but I had trouble reading it because your penmanship is so poor. It's always hard to read what you write. Next time, take more care forming your letters for this old lady. Love and kisses, Tata."

My eyes burned, and a trembling pain started in my gut and moved out, like water into an overfilled glass.

"Oh good!" Mami exclaimed as she read her letter, a happy expression on her face. She turned the page with an eager smile, her right hand over her heart.

I crumpled Tata's letter and threw it into the yard.

Mami looked up. "What's the matter?"

"Nothing," I collapsed into her lap.

"What's wrong? What did the letter say?" She was as upset as I was, her eyes darting from my sobbing face to the balled-up letter in the yard. "Héctor!" she called to my brother, who was practicing marble shots into a hole in the ground. "Bring me that piece of paper." She read it, took in a breath, and put the paper under her thigh so the breeze wouldn't blow it away. She held me for a few minutes then raised my face up and wiped my cheeks with the hem of her dress. "From now on, when you write to Tata," she said with a smile, "print."

꙰ That night, as Felipe Rodríguez sang that his love had left him with nothing to keep him company but a bottle of rum, I heard Mami and Papi murmuring in their bed. The noise coming from the bar made it impossible to hear everything they said, but after a while Papi was angry and rolled out of bed. I heard him open the door to the outside, and go out into the night. He didn't come back for days.

❧ Because of all the running around she had to do with Raymond, Mami couldn't work a steady job anymore. Still, his medications and doctor visits meant we needed money, so Mami talked our landlord into paying her for cooking a daily *caldero* of rice and beans and a stack of fried chicken pieces or pork chops, which he then sold at the bar. Sometimes she left the house, not in her work clothes but dressed a little better than what she wore around the house. She didn't tell us where she was going on those days, and it was years before I learned that she went to clean other people's houses. One day I came back from school to find a rope stretched across the front room and men's white shirts, clean and crisp, hanging in a row.

"Don't touch them. They're not ours."

"Whose are they?"

"They belong to the laundry down the street."

She spritzed some water from a bottle onto the cuff of a shirt and pressed the iron against it, making the steam rise up to her face.

"How come you're doing their ironing?"

"They were very nice and let me bring the work home instead of do it there." She finished the shirt and put it on a wire hanger alongside the others.

Of all the things in the world Mami had to do, this was her least favorite. She liked cooking, sewing, mopping, even dusting. But she always complained about how much she hated ironing.

"Can I try?"

"To iron?" Her eyebrows formed a question mark over her round eyes. Her mouth toyed with a smile. This was probably the first time I'd ever volunteered to learn anything useful.

She turned off the iron and looked for one of Papi's old shirts in her clean laundry hamper. "We wouldn't want you burning a customer's shirt," she chuckled. She stretched it on the board.

Quietly she showed me how to set the temperature for linen or cotton, how to wet my finger on my tongue and listen for the sizzle when I touched the flat bottom of the iron, and how to keep the electric cord from touching the hot metal, which could cause a fire. She turned over the bottle of cold water and sprinkled the inside of my wrist.

"This is how little moisture you need to get the steam to rise." She curved my fingers around the handle, pressing the iron against the fabric while with the other hand she pulled the cloth taut.

"Always iron the inside button and hole plackets first, then the inside and outside collar, then the cuffs." We danced around the ironing board, with Mami guiding my hand, pressing down on the iron, and standing away for a minute to see me do as she'd taught. The steam rose from the shirt and filled my head with the clean fresh scent of sun-dried cotton, and bubbles of perspiration flushed along my hair line and dripped down my neck. But I pressed on, absorbed by the tiny squares in the weave, the straight, even stitches that held the seams in place, the way the armhole curved into the shoulder.

"You're doing a good job," Mami murmured, a puzzled expression on her face.

"This is fun," I said, meaning it.

"Fun!" she laughed. "Then from now on you do all the ironing around the house." She said it with a smile, which meant she was teasing. And she never asked me to do it. But after that, whenever I wanted to feel close to Mami, I stacked wrinkled clothes into a basket, and, one by one, ironed them straight, savoring the afternoon when she taught me to do the one thing she most hated.

❧ In early December our landlord fenced in a corner of the yard and led a squealing pig into the enclosure.

"Christmas dinner," he said with a grin. With Papi's help, he dug an oval pit near the back fence, lined it with rocks that we children gathered, stuck two Y-shaped sticks at the edges of the hole, and laid a sturdy rod between them. "This should do," he smiled.

A couple of days before Christmas we gathered by the pig-sty. Mami held a large white porcelain bowl, Papi a rope, our landlord a long butcher knife. Our next-door neighbor and her sons had set up a table on sawhorses nearby, and a caldron of water bubbled over the fire in the pit, tended by some people I didn't recognize.

Papi tied the squealing pig by its legs and, with the help of one of the men, turned it over and carried it to the table. Our landlord drew a necklace on the pig's neck with one swift arc of the knife, and blood gushed into Mami's porcelain bowl, squirted droplets onto her apron, bright red spots that jelled into maroon dots.

"The tail is mine," I announced, and the grown-ups laughed.

"You have to earn it," our neighbor said. She handed me a bowl into which the pig's guts spilled like syrup, quivering pink, blue, and yellow, warm and musky, alive, hard to imagine as solid, piquant, brown sausages.

While the men dressed and roasted the pig, Mami and the women made *pasteles*. They grated plantains, green bananas, *yautías*, and yucca, into bowls, seasoned the mixture, spooned mounds of it onto roasted banana leaves, and dropped chunks of savory meat into the centers of the mounds. They then folded the banana leaves into rectangles, tied them with cotton twine, and dropped the *pasteles* into a huge pot of boiling water. They split ripe coconuts open, broke the thick white meat into chunks that we children grated when we weren't munching. The flakes were squeezed for coconut milk, to be used for *arroz con dulce* and *tembleque*. Some of the coconut milk was mixed with sweet evaporated milk, sugar, egg yolks, and rum to make *coquito*. I helped Papi string colored lights across the yard, and we decorated an eggplant bush with crêpe paper flowers and cutout figures. For once, the music coming from the other side of our wall was festive and hopeful, with only one or two songs blaming women for men's troubles.

On Christmas Eve the bar was closed, and neighbors came out of their houses dragging tables, which were lined up along one end of our yard and then laden with food made by women

I'd never seen, who came in and out as if they were long-lost relatives, stroking our hair, smiling at me and my sisters and brothers as if we were the most wonderful creatures on earth. A group of men showed up with a *cuatro*, a guitar, *maracas*, and *güiros*. The middle of the yard was cleared and swept for a dance floor. We all sang *aguinaldos*, and for the rest of the night people danced and sang and ate and drank and celebrated as if we were all friends and had only needed an excuse to get together.

⮞ "Tomorrow I'm taking you to visit your cousins," Mami said some weeks later.

"What cousins?"

"Gladys and Angie. They're really my cousins, but they're your age. You're spending a few days with them."

They lived in a cement house with a blue and white porch next to Lalo's Cafetín, a landmark in the area known as La Parada 22. Mami had grown up on this street, and Tío Lalo had built his fortune here, in a store that specialized in homemade sweets and Puerto Rican fast food—codfish fritters, fried plantain balls, and his famous stuffed potatoes.

We were greeted by his wife, Angelina, and their two daughters. On the way to their house Mami had told me to be especially nice to Gladys and when I met her, I understood why. She was tall and gaunt, with huge black watery eyes and a timid manner that told me she would remain *jamona* the rest of her life. Her sister, Angie, was pretty, lively, with a quick sense of humor and the air and manner of someone who was used to getting her way. I liked Gladys better, but I could see that Angie was more fun.

"Girls, take Negi and show her your rooms," Angelina said. Angie bounded off behind a curtain, and I followed Gladys, who walked at a leisurely pace, as if counting seconds.

"This is where we will sleep," Gladys said, stepping into a narrow room by a neatly made bed that took up most of the floor space. A small Miami window looked out on a cement yard and the wall of the next house. There was a small rug in front of the bed, and a long bare dresser across from it, near a door to another room patched with pictures of singers and movie stars.

"Those are her pictures," Gladys muttered in a voice that reminded me of the sound from a comb harmonica.

"You can come in now," Angie sang and opened the door a crack. "Not you!" she said to her sister. Gladys backed away and lay on her bed, hands on her chest, her huge eyes fixed on the ceiling.

Angie's room was pink and ruffled, carpeted, and decorated with stuffed animals, dolls, and pictures of American movie stars. She had her own pink record player and a collection of albums. Books and magazines were stacked in a basket near her bed. The dresser held a matched comb and brush set, a mirror tray with tiny perfume bottles shaped like kittens and bunnies. On the night table a ballerina held aloft a lamp shade, and a soft pink light bathed her porcelain tutu, accentuating the curves of her strong legs.

"Wow!" I couldn't help myself. Even Jenny's room wasn't this nice.

"You can't come in here unless I ask you," Angie said, and I backed away, afraid that if I touched anything I would stain, or break, or somehow contaminate the feminine air of this fragrant room. Angie closed the door. I retreated to the edge of Gladys's bed and stared at the curtain leading to the room where Mami and Angelina murmured in soft cadences.

"She's so mean," Gladys muttered. "Mamita and Papito spoil her just because she's the youngest." It seemed strange that Gladys should call her parents by the diminutive, which was usually reserved for small children. "They insist we call them that," she said, as if she had read my mind. "I know it sounds babyish, but they make us do it."

I looked around her room, the only decoration in it a framed copy of the Lord's Prayer. Soft music came from Angie's door so faintly that it could have been in the house next door.

"Don't you have a radio?" I asked.

"No. My mother is Evangelical. She doesn't like the radio, unless it's preachers."

A wave roiled inside my stomach, and my fingertips and toes felt cold. In Macún many of our neighbors were Evangelicals. The men dressed in neat white shirts and ties, and the women wore sleeved blouses and long skirts in solid, dull colors year-round. They never cut their hair and didn't wear makeup, shorts, or jewelry. They didn't dance, drink, or read popular novels. Every other word out of their mouths was "Blessed be the Lord" or "*Aleluya*," and they went around door-to-door every Sunday selling religious magazines. From what I could see, they lived dull, inhibited lives. But they lived them with a fervor that was frightening. Our family never went to church, and I worried that people who did were infallible and we were wrong in our willful resistance to religious guidance. Mami had not told me Uncle Lalo and Angelina were Evangelicals, and I worried that she didn't know and that they would try to convert me. Then I wouldn't be any fun and would spend the rest of my days selling *The Watch Tower* and brushing my long hair into a single braid that dangled down my back.

"I want to see my mother," I said to Gladys and stepped through the curtain. Mami and Angelina were in the kitchen cooking. "Mami can we go now?"

"No, silly. You're spending a few days here." She said it with an edge to her voice, letting me know I was being disrespectful by asking to leave when we hadn't even eaten. Angelina smiled.

"And you haven't seen your Tío Lalo's store yet. Come, and you can choose a dessert for after dinner." She led me through a door into a room with a long table and a sink on either end. There were shelves along the wall, and a refrigerator. Against a corner there was a stack of burlap sacks with fancy black lettering: POTATOES. We stepped down twice into another room dominated by glass-front refrigerator cases that served as the counter for the store. On either side of the narrow center aisle there were more refrigerated cases for ice cream and sodas, and the walls of the store were dappled with candy in shiny cellophane wrappers clipped to metal skeletons.

Tío Lalo stood behind the counter. Every second we were there he was serving people lined up to buy his stuffed potato balls or his creamy *tembleque.*

"Hello!" he murmured, his solemn face not giving any hint that he was happy to see me. "Pick any sweet you like," he said. I looked around, unable to decide, until he pulled a Hershey's Milk Chocolate Bar from the wall. "Take this one," he said, "and get back to the house." Even though I wouldn't have chosen that one, I took it and scrammed, sensing that the store, with all its colors and things to make a child happy, belonged to Tío Lalo alone, and not even his family was allowed to go in there.

&❧ Angelina's cooking was bland and colorless. Before we could eat, she offered a prayer, and we had to bow our heads to hear it. At the end, Mami elbowed me so that I would say "Amen" along with everyone else.

"So how long will you be in New York?" Tío Lalo asked.

Everyone looked at me. Mami wore a frightened expression. "A couple of weeks," she said.

"You're going to New York?" I couldn't believe she hadn't told me. Now I knew why I had to spend time in this quiet, cheerless house.

"Your grandmother made an appointment for Raymond to see a specialist. Maybe they can save his foot." It was an apology, not a reason.

"But why didn't you tell me?" I couldn't help the whine in my voice, the tightness that closed my throat, making it difficult to speak without pain. "Why can't I go with you?"

"Your Mami can't afford to take both of you," Angelina said. "It's very expensive to go to New York. Besides, we're so happy to have you. You've never been to visit us," she said, as if it were my fault.

"Come on," Tío Lalo muttered, "don't make it hard for your Mami."

Mami had never needed anyone to defend her, and all of a sudden it was as if she were the child and I the grown-up who was exacting justification for something that should have been obvious.

"I'll come for you as soon as I get back," she said.

"When?"

"A couple of weeks."

"But when? Which day?" I didn't care if they all thought I was a spoiled, disrespectful, impertinent brat.

Mami took in a long, deep breath that doubled the size of her chest and cleared the flush from her cheeks. "Sunday after next." She was embarrassed by my behavior, but she wasn't going to do anything about it in front of her uncle.

"What time?" I pushed.

"One-thirty in the afternoon," she said through her teeth.

"Your beans are getting cold," Angelina murmured, her voice a miaow.

I ate the tasteless beans, the sticky rice, the greasy fried chicken. To my right Mami felt tense and tight, but she talked to Angelina and Tío Lalo as if nothing special was happening, as if disappearing into the sky for weeks was something she did all the time, like killing chickens and washing her hair. Across from me, Angie toyed with her food, dispersing it over her plate so that it would look as if she'd eaten it. Gladys munched as slowly and deliberately as a cow, her huge black eyes fixed on me, her lips curled into a slight smile.

☙ That night I lay next to Gladys, unable to sleep.

"If I ever talked to Mamita like that," Gladys whispered, "Papito would beat me until I had no skin left."

I felt no sympathy, no desire to accept hers.

"Once I talked back, and Papito took me behind the kitchen and beat me with his belt."

I had no idea where my sisters and brothers were, who was

watching them while Mami took Raymond to New York. I wondered if Papi had to stay home from work. Why couldn't I stay with him and the kids? After all, I was the oldest.

"Angie talks back all the time, but they never hit her."

Mami probably didn't trust me with my sisters and brothers. After Raymond's accident she never left me alone with them for more than an hour. Maybe she knew his accident was my fault.

"Papito favors her because she's named after Mamita. I don't know why they didn't give me her name. I'm the oldest. I should have my mother's name."

Mami was probably planning to stay in New York and leave us in Puerto Rico. Maybe she had given us away, the way people who couldn't take care of their kids did. Maybe she gave me away to Tío Lalo and Angelina because they were so strict.

"They make me peel all the potatoes. She always has an excuse. Now they'll probably make you peel her potatoes while she sleeps late."

"What potatoes? What are you talking about?"

"For the stuffed potato balls. Papito is famous around here for them."

"What does that have to do with me?"

"You're here to peel potatoes. Every morning he boils two sackfuls, and we can't do anything else until they're clean, or Papito gets mad."

"Why do we have to do it?"

"Who else? He has to tend the store, and Mamita has to clean the house."

It wasn't fair. Mami had given me away to Evangelicals who would make me peel potatoes all day long. I scrunched the pillow over my head and let the sobs out. It seemed like more punishment than I deserved for letting Raymond have an accident.

     ❧ Tío Lalo set the potatoes to cook as soon as he woke up, and he had drained them by the time Gladys and I sat down to breakfast. No sooner did we finish eating than he called us into the room behind the store.

"Show her how it's done," he said to Gladys.

She speared a steaming potato with a fork and showed me how to peel it until there wasn't a spot on it. "If there are any peels left," she said, "the balls come out gritty and the customers complain."

The potatoes had to be peeled while they were hot, she explained, because the skin stuck if they got too cold. Papito, she said, didn't want a lot of waste.

Every so often, Tío Lalo came and stood behind me to see how I was doing. Whenever he did, I shook inside but let my fingers fly over the potatoes, stripping off every centimeter of skin until they were clean, yellow, and unblemished.

&ra Two Sundays later I woke up early, peeled potatoes, then packed my bag. I showered, braided my hair with ribbons, and sat in the living room reading a religious magazine while I waited for Mami to pick me up. Angelina had taken the girls to church, as she did every Sunday. To my relief, Angelina didn't seem intent on converting me. She had probably given me up for lost to the Devil the first day we met.

I sat in my nice dress, with my good shoes on, trying to look as innocent and good as I possibly could so that when Mami came she would see that I had learned my lesson. But Mami didn't come. Angelina and the girls came back from church, and we sat down to Sunday supper, and Angie disappeared into her room and Gladys into hers, and I waited, feeling more and more abandoned as afternoon lengthened into evening, then night.

Tío Lalo closed the store, came inside the house, found me sitting on the same chair, my bag at my side, the religious magazine crinkled from having been read so many times.

"She's not coming."

"How do you know?"

"She wrote me a letter that says she's coming next Friday." He smiled.

He was lying, even though he was Evangelical and they were supposed to tell the truth. He had waited until I was humiliated before bothering to tell me she wouldn't be coming that day. But his lie about the letter was only covering up for what we both knew: Mami wasn't coming today and no one knew when she would return.

I picked up my bag and sidled past him, my eyes flooded with the tears that were lately so close to the surface. I heard him chuckle as I went into Gladys's room and undressed, crumpling my dress and pretty ribbons into a ball as solid and round as his stuffed potatoes.

➤ She came with presents wrapped in *The Daily News*. For me, a yellow handbag with a small mirror on the flap. "And at home I have a lot of clothes sent by your New York cousins." She was excited and handed Angelina, Tío Lalo, Angie, and Gladys their presents while she chattered about Tata and Ana and Margot and Gury and Chico and all our relatives in New York. The doctors who had seen Raymond were the best in the world, she told us, and had assured her that with the proper treatment, his foot would heal as good as new.

I hung on to her, afraid that when it was time to leave she would forget me. But she didn't. She helped me pack my bag, put a couple of pennies in my yellow handbag, and we walked away from Tío Lalo's laden with sweets for my sisters and brothers and a dozen freshly fried stuffed potato balls.

On the bus Mami told me how tall the buildings were in New York, and how she had travelled around on trains that were much faster and nicer than our crowded, stuffy buses. We got off at a different stop, and when I told her we'd made a mistake, she said, "No. It's all right. We've moved."

CASI SEÑORITA

Con la música por dentro

With the music inside

I didn't mean to steal the nickels from the baby's glass piggy bank. But they left me alone with her, and the pig sat right there on top of the dresser as she slept. I had no idea an old lady was peeking in the window and saw me tip the pig over and slide out one nickel, two, three at most. When Papi gave me a talk about being trustworthy, and Mami a few *cocotazos*, I wasn't sorry I stole the money. I was mad that no one asked why the neighbor had been looking in the window.

That snoopy old lady in our new neighborhood put an end to my baby-sitting career. And the well-intentioned neighbor next door ensured that I would never go to church.

"Even if you don't accept the Lord," she told my mother one day as they chatted on opposite sides of their fences, "you can send your children to Sunday school. At least it gives you a free morning."

Mami lined us up for a bath, and, in keeping with the occasion, checked behind our ears and around our necks so that, even though people might complain we were heathens, no one could say we weren't clean. Héctor and Raymond were buttoned into their school assembly shirts, and us girls put on our good dresses, while Mami combed our hair into tight braids held at the nape with modest white ribbons.

"No picking your nose. No sucking your thumb. No speaking unless spoken to." She pulled up Delsa's socks and buckled Alicia's shoes. "No pushing or shoving each other. Say 'with your permission' and '*muchas gracias*' and 'you're very welcome.'" She pulled up Héctor's pants and tucked in his shirt. "If you need to use the bathroom, aim so you don't make a mess, and wash your hands afterwards."

She didn't really need to go through all the rules on behavior. They were engraved on our brains from constant repetition

and the painful results of not following them to the letter. But
Mami was not one to take chances with our natural high
spirits and tendency to ignore what she told us the minute she
turned her back.

"Doña Susana will be there watching you," Mami warned,
unnecessarily, since we expected another pair of eyes as stern
and unforgiving as hers to watch our every move when she
wasn't around. "Now go along to church."

The Iglesia San Juan Bautista de Paz y Misericordia was up
the street from our house. It had once been a private home, but
its owner went off to train as a minister, and when he came
back he held services in his living room. Before long, the congregation had grown so large that he moved elsewhere and
refurnished the house with rows of wooden pews and a tiled
fountain in the place once occupied by the family's television set.

"*¡Ay, qué lindos!*" Doña Susana exclaimed when we paraded
into the churchyard. She tugged on the sleeve of a thin young
woman. "Sister Dolores, these are the children I was telling
you about."

Sister Dolores led us to the rear of the house, where she seg-
regated us by age into small groups led by bespectacled young
men and well-scrubbed young women.

"You," she said to me, "are old enough to sit with the congregation." I joined the older children in the back of the church
just as the service began.

In contrast to Abuela's opulent church, this *iglesia* was plain,
with nothing to divert attention from the service. The white
walls were unadorned; the fountain looked like a tile bathtub.
The preacher, Don Joaquín, was slight, with child-size hands,
delicate shoulders, and a thin neck trapped inside the collar of
a starched shirt.

"Sisters and Brothers," he began in a voice so deep I looked
around to see where it came from. But Don Joaquín stood
alone in front of his congregation.

In less time than it took me to say the Lord's Prayer, he
had worked himself into a frenzy that sent the congregation

to its feet, moaning their repentance and the ecstasy of re-demption.

Don Joaquín called on sinners to cast off evil and come to Jesus. Men and women who until that day had been sedate citizens—a solemn storekeeper, the unsmiling man who delivered the mail, the stern school crossing guard, the methodical newspaper vendor—stood up in rapture, ran to the front of the room, knelt in front of Don Joaquín, grabbed for his hand, waved their arms about in jerky motions. Tears streamed down their cheeks, their voices charged with sobs, choked laughter, unfinished prayers, joyous gratitude. These proper folk, who had always maintained an appearance of peaceful reserve, now rolled in the aisles with abandon. Don Joaquín's voice rose in timbre and pitch, until he seemed to disappear and only his words remained, reverberating against the cement walls, piercing the assembled into delirious convulsions and ecstatic trances.

Every hair on my body stood on end as I witnessed these transformations. A bristling sweat seeped into my clothes, dribbled behind my ears. I wanted to wail, to wave my arms in exuberance, to give myself up right then and there to the un-explainable force that overpowered the others in the room.

But my fear was too great, my conscience too precocious to allow me to relinquish control of my well-guarded soul. I was alone, isolated in a bubble of resistance, watching this surreal scene magnified beyond comprehension. I crumpled onto the hard pew and hid my face behind my hands, through which bright specks of light still danced in circles.

※ "If she wants to play the piano, let her," Papi argued, pride in his voice.

"How can we afford a piano?" Mami asked. "We don't even have a television set."

"She doesn't need a piano while she's studying. Don Luis said she can come over and practice there any time."

Mami turned up her nose. "That buttery old man!"

"He's the principal of the school, Monín. Everyone else holds him in high regard."

"He has shifty eyes, and he can't sit still."

"He's a musician. Those people always seem nervous to the rest of us."

I had not meant to start a contest of wills between my parents when I mentioned my dreams of playing the piano to Papi. My hands seemed to yearn for action, moving constantly as I talked, seeking textures when I sat reading a book, digging fearlessly into holes on walls, dipping into containers, drawers, boxes with lids that didn't quite close. Since I loved music, learning to play piano seemed like a good choice, even though I'd never actually seen a piano, let alone had any idea of what it took to play one.

When I mentioned it to Papi, he was excited. The idea of a concert career for me appealed to his vision of himself as a poet and of me as more than a spunky tomboy. He took it upon himself to find me a teacher and came up with the principal at my new school, an elderly gentleman with thinning hair and a thick mustache that seemed pasted on his delicate features. We wouldn't have to pay anything, Papi said, because "he's willing to give you lessons in exchange for some carpentry on his porch."

On Sunday afternoon I set off with Papi for my first piano lesson. I had never seen a teacher outside of school, and as we neared Don Luis's house, I was scared and dug my thumbnail into the other nails to scrape out any dirt that might have escaped the scratchy bristles of Mami's vegetable brush.

"¡*Buenas*!" he greeted us. I held on to Papi's hand as to a lifeline, not trusting my knocking knees to hold me up. But Don Luis's warm smile soon melted my fear into awe at finding myself in his house, away from the unpleasant implications of a student face-to-face with the school principal.

His house was detached from those around it, surrounded by flowers that bloomed in splendid colors and overwhelming fragrances. The inside was small but as ornate as the yard, with lace curtains, glass-topped tables, invitingly curvy furniture, and, dominating the back wall, an enormous reddish-brown piano, lustrous and dust free, majestic against a fabric-covered wall. I looked at Papi, who winked at me and smiled. We shared the joy of being in this room, in the home of an artist, a person whose life was gracious and carefree, whose furnishings and decorations were as impractical as ours were utilitarian.

"Well," Papi said, "I'll get to work outside." He left me in the room, which suddenly became as foreign as another country.

Don Luis led me to the piano and showed me how to open it to reveal the gleaming white and black keys that welcomed me to a world as removed from my everyday life as I could ever hope to get. He ran his fingers across with a light touch, and I noticed how long and tapered they were, how feminine. "You place your hands on the keys like this."

He led me through the lesson. In the background, Papi sawed and hammered in a rhythm much more musical than what I conjured from the piano. But when the hour was over, Don Luis insisted that I showed aptitude and suggested that in the future I should come at a different time because Papi's hammering interfered with my timing.

After that, Mami walked me to Don Luis's house then let me come home by myself. She didn't insist that I dress up, as long as my clothes were neat and clean. But Don Luis cared what I wore. He often commented on the color of a blouse or the cut of a skirt, and once he suggested that next time I wear the same sleeveless scoop-neck dress. Its blue flowers, he said, were pretty. When I told Mami she made a face, and that night she muttered to Papi about "what that dirty old man is up to. You know she's *casi señorita*."

Until then Mami had used the excuse that I was almost pubescent to warn me against playing with boys, to insist that I do something useful like housework or cooking, and to remind me to sit with my legs together. But now she was using the familiar phrase as a warning to Papi, not to me, as if it were he who had to do something about my semistatus. It excited me that being "*casi señorita*" meant my piano teacher saw me as more than a gifted student. The next time I went for my lesson I wore the sleeveless scoop-neck dress, which until then had been a favorite only because it kept me cool, and its broad skirt made it possible to sit cross-legged without my panties showing.

"So pretty," Don Luis said as I came in. "So nice."

We began the lesson with my tortured scales, but he interrupted to put his arm around me, to demonstrate, he said, the proper position of my wrist. He was as fragrant as the flowers outside his window, as slight, but he trembled with a warmth I'd never felt before, an almost imperceptible tremor that somehow transferred to me. I nudged him, respectfully, as if by accident. He returned his arm to his own body and slid over.

"Ahem," he said and straightened his collar.

I continued playing but was unable to concentrate because I kept the corner of my eye on his restless hands, the elegant fingertips that danced against the pale blue fabric of his pants.

"No, no, no!" He took my fingers into his left hand and, with the right, slapped me hard.

I hopped off the bench, humiliated. "Why'd you do that?"

"You're striking the keys like they're conga drums. This is a very delicate instrument. The touch has to be light, light. . . ." He wiggled his fingers in the air. "Now sit down and try again."

I sat as far away from him as possible without falling off the bench, elbows butterflied to give me even more room. He stood up, walked behind me, bent over, and gently pushed my arms close to my ribcage, held them there.

"Better," he said softly.

He hovered above me, his fingers on my elbows as light as flour, his skin shivering against mine. I pounded my unease into the keys, hoping the discordance would drive him away, but he held on. His breath fanned my hair as he bent closer. I hunched away from him and saw how the neckline on my dress puffed out for a clear view, to anyone standing above, of the slight mounds, like egg yolks, that had recently begun to ache on my chest. I jumped up and pulled the neckline of the dress up until my fists were against my chin. He stepped back, hands in front of him in a position similar to the one I used to keep Mami from striking me. His eyes were wide, his skin mottled pink and white, his mouth invisible behind his mustache.

"¡*Viejo asqueroso*!" I screamed in a voice and tone borrowed from my mother. "Filthy old man!"

Shame rose from the ground and wrapped me in a hot, turbulent funnel that I wished would lift me out of this room, away from my school principal's startled blue eyes and quivering, elegant fingers. I shuddered with fear and rage. I felt soiled, as if his gaze had branded my naked chest. He spoke, but I couldn't make sense of what he said, nor did I stay to listen. I backed out of his house, confused, arms wrapped around myself, head heavy, as if it had grown until I felt I had no body.

That night, when I told them what happened, Mami and Papi had a loud fight. I was not to study piano anymore, and Papi was to have a talk with Don Luis. As if she didn't trust Papi to do it right, Mami went to school the next day to have her own discussion with the school principal. And for the rest of the year, whenever we passed in the hall, Don Luis sought the distance directly above and beyond me, as if I had become invisible as dust.

> If I stepped out of our new house on Calle Castro Viña, up the block and to the left, I could walk through a quiet, shadowy street that curved in and out of unpaved alleys and, within minutes, be sitting at my grandmother's table, eating *guanimes*, which were cornmeal patties stuffed with cheese, wrapped in a banana leaf, and then boiled. Mami didn't make *guanimes*.

"Too much work," she said.

Abuela didn't think they were too much work. Every Friday she made them and served them with a clear fish head broth on the surface of which floated fresh cilantro.

My grandfather had died the year before, of old age. When I came to Abuela's house, I mourned the emptiness of his room, from which he had emerged dressed in his white long-sleeve shirt and pants, his feet bare, his platinum hair cropped to a stubble.

Once, while Abuela was in the kitchen, I stepped inside Abuelo's room. Everything looked the same: the narrow cot, the colorful picture of Jesus' bleeding head crowned with thorns, a palm frond nailed above it, the simple table and chair. The room was cold, its cement walls whiter than I remembered, the window shaded by a breadfruit tree, its large leaves shedding pale reflections against the ceiling. I touched the small pillow where Abuelo's head had rested and had an image of him deftly peeling an orange in a long ribbon to his bare feet, which were brown, calloused, and delicately shaped.

"He's in Heaven, with Papa Dios," Abuela said behind me, startling me out of the brooding sorrow that pressed against my chest. I let her lead me to the table, where the hot broth and gritty cornmeal soothed the ache.

"I hope when your Mami is in New York you will come visit me," she said as we washed dishes.

"Mami already went to New York . . . last spring."

"I think she's going again. Generosa will stay with you for a few weeks."

I dried my hands on the hem of my dress and leaned against the sink. I took the emptiness of Abuelo's room inside myself, the cold, stippled walls desolate and hard.

"You know your little brother's foot is still giving him problems."

I knew that. But it didn't matter. His pain meant he got to spend more time with Mami than any of us did. He got to travel to New York, a place Mami spoke of with reverence.

"You have to be a help to your Mami," Abuela said. "You're the oldest. She depends on you."

I caved in to my misery. Mami was leaving, and once more she hadn't told me, hadn't included me in her plans.

"I don't like it when she goes away," I cried into Abuela's shoulder, the only place where I could express my loneliness, my fears. To have told Mami would have been wrong. She was overwhelmed by what she called "the sacrifices I have to endure for you kids," and my love, expressed in demands, added a greater burden. I was keenly aware that she wasn't *my* mother: I had to share her with Delsa, Norma, Héctor, Alicia, Edna, and Raymond. But it seemed that somehow my share was smaller because I was the oldest, because I was *casi señorita*, because I ought to know better.

I walked home from Abuela's house feeling Mami's absence as if she had already left. By the time I got home, I had wrapped myself in the blanket of responsibility she was about to drop on me. It felt heavy, too big for me, yet if I made the wrong move, I was afraid it would tear, exposing the slight, frightened child inside.

❧ It wasn't that when Mami was gone we misbehaved more. It was simply that I couldn't muster her authority, couldn't manage to keep my sisters and brother in line with her strict rules of behavior. Not when I, too, saw an opportunity to break them.

"What do you kids like to eat?" Titi Generosa asked us, her voice scratchy as a *güiro*.

"Oatmeal!" Héctor sang.

"Oatmeal!" Delsa and Norma agreed.

"What else?" Titi Generosa asked.

"Pork chops and fried potatoes," I said.

"I don't like fried potatoes." Edna pouted.

"And I don't like the pork chops if they're too crisp," Alicia said, her blank-toothed grin an explanation.

"But you all like oatmeal."

"Yeay!" we shrieked, as if she had just answered the question that won the jackpot.

"All right," she mumbled. "Oatmeal it will be."

I liked Titi Generosa. Her voice, which everyone said sounded as if she were hoarse, came forth in the rhythmic *jíbaro* dialect I loved. But there was one thing Mami had warned us about, a habit we were not to pick up from her under any circumstances. Titi Generosa had a foul mouth.

She lived next to her mother, my *abuela*, whose every other word had God in it, was sister to my father, who wrote poems, and to Tío Vidal, who recited poetry as he clipped men's hair in his barbershop. But Titi Generosa wasn't inclined toward elegant speech, nor toward euphemisms. She spoke her mind in the most crude language I'd ever heard, as if there were nothing shameful in it, as if calling a woman a *puta* were not embarrassing. I loved that about her and wished for the courage to express myself in the hard language she used. But just thinking such words made me look around guiltily, as if Mami were standing behind me with a hot pepper, set to rid me of the habit of vulgar speech.

The other thing we liked about Titi Generosa was that even though she was a mother herself, she believed everything we told her, no matter how farfetched. We told her Mami didn't mind if we wandered around the neighborhood, when in fact Mami didn't allow us out of the front gate without permission, instructions for the exact route we were to take, and a promise to return at a strictly enforced time. We told Titi Generosa we didn't have to bathe daily, that we had no chores, that we could eat candy for lunch, and that we could wear whatever we wanted whenever we felt like it.

Delsa and Norma, who liked to dress like princesses whenever possible, wore out their three good dresses in no time. Héctor, who had a gift for talking people into doing things they weren't sure they wanted to do, ingratiated himself with the candy store owner down the street and spent most of his day "helping" the owner and himself. Affable, placid Alicia whiled away her days in bed, playing with dolls in tents constructed from Mami's sheets. And Edna tagged along with whoever seemed to be having the most fun. I disappeared on long walks through forbidden streets, free of Mami's vigilance.

A couple of blocks from our house, on busy Avenida Roosevelt, I came upon an enormous round building, its zinc roof bright red, its walls adorned with murals of fierce fighting cocks with sharp beaks and murderous round eyes. It was ringed by hurricane fencing; a padlock sagged from a chain wrapped around the gate. From the rear of the building cocks screeched furiously, their cries mingling with the roar of the avenue, their cries interrupted every so often by the lilting *qui-qui-ri-quí* of the roosters they once were. I felt sorry for those trapped birds, whose skinny legs were plucked to reveal spurs sharpened into lethal spikes.

Across the avenue, which was so busy I was afraid to cross to the other side, a development was going up. From backhoes, cranes, cement-mixing trucks, and men in hardhats came a roar of clanging metal, grinding gears, sliding gravel—and the occasional whistle at a passing woman.

Further down, behind a new shopping center with FOR RENT signs in the plate-glass windows, a neighborhood of *parcelas*, little farms, slept within the rustle of mango and avocado trees. Skinny dogs lay in the sun of the unpaved road; open sewers at either side obliterated the spicy smells wafting from cooking fires.

Boys played stickball in dusty yards, while girls strolled in giggly groups of two and three. I heard them whisper at the impropriety of my roving about unaccompanied, but I didn't care. Unlike them, I had no one to whom I needed give account. The freedom I had gained from Titi Generosa's ingenuousness was usually given only to boys, and it set me apart from any friends I might have had at the time, whose mothers were as cautious as mine. I savored it, as I might savor an expensive piece of candy given only at Christmas.

Behind Titi Generosa's back we called her Titi Avena, Auntie Oatmeal, because oatmeal was all she cooked for us. Papi once asked why it was that there was never any food in the house, and we told him. He rubbed his chin and looked at us suspiciously but didn't say anything.

Another day he gathered us on the back steps and told us that Titi Avena said we fought too much and gave her too many problems.

"You must behave yourselves," he said, "or she won't come to watch you anymore."

This was no threat, since the only choice would have been, we thought, Mami's speedy return from New York. We didn't have to consult each other or come up with an elaborate plan. We simply did the exact opposite of what was expected, knowing we would be punished by Mami when she returned but willing to take the chance to have her back.

We took every opportunity to make Titi Avena miserable. We played Caribs and Spaniards in the house, whooping and pretend-dying around her as she stirred our oatmeal. Delsa, who had a more disciplined conscience than I did, tried to take over the role of responsible older sister, but we turned on her, sending her in tears to sit resentful and hurt in the corner of the yard while we broke furniture, tore bedding, and fought one another until we drew blood. I knew what we were doing was wrong, but it was fun, even though every night I went to bed worried that Mami would show up and see the dirty house, the torn sheets, the disorder that Titi Avena tried to prevent but couldn't because she was outnumbered.

At first Papi didn't seem to notice what we were doing. He worked seven days a week, dawn to dusk, and when he came home, he gave a look at the confusion in what was once an orderly, neat three-room house and shook his head but didn't say much.

One morning, however, he didn't go to work. When Titi Avena came, she helped me pack a bag, and Papi took me to Tío Lalo's house.

"Why do I have to go there, Papi?" I cried on the bus.

"Because your *titi* can't watch you kids. And I have to work, so I can't stay home and take care of you."

"Why doesn't Mami come back?"

"I don't know." He said it as if he didn't care if she ever returned.

He had a cup of coffee and a piece of Tío Lalo's rice with coconut and raisins then kissed me on the forehead. "You be a good girl now, until your mother comes."

I stood on the threshold of Tío Lalo's house, Gladys's watery eyes fixed on me, Angie's face hiding a smile, Angelina's catlike voice miaowing assurances that Mami would be back soon, and then I could see my sisters and brothers again.

⇛ The visit with my cousins took on a routine as dull and uninspired as the previous days had been exhilarating. Gladys and I rose early to peel potatoes, then we sat for hours in the front porch playing jacks or jumping rope to made-up rhymes. Occasionally, Angie joined us, but most of the time she remained sequestered in her pink room, listening to the music we were forbidden in the rest of the house. I once considered running away and packed my belongings in the ragged bag Mami had given me, but I didn't have the courage to step out of Tío Lalo's house into the large world beyond his stoop. I counted the days by the sacks of potatoes that Gladys and I peeled. Fingers burning, I stripped the hot skin off potatoes in silence, swallowing hurt and resentment with the same outward resignation that Gladys manifested. But although it seemed that Gladys had simply accepted her lot with meekness, I seethed, playing Titi Avena's dirtiest words inside my head as I dropped potato after potato into the bowl where they would be mashed. One potato, *coño*. Two potato, *puñeta*. Three potato, *carajo*.

DREAMS OF
A BETTER LIFE

Adiós Candelaria hermosa
las espaldas te voy dando,
no siento lo que me llevo
sino lo que voy dejando.

❧

Goodbye lovely Candelaria,
I turn my back to you,
I feel not for what I take,
but for what I leave behind.

"I couldn't believe it! I get home, and everything's gone. The house is locked. The windows are shuttered. There's no sign that anyone lives there. So I ask the neighbor, who tells me Pablo moved! Didn't even write to me in New York. He just sold everything, packed off the kids, and went back to Macún."

Angelina gasped. "How did you find them?"

"I went to Doña Margara's house. She told me." Mami stroked my head, which lay relaxed and at home on her lap.

"Are we going back to Macún?" I asked, hopeful.

"Nah! I'm not living there again."

"Is Papi going to live with us?"

She tightened her lips. "Yes, of course." She stood up. "Go get your things. We have to go."

I stuffed my belongings into a bag, fingers shaking so hard I couldn't zipper the top. Mami had come back from New York with cropped hair that formed a curly black ring around her face. Her nails were long and painted deep pink. She wore high heels and stockings that shadowed the blue lines on her legs.

But besides her appearance, there was something new about her, a feeling I got from the way she talked, the way she moved. She had always carried herself tall, but now there was pride, determination, and confidence in her posture. Even her voice assumed a higher pitch that demanded to be heard. I was puzzled and frightened by this transformation but at the same time enthralled by it. She was more beautiful than before, with eyes that seemed to have darkened as her skin glowed paler. Even Angelina remarked on this. "*¡Qué bonita te ves!*" she had exclaimed, and we all had to look and agree that yes, she looked very pretty.

On the way to the bus, men stared, whistled, mumbled *piropos*. Eyes fixed straight ahead, she pretended to ignore the gallantries, but a couple of times her lips curled into a smile. I strolled next to her half proud, half afraid. I had heard men speaking compliments in the direction of women, but I'd never been aware of them going to my mother. Each man who did a double take or pledged to love her forever, to take her home with him, to give his life for her, took her away from me. She had become public property—no longer the mother of seven children, but a woman desired by many. I wanted to jump on those men and punch their faces in, to quiet the promises and the seductive looks, to chill the heat they gave off, palpable as the clothes I wore. During the entire bus ride home I was miserable, wrapped in a rage I couldn't explain or think away. Mami chatted about New York, my cousins, movies, and tall apartment buildings. But I didn't listen. I kept replaying the walk to the bus stop, her proud bearing, the men's stares, their promises, and the nakedness her accessible beauty made me feel.

❧ Our new place in Sabana Grande was a pretty *finca* at the end of a cul-de-sac by a golf course. A creek ran at the side of the property dividing us from the large house next door, which Mami said belonged to "*una gente rica*"—rich folks. On the other side of us was the home of Doña Lina and Don José, their children, and their television set.

We had seen television before, but this was the first time we were captivated by the figures on the screen. Tom and Jerry, El Pato Donald, and El Ratoncito Mickey Mouse delighted us with their adventures. Superman burst through walls, lifted cars, and caught people falling out of buildings before they hit the ground. Tarzan let out mighty yelps and swung from limb to limb on vines that looked suspiciously like ropes decorated with sweet-potato vines. All the male characters, cartoon or live action, sounded like the same two people—José Miguel Agrelot or Jacobo Morales, two of my favorite radio voices. It took me a long time to figure out that the programs were actually in English dubbed into Spanish, and after that I enjoyed them less because I spent most of my time watching the mouths move out of synchronization with the voices.

Papi was never a part of this entertainment. He had converted what used to be a tool shed into his private world, with a padlock on the door and curtained windows from which sometimes rose sweet-smelling smoke. He came home, ate dinner, and disappeared into his room with a lit candle and books and magazines. We knew better than to disturb him. He was as withdrawn as a person can be and still live in the same household: morose, preoccupied with matters that were none of our business.

Once, while he was in the latrine, I sneaked into his spice-scented hideaway and rifled through a stack of Rosicrucian literature and a book by Nostradamus. Just touching the pages gave me the creeps. Illustrations of disasters and holocausts bloomed over the turbaned heads of men with bulging eyes of frightening intensity. The texts were in formal Spanish, with *thee* and *thou*, and grammar that was hard to follow. On a small table by the window, an unmarked bottle of amber liquid sparkled next to a chipped bowl with ashes. A strange energy shadowed the corners of the room; the air seemed to circle on itself, confined by the narrow walls. I ran out, breathless, my heart beating fast, chills curling my tailbone.

❧ I got my own room, off the kitchen, with a curtain for a door. In it Mami put a cot with its own mosquito net, a small table and chair, and a basket for my underclothes. Papi nailed a rod in the corner, where I hung my uniform and good clothes.

"Now you keep this room neat," Mami said. "You know

you're almost *señorita* and should learn how to take care of things."

From his toolbox, Papi pulled out a package of green thumbtacks. "You can use these to pin pictures and poems on the wall," he said, handing me a portrait of the governor.

I clipped out flowers from cans of Carnation milk and pinned a wreath around cutouts of the little girl under an umbrella from the salt box and of Mr. Quaker from the box of oatmeal. Edna drew me a horse, and Héctor gave me one of his best marbles, which I set on a small pedestal carved from a dried avocado pit.

The first night, I couldn't sleep. The floorboards were pocked with holes where knots had fallen out. Cold air blew in, whistling a mournful tune like the dead singing. I pulled the sheets up to my chin and tucked my head between my arms. Under the house, hens cackled softly, while the flapping of wings above sounded like secret applause. I rolled into a ball in the middle of the mattress, cold sweat nipping my back. I missed Delsa's warmth, the secure feeling of sleeping in a room full of people. I tossed until dawn, unused to so much room on the bed, while on the other side of the wall, my sisters and brothers slept, their bodies gently rising and falling in rhythm with one another's breathing.

I woke to the cock's song. Outside the air glistened misty grey, and in the dark recesses of the yard, toads and tree frogs still serenaded the night. Inside, my sisters and brothers curled against each other like newborn kittens. From Mami and Papi's room came a rustle of sheets and hushed mumbles. I tiptoed to their door and a board creaked.

"Who's there?" Mami called out.

"It's me," I whispered, walking in. Mami lay in Papi's arms, her head on his shoulder, his left hand cradling her face. He quickly pulled their covers up, but I saw she was naked. She blushed, and even though Papi's skin was too dark to show it, I knew he blushed too by the startled expression on his face.

"What are you doing up so early?" Mami asked sitting up. Her hair was matted against her neck, and she brushed it away with one hand, while with the other, she held the covers up to her chest.

"I don't know. I just woke up."

"Go back to bed. It's too early." She lay down against Papi's shoulder again, and I backed out of the room, feeling left out. I stood on the other side of the door a while, but there was no sound from their room until I'd crossed the creaky floor. The rustles resumed, and the throaty whispers. I lay on the living room couch and was lulled to sleep by the sound of my parents making love.

⭮ Papi and Mami started a business. We called it a *cafetín ambulante*, a small truck with compartments and shelves in the back, a refrigerated section, and a hot plate. From the truck he sold coffee and pastries, the hot lunches Mami cooked daily, and the bark cider he made by the gallon. The shelves were laden with snacks and sweets, which we were not allowed to touch. He drove to construction sites and broadcast the menu of the day through a loudspeaker. His rich baritone could be heard a mile away reciting poems about the food on the back of his truck:

> *They say my* arroz con pollo *is good,*
> *Especially when enhanced by red beans*
> *Soaked overnight,*
> *Cooked at low heat with ham and delectable spices.*
> *The plantains are ripe, fried until just right.*
> *The coffee steams hot like Vesuvius.*
> *The milk pasteurized, sugar* del país,
> *So you know it's sweet.*
> *Come see for yourself.*
> *Give your mouth a treat.*

The business didn't last very long. The truck was expensive to maintain, bandits tried to mug him a few times, and he didn't have the heart to say no to men who bought on credit then never paid him back. The truck was returned to wherever it had come from, and Papi went back to his work fixing other people's houses.

⮎ Love made people do crazy things. Husbands shot wives in fits of passion then turned the gun on themselves and splattered their brains all over the walls. The newspapers printed photographs of dismembered bodies, bloody sheets, rooms in which all the furniture had been upended and strewn as if by a hurricane: SCENE OF THE CRIME, the headlines read.

On the radio, love was different. Men with rich voices, who were always tall and dark, won the hearts of young women who were always petite and innocent. Even if poor, the men were decent, worthy of respect, accomplished in the manly arts of riding and pistol shooting, but not reckless with either animals or firearms. The women suffered. Frequently they were orphaned, brought up by nuns or stepmothers who made them do all the housework. In spite of this, they were cheerful and optimistic, never doubting that if they were pure of heart, life would eventually get better.

I rushed home from school every day to sit by the radio for hours listening to the romantic tales of women with names like Mariana and Sofía, and men such as Armando and Ricardo. The more convoluted the story lines, the more I liked them, and I imagined that all the long-suffering heroines looked like me, or rather, that I looked like them. At night I played out the fantasies, seeing myself race across a flower-strewn field, hair blowing wild, arms outstretched toward the waiting arms of a tall, dark Armando or Ricardo who kissed me passionately in a frenzy of violins. I always fell asleep just as Armando or Ricardo touched my lips, and mornings, I woke to the same embrace, and a warm feeling between my legs that I savored until it faded like morning mist.

According to the soap operas, someday I would fall in love at first sight, but my love and I would suffer before we could be happy. There would be illnesses, from which I would recover just at the point of death. There would be evil women who would lie, cheat, and try to maim me just to get their claws into my sweetheart. There would be wars and earthquakes, tornadoes, hurricanes, epidemics, which I would survive by nursing those less fortunate, only to discover my beloved among the dying and revive him with the power of my brown eyes. All this I dreamed during those restless nights in my own room.

At the same time, Mami and Papi battled each other, intruding into my fantasies with their real-life love-hate relationship. Even though they'd lived together for fourteen years, they weren't married, but it hadn't been an issue in our lives until Mami returned from New York. All of a sudden, it seemed important to her that she and Papi be legal. They fought about it constantly. One minute they were just like any other couple, doing things together, playing with us kids, boasting about our virtues to the neighbors. The next they called each other names, spewed out ugly lists of offenses on both sides, with the recurrent theme of Mami's uncertain status as a common-law wife.

I disappeared into my room the minute the air tensed and wrapped myself in a thin sheet that didn't silence their insults but made me invisible to the hate that clouded their eyes. I called up the images of Armando or Ricardo, and with Papi and Mami's shrill fights as background, I imagined a man and woman touching one another gently, discovering beauty in a stubbled cheek or a curl of hair, whispering adoring words into each other's ear, warming one another's bodies with love.

∾ Johannes Vélez noticed me, even though Maritza Ortiz said I was so ugly that no boy would ever want me. She was the most popular girl in seventh grade. I was nobody. Her reasons for picking on me were as mysterious as Johannes's reasons for catching up with me one day after school and offering to carry my books.

"I can carry them myself," I snapped.

"Aw, come on, Esmeralda," he mumbled, standing closer. "Don't make me look bad."

A group of boys leaned against the wall of the school, pretending not to watch us. Maritza and her retinue giggled near them. I had not fallen in love at first sight with Johannes Vélez, but his eyes on me felt good, and I wanted very much to give him my books to carry. But I felt as if by handing them over I would be relinquishing something more precious than my math homework, only I didn't know what that something might be.

"You can do it tomorrow," I said and walked off in a haze of fear and anger at my own stupidity. That night Armando and Ricardo blended into the mournful face of Johannes Vélez. I replayed our encounter, only this time I was charming, confident, able to carry on a conversation that dazzled him while Maritza and her friends watched enviously.

❧ "Mami, what should I do if a boy wants to carry my books?" I asked the next morning.

"Let him," she said as she flipped an egg. She went to the door, pan in hand. "Delsa, Norma, Héctor, you'd better get dressed fast or you'll be late for school." She slid the egg on my plate. "Who wants to carry your books?"

"Johannes Vélez."

"What kind of a name is that?"

"I don't know."

"Is he American?"

"He's from around here."

"Who's from around here?" Delsa asked hopping to her chair.

"Negi's boyfriend," Alicia said from across the table.

"He's no such thing!" I yelled. Norma and Héctor pushed each other to sit near the window.

"Stop that!" Mami hollered. She broke three eggs into the pan, "Uhmm . . . Vélez. . . . I don't know a Vélez family." As if everyone in the world had to check with her before moving to town.

"There's a Vélez in my class. Sarita Vélez. She's a pest."
Norma turned up her nose.

"Not the same family," I bit back, possessive all of a sudden.

"Negi has a boyfriend!" Héctor sang.

"I do not!"

"Do so!" Delsa and Norma joined in the chant, and Edna
and Raymond appeared out of nowhere to torture me.

"Mami, make them stop!"

"You kids leave your sister alone."

But they just lowered their voices to a whisper when Mami
turned her back. "Negi has a boyfriend!"

"Mami!" I was embarrassed by their teasing and would have
bopped them on the head if Mami hadn't been right there.

"You kids get ready for school. Scram!" They left the table
one at a time, Mami taking threatening steps toward them
each time they stopped to look back with mischievous expres-
sions and a mouthed "Negi has a boyfriend."

I was humiliated. Tears formed in my eyes, making Mami's
face look out of focus.

"If there's a boy who likes you," she rubbed my hair, "and
you like him, ask him to visit you at home. That's the proper
thing to do."

"It's not like I'm getting married or anything. He just asked
to carry my books."

"I know . . . But you're *casi señorita*, and boys are interested.
The thing is, no boy will respect you if you don't bring him
home to meet your parents."

I should never have asked her. She had no clue about my
feelings. All she cared about was the boy, not me.

"Why do you keep saying I'm *casi señorita*? When am I
going to be a *señorita*, without the *almost*?"

"Negi, don't take that tone of voice with me."

"But when, Mami? You keep saying I should do this, I
shouldn't do that, I should do the other. All because I'm almost
a *señorita*. What does that mean? What does it have to do
with anything?" I heaved out sobs so full they scared me. She
held me for a few minutes then sent me to my room.

"Take off your uniform before it gets wrinkled."

"But I have to go to school," I wailed as if she'd just given me awful news.

"You can be a little late. Lie down for a while, and I'll send a note that you weren't feeling well."

I unsnapped my skirt and unbuttoned my shirt, tears streaming down my cheeks, sobs racking my chest so that I had to lean against the wall as I undressed. The world was a terrible, cruel place, a dark pit jawing open to swallow me in perpetual despair.

Mami sent Delsa, Norma, Héctor, Alicia, and Edna to school, their protests proving my point, making me cry even harder. Raymond rubbed my leg gently, but I kicked him away, unwilling to accept pity. In the kitchen Mami scrubbed the dishes, sighing, "*Ay Dios Mío Santo*, help me make it through their puberties!"

↲ Our house sat on concrete stilts that allowed enough headroom underneath for us to stake out play areas with clearly defined boundaries. Discarded pieces of zinc, chicken wire, cardboard, torn sheets that Mami had given us, and dried palm fronds formed the walls of our very own *barrio* under the house. My spot was on the back corner nearest the kitchen, where the land sloped toward Papi's shed. I couldn't quite stand up, but I could crawl in and kneel or squat comfortably. I had swept the ground smooth and placed mismatched tiles in the center for a colorful mosaic floor. It was there that I went when I was sick and tired of everybody, which was most of my twelfth year.

Through a hole in the burlap bag that served as the door of my hideaway I had a view of the creek, the *malanga* and bananas growing on the slope, and the gardenia near the porch. The more I looked at it, the more I loved that bush that had never flowered. It was oval shaped, with branches sticking out here and there like a woman who had not combed her hair.

"Papi," I asked one night as he sat on the porch reading the paper, "how come the gardenia never blossoms?"

"It probably needs water," he said.

So every day I filled an old coffee can two or three times and watered around the roots of the bush, moistening the earth until it became spongy. The bush grew rounder, taller, its leaves thick and green.

"If you prune the tips," Mami said, "it will grow faster and fuller."

With a rusty pair of scissors, I trimmed the branches. "I'm sorry, little tree," I murmured so no one else could hear, "but I want you to grow and give us flowers." Whatever I cut off, I put under the bush, to feed the roots.

"I've taken real good care of it," I said to Papi, "but it still won't bloom."

"It takes patience. You've only been doing it for a week. Give it time."

"It won't flower when you want it to," Mami said. "Keep taking care of it and you'll see. One day it will surprise you."

I stopped asking the bush to give me gardenias but continued watering it and clipping its branches. The leaves grew larger, greener, veined underneath in pale chartreuse, the blades thick and full of liquid that I kept expecting to smell like gardenias, but it didn't.

"It's probably a *macho* tree," Papi said. "It needs a female to blossom."

"There's no such thing, Pablo," Mami chided. "Gardenias are not like people."

"But some plants need a male and a female before they can give fruit. Plantains, for instance."

"Yes, plantains. But not gardenias!" She laughed, and Papi didn't say any more.

❧ Johannes Vélez didn't ask to carry my books after I brushed him off, but during math class he stared at me. I smiled, but he looked at his notebook and seemed to be concentrating on the problems Mrs. Nuñez had given us to solve. Every day for a week I stopped to buckle my shoe, or to drink from the hall fountain, so that Johannes Vélez would have enough time to catch up. But he didn't, and I couldn't bring myself to be the first to speak. One Saturday, as I watered my gardenia bush, he showed up.

"*Hola.*" He stood stiffly on the other side of the gate, sleepy eyes begging me to ask him in. My first instinct was to run and change my tattered dress for something nicer. At the same time I was furious that he had just appeared uninvited.

Mami materialized on the porch steps as if she'd been expecting him. From every corner of the world my sisters and brothers emerged to stare at us as though at animals in a zoo.

"*Buenas tardes,*" Mami said, wiping her hands against her hips. "Negi, is this your friend from school?"

I wished a bolt of lightning would strike me dead right then and there. The idea that he now knew I talked about him to my mother, my mother!

"*Sí.*" I growled.

"Aren't you going to ask him in?" She was as cheerful as a sparrow, while I wanted nothing more than to be swallowed by the earth in one gulp.

"Come in," I mumbled and raced up the porch steps.

He sat on the sofa, silent and dignified, while Mami fed him crackers and lemonade. My sisters and brothers casually arranged themselves around the room, pretending to read or play jacks while keeping an eye on everything that went on. I wanted to swat them away like flies.

"I know some Vélezes in Bayamón," Mami said. "And there are some in Caguas." I bet there were Vélezes in every single town of the island. But she acted as if she knew them all.

"My family is from Ponce, but my dad is stationed at the Roosevelt Base."

"Oh." She was impressed. His father was a military man with a steady job.

"Where did you get such a funny name?" I asked, evil as the radio vixens.

His chocolate skin reddened. Mami glared at me. My sisters and brothers stifled giggles.

"I . . . I guess my Dad chose it. . . . I was born in Kentucky."

"Kentucky!" Mami murmured. An American as my first suitor!

"There's a Johannes-burgh in South Africa. Is that what you're named after, a city?"

The kids laughed, and Johannes bit his lip.

"Negi," Mami commanded, "come into the kitchen a minute."

As soon as we were on the other side of the wall she grabbed my arm. "You're being very rude to your friend!"

"He's not my friend. I didn't ask him to come. He just showed up."

"Well, he's here, and you must treat him with respect. Now get in there and behave like a proper *señorita*."

"All the kids are watching. . . . They'll make fun of me."

"See if he wants to go outside. Show him your gardenia bush or something. I'll keep the kids here. . . . Wait a minute." She moistened a rag and wiped my face and neck. "Scrub those grimy hands before you go."

We went back to the living room, where Johannes sat examining Héctor's new red and yellow top.

"Wanna see a tree?" I asked. Mami rolled her eyes.

We stepped into the yard, trailed by Delsa, Norma, Héctor, Alicia, Edna, and Raymond. "You kids stay with me!" Mami called.

"I have to get my marbles!" Raymond wailed.

"Get them later. Come in here now."

I led Johannes to the creek, away from the house but within view of Mami who would be watching.

"Your mother is very nice," he said.

"What are you doing here?" I couldn't help myself. He was the cutest boy in seventh grade, and I liked him. But every time

I opened my mouth, something nasty came out, as if the part of me that spoke was different from the part of me that felt. I tried to remember what soap opera heroines said to their lovers, but I couldn't compare this boy in shorts and knee socks to the manly Ricardos and Armandos. And I was no heroine. Not in my faded dress and worn shoes.

We stood by the creek, Johannes telling me about his dad's work as a sergeant in the army, the many places he'd lived, how they were moving again, to Colorado. But I didn't want to hear any of that. I wanted to hear a man's soft voice telling me I was beautiful, that he would love me forever, that life would mean nothing without me. I tuned in to the creek's gurgle, imagining a pristine river on a deserted island, its shore lined with orchids and gardenias, with birds warbling sweet melodies. I wanted to dance to this music in my head, but when I took a step, I tumbled into the creek with a wild splash. Johannes stood on the bank, stupefied. I fought the sucking mud and crawled out like some prehistoric creature from an ancient lagoon just as Mami and my sisters and brothers came running.

"You'd better go home now," I told Johannes through my tears. The last I saw of him was his straight back convulsed in laughter, his khaki pants and knee socks spattered with mud.

❦ Mami took Edna and Raymond to buy shoes, and I sat on the porch reading a Corín Tellado romance instead of watching my sisters and brother, who disappeared whenever I was in charge. A man came out of the house where "*una gente rica*" lived, his eyes shaded by a straw sombrero. He wore a yellow shirt tucked into white pants, and something about the way he moved reminded me of Jorge Negrete, the Mexican movie star. His broad shoulders tapered to a narrow waist, and he walked with the swagger of someone who wore a six shooter on each hip. He sat on a rock, dangled his hands between his knees, and stared at the quickly flowing water as if it held a secret. My heart thumped the name "Armando," whispered hoarsely as in the radio soap operas, and I willed him to look up and fall in love with me at first sight. But he just stared numbly at the stream, his face invisible under his hat. I ran inside, combed my hair, washed my face, and tugged here and there so that the bodice of my dress lay flat against the bumps on my chest. With trembling fingers, I undid one of the buttons to show an inch more skin where the cleavage should have been.

When I returned, he was on his back, hands under his neck, *sombrero* over his face. The afternoon was quiet, disturbed only by the rushing stream and the buzzing of a *colibrí* around my gardenia bush. A flower now bloomed on the side of the bush facing the water, the first to bloom of hundreds of buds that studded the tree like pale gems. I nipped it, brought it to my face, and buried myself in its fragrance. He rose and looked across to where I stood. I felt dangerous, bold, older by years, inspired by all the Marianas and Sofías whose emotional ups and downs had fed my romantic fantasies. I looked at him, and my gaze was met by an amazingly blue pair of eyes against cinnamon skin and a faint smile tickling white teeth. He tipped his hat in greeting. I nodded then stuck the stem of the gardenia in the open buttonhole, where it flopped in the wide space between my soon-to-be breasts. He chuckled, but I didn't mind. I took the gardenia out, pinned it behind my right ear, where, I thought, it accentuated my intensely black eyes. I felt beautiful, fragrant, warm as the morning sun. I leaned against the mango tree, throwing my chest up the way I'd seen María Félix do in movies when Jorge Negrete was about to kiss her. The man across the way folded his arms across his chest and smiled broadly. I closed my eyes.

"Negi, what are you doing?"

Mami stood outside the gate staring, with Edna and Raymond snickering behind her. She scraped open the gate against the cement walk, and I quickly buttoned my blouse. She stared at the man walking up the bank toward the big house on the corner.

"Who was that?"

"Who?"

"That man across the creek." He'd gone into the house as quickly as he'd appeared.

"I don't see anyone."

"Get inside and help me with these bundles," she said, dropping a shopping bag into my arms. "And I don't want you out here again when that man is out." On the rocking chair my Corín Tellado book flapped in the breeze. "I wish you'd stop reading this trash," she said and flung it inside, where it fell under the sofa, to be retrieved later.

  Mami and Papi's arguments became unbearable. They screamed at each other, ruptured the night with insults and hate-filled words that echoed in my head for days. I lay in bed crying, afraid to step into the room where I heard things breaking, but the next morning there were no mismatched pieces, no chips or fragments, nothing to sweep away. We had breakfast in silence long after Papi left for work, Mami distant as another country, shrouded by something dark and grievous that we couldn't break through. She served us, helped us dress, sent us off to school, and left for her own job in a fog of pain that obliterated all hope, all romance. I tried to disappear within the hallways of Ramón Emeterio Betances School, where children from happy homes crowded in cheery groups. The school library became a refuge from would-be friends, and I sat for hours reading fairy tales, diving into them as into a warm pool that washed away the fear, the sadness, the horror of living in a home where there was no love.

  "Don't be so dramatic!" Mami scolded as she wrestled with a chicken whose neck she was about to wring.

"But it's true," I sobbed. "Nobody loves me. I have no friends. Kids tease me all the time. And you and Papi . . ." My throat closed.

The chicken flapped its wings wildly; downy feathers floated around Mami like a nimbus. "Oof! This one doesn't want to be eaten!" She tugged hard, and the chicken's neck cracked. She grinned. "There!" The bird's wings slowed as if it were flying through water.

"You're not even listening," I whined.

She sighed deeply, hung the chicken on the side of the house, and wiped her hands on her dress. "Negi, we love you. But what goes on between me and your Papi is our business. We have our problems, just like every other couple."

"I don't hear all the neighbors yelling and screaming at each other like you do!"

"Now you're being disrespectful." The warning in her voice made me back down.

"It's not fair," I mumbled.

"What's not fair?"

"Nothing's fair. Life's not fair!" I wailed in a fresh fit of tears.

She sat next to me on the steps and draped her arms around me. Her body jiggled, and when I looked up, tears streamed down her cheeks, but her mouth was curled into a smile that she was trying hard to conceal.

"What's so funny?" I cried, on the verge of catching her giggles.

"Nothing," Mami said, laughing and kissing the top of my head. "Nothing's funny."

We sat on the steps holding each other, laughing and crying at nothing, the chicken's wings thumping against the side of the house.

☙ "Next week you will be a *teeneyer*," Papi said as we sat on the porch smelling the night air.

"What's that?"

"In the United States, when children reach the age of thirteen, they're called *teeneyers*. It comes from the ending of the number in English. *Thir-teen. Teen-ager.*"

I counted in English to myself. "So I will be a *teeneyer* until I'm twenty?"

"That's right. Soon you'll be wanting to rock and roll." He laughed as if he had told a very funny joke.

"I don't like rock and roll," I protested. "Too noisy. And it's all in English. I don't understand the songs."

"Mark my words," he said. "When you're a *teeneyer* it's like something comes over you. Rock and roll sounds good. Believe me." He laughed as if I knew what he was talking about. I hadn't seen him this happy in a long time.

"Well, it's not going to happen to me." I pouted and ignored his chuckles at my expense.

"Just wait," he said. "Once you're in New York, you'll become a regular *teeneyer Americana*."

"I'm not going to New York."

"Your mother's talking about moving there."

My stomach fell to my feet. "What?!"

"Didn't you tell them, Monín?" He called into the house, where Mami and the kids watched a program on our very own black-and-white television set.

"Tell them what?" She came out to the porch, hands on hips.

"That you're moving to New York." He didn't look at her; he just spit out the words like phlegm into the night.

"Pablo . . . ," she said as one might murmur a prayer.

"Is it true Mami?" Laughter came from the living room where my sisters and brothers watched Don Cholito's slapstick.

"How can you be so cruel?" She said to Papi. "You know I have no choice."

"You have a choice," he growled.

"Stay here? Put up with your *pocavergüenzas*?"

"I've given you a home. I'm not a rich man, but we've always had enough to eat."

"Do you consider that enough?" Her voice was tense and rising in pitch.

"I don't know what you want from me, Monín. I just don't know."

"I've lived with you for fourteen years. We have seven children together. You won't marry me. You won't leave me alone."

"Is that what you want? Marriage? What would that do? I've recognized them all. They all have my last name . . ."

"Mami, Papi, please . . ."

Rage transformed them; a red fury choked the good in both of them and bottled the love they once felt into a dark place where neither could find it.

"Please stop . . ."

Their hands formed into fists; their eyes squinted into slits that sent out invisible daggers.

"Please, Mami and Papi . . ."

They growled words that made no sense, echoes of all the hurts and insults, the dinners gone to waste, the women, the abandonments.

I crouched against the wall and watched them injure each other without touching each other, hurling words that had the same effect as acid on metal. Each word diminished them, flattened them against the night until they were puppets, pointing fingers in each other's faces. Their voices extinguished night sounds, and darkness swallowed everything but these two people I loved, the overhead light a dim spotlight that disfigured their features into grimaces. One by one Delsa, Norma, Héctor, Alicia, Edna, and Raymond came out on the porch, their eyes round as guavas, tears glistening the tips of their lashes. In their passion Mami and Papi had forgotten about us. They were real only to one another. We huddled in a corner, afraid that if we left them, they might eat each other.

➣ August marked the beginning of hurricane season. Thunder and lightning broke overhead, while in our house, a dreadful calm settled like clear water in a tainted pool. Mami prepared for our trip with the steady resolve of someone who never looks back. She bought suitcases and filled them with our good clothes, allowing us to wear only the faded dresses and shirts that we would leave behind like butterflies a cocoon. Edna, Raymond, and I were to go with her. Delsa, Norma, Héctor, and Alicia would stay with Papi until Mami could save enough money for their airfare.

"Does this mean you're divorcing Papi?" I asked.

"We were never married," she answered. "We can't get divorced."

"Why doesn't he marry you?"

"He says he doesn't love me anymore."

"Do you love him?"

"It doesn't matter. . . ."

She was a stone packed inside a shell that wouldn't crack. Papi was numb, detached even from himself, his voice flat, his step so light it was difficult to know he was there at all. We tiptoed around them and saved our voices for play far from the house, where even our laughter was received by Mami and Papi with a stare, a quizzical look, a warning glance.

"Your father is a good man," Mami told me. "Don't you ever think otherwise."

It didn't seem possible that he was a good man when he wasn't fighting for her or for us. He was letting us go to New York as if it no longer mattered where we were, as if the many leavings and reconciliations had exhausted him, had burned out whatever spark had made him search for us in swamps and fetid lagoons.

"No, I'll never go there," he said when I asked, and a wound opened in my heart that I was certain would never heal. He brought me magazines with pictures of Fabian and Bobby Rydell and encouraged me to accept what was coming with no questions, no backward glances. As if these teenage idols could ever take the place he was so willingly giving up. I tacked the pinup photos on my wall next to Don Luis Lloréns Torres, whose poems had inspired me to love my country, its *jíbaros*, and the wild natural beauty that could be found even in the foul air of El Mangle.

ê When the day finally came, he drove us to the airport, the radio tuned to the American radio station, where Brenda Lee sang her regrets. He hummed along with her, his eyes focused on the road, the rest of us silent as fog. At the airport he unloaded our bags, helped us verify our tickets. I kept expecting him to change his mind, to get down on his knees and beg Mami not to leave. But he didn't. When it was time to go, he kissed us good-bye, held us for a long time. I grasped his neck and pressed myself against his chest, smelled the minty fragrance of his aftershave, tickled my fingers through his kinky hair. Behind him Mami gathered Edna and Raymond, her eyes focused on the door to the tarmac, her mouth set in a solid line. I didn't want to give up either one of them. But it felt as if I were losing them both. Papi pushed me away, kissed both of my cheeks, and brushed the hair from my eyes.

"Write to me," he said. "Don't forget."

Edna, Raymond, and I followed Mami outside the terminal, down the strip to the waiting plane, gray and cold in the dusk. I looked behind me at Papi, his face inscrutable, at Delsa, Norma, Héctor, and Alicia huddled against the terminal window. Several times I bumped into Mami as I walked backwards, unwilling to face the metal bird that would whisk us to our new life. She tugged on my arm and swung me around to face forward, but I kept turning back to the horizon dotted with palm trees in front of moss green mountains that rose to an innocent pink sky. Mami pushed me into the plane, down a long aisle lined with seats dead-ending against a wall—my first glimpse of what New York would be like.

Across the aisle, Mami's eyes were misty. She stretched her fingers toward mine, and we held hands as the plane rose above the clouds. Neither one of us could have known what lay ahead. For her it began as an adventure and turned out to have more twists and turns than she expected or knew how to handle. For me, the person I was becoming when we left was erased, and another one was created. The Puerto Rican *jíbara* who longed for the green quiet of a tropical afternoon become a hybrid who would never forgive the uprooti

ANGELS ON THE CEILING

Ahí fué donde la puerca entorchó el rabo.

❧

That's where the sow's tail curled.

Uniformed women with lacquered hair, high heels, and fitted skirts looked down on us, signalled that we should fasten our safety belts, place parcels under the seat in front of us, and sit up.

"Stewardesses," Mami said, admiring their sleek uniforms, pressed white blouses, stiff navy ribbons tied into perfect bows in their hair. None of them spoke Spanish. Their tight smiles were not convincing, did not welcome us. In our best clothes, with hair combed, faces scrubbed, the dirt under our nails gouged out by Mami's stiff brush, I still felt unclean next to the highly groomed, perfumed, unwrinkled women who waited on us.

"Someday," Mami mused, "you might like to be a stewardess. Then you can travel all over the world for free."

The stewardesses minced up and down the narrow aisle, glancing from side to side like queens greeting the masses. I tried to read in their faces where else they'd been, if their travels had taken them to places like Mongolia, Singapore, Timbuktu. That's where I'd want to go if I were a stewardess. Not New York, Paris, or Rome. I'd want to go places so far away that I couldn't even pronounce their names. I'd want to see sights so different that it would show on my face. None of the stewardesses seemed to have been anywhere that exotic. Their noncommittal smiles, the way they seemed to have everything under control was too reassuring, too studied, too managed to make me comfortable. I would have felt better had there been more chaos.

"Do these planes ever just fall from the sky?" I asked Mami, who sat across the aisle from me.

The woman sitting in front of her shot me a fearful look and crossed herself. "*Ay, nena*, don't say such a thing," she said in a hoarse whisper. "It's bad luck."

Mami smiled.

We were high over thick clouds, the sky above so bright it hurt my eyes. In the window seat, Edna pressed her face flat against the pane. She looked up, eyes shining. "There's nothing there!" She stretched over my lap and reached out her hand to Mami. "I'm hungry."

"They'll serve us dinner soon," Mami said. "Just wait."

The stewardesses brought us small trays fitted with square plates filled with sauce over chicken, mushy rice, and boiled string beans. It all tasted like salt.

The sky darkened, but we floated in a milky whiteness that seemed to hold the plane suspended above Puerto Rico. I couldn't believe we were moving; I imagined that the plane sat still in the clouds while the earth flew below us. The drone of the propellers was hypnotic and lulled us to sleep in the stiff seats with their square white doilies on the back.

"Why do they have these?" I asked Mami, fingering the starched, piqué-like fabric.

"So that people's pomade doesn't stain the seat back," she answered. The man in front of me, his hair slick with brilliantine, adjusted his doily, pulled it down to his neck.

I dozed, startled awake, panicked when I didn't know where I was, remembered where we were going, then dozed off again, to repeat the whole cycle, in and out of sleep, between earth and sky, somewhere between Puerto Rico and New York.

❧ It was raining in Brooklyn. Mist hung over the airport so that all I saw as we landed were fuzzy white and blue lights on the runway and at the terminal. We thudded to earth as if the pilot had miscalculated just how close we were to the ground. A startled silence was followed by frightened cries and *aleluyas* and the rustle of everyone rushing to get up from their seats and out of the plane as soon as possible.

Mami's voice mixed and became confused with the voices of other mothers telling their children to pick up their things, stay together, to walk quickly toward the door and not to hold up the line. Edna, Raymond, and I each had bundles to carry, as did Mami, who was loaded with two huge bags filled with produce and spices *del país*. "You can't find these in New York," she'd explained.

We filed down a long, drafty tunnel, at the end of which many people waited, smiling, their hands waving and reaching, their voices mingling into a roar of *hello*'s and *how are you*'s and *oh, my god, it's been so long*'s.

"Over there," Mami said, shoving us. On the fringes of the crowd a tall woman with short cropped hair, a black lace dress, and black open-toed shoes leaned against a beam that had been painted yellow. I didn't recognize her, but she looked at me as if she knew who I was and then loped toward us, arms outstretched. It was my mother's mother, Tata. Raymond let go of Mami's hand and ran into Tata's arms. Mami hugged and kissed her. Edna and I hung back, waiting.

"This is Edna," Mami said, pushing her forward for a hug and kiss.

"And this must be Negi," Tata said, pulling me into her embrace. I pressed against her and felt the sharp prongs of the rhinestone brooch on her left shoulder against my face. She held me longer than I expected, wrapped me in the scratchy softness of her black lace dress, the warmth of her powdered skin, the sting of her bittersweet breath, pungent of beer and cigarettes.

Behind her loomed a man shorter than she, but as imposing. He was squarely built, with narrow eyes under heavy eyebrows, a broad nose, and full lips fuzzed with a pencil mustache. No one would have ever called him handsome, but there was about him a gentleness, a sweetness that made me wish he were a relative. He was, in a manner of speaking. Mami introduced him as "Don Julio, Tata's friend." We shook hands, his broad, fleshy palm seeming to swallow mine.

"Let's get our things," Mami said, pulling us into a knot near her. "You kids, don't let go of each others' hands. It's crazy here tonight."

We joined the stream of people claiming their baggage. Boxes filled with fruit and vegetables had torn, and their contents had spilled and broken into slippery messes on the floor. Overstuffed suitcases tied with ropes or hastily taped together had given way, and people's underwear, baby diapers, and ratty shoes pushed through the stressed seams where everyone could see them. People pointed, laughed, and looked to see who would claim these sorry belongings, who could have thought the faded, torn clothes and stained shoes were still good enough for their new life in Brooklyn.

"That's why I left everything behind," Mami sniffed. "Who wants to carry that kind of junk around?"

We had a couple of new suitcases and three or four boxes carefully packed, taped at the seams, tied with rope, and labelled with our name and an address in New York that was all numbers. We had brought only our "good" things: Mami's work clothes and shoes, a few changes of playclothes for me, Edna, and Raymond, some of them made by Mami herself, others bought just before we left. She brought her towels, sheets, and pillowcases, not new, but still "decent looking."

"I'll see if I can find a taxi," Don Julio said. "You wait here."

We huddled in front of the terminal while Don Julio negotiated with drivers. The first one looked at us, counted the number of packages we carried, asked Don Julio where we were going, then shook his head and drove along the curb toward a man in a business suit with a briefcase who stood there calmly, his right hand in the air as if he were saluting, his fingers wiggling every so often. The second driver gave us a hateful look and said some words that I didn't understand, but I knew what he meant just the same. Before he drove off, Mami mumbled through her teeth "*Charamanbiche*." Don Julio said it was illegal for a driver to refuse a fare, but that didn't stop them from doing it.

Finally, a swarthy man with thick black hair and a flat cap on his head stopped, got out of his taxi, and helped us load our stuff. He didn't speak Spanish, none of us spoke English, and, it appeared, neither did he. But he gave us a toothy, happy smile, lifted Raymond into Mami's lap, made sure our fingers and toes were inside the taxi before he closed the doors, then

got in with a great deal of huffing and puffing, as his belly
didn't fit between the seat and the steering wheel. Tata and
Don Julio sat in the front seat with the driver, who kept asking
questions no one understood.

"He wants to know where we're from," Mami figured out,
and we told him.

"Ah, Porto Reeco, yes, ees hot," he said. "San Juan?"

"Yes," Mami said, the first time I'd ever heard her speak English.

The driver launched into a long speech peppered with familiar words like America and President Kennedy. Mami, Tata, and
Don Julio nodded every once in a while, uh-huhed, and laughed
whenever the taxi driver did. I wasn't sure whether he had no
idea that we didn't understand him, or whether he didn't care.

&> Rain had slicked the streets into shiny, reflective tunnels
lined with skyscrapers whose tops disappeared into the mist.
Lampposts shed uneven silver circles of light whose edges
faded to gray. An empty trash can chained to a parking meter
banged and rolled from side to side, and its lid, also chained,
flipped and flapped in the wind like a kite on a short string.
The taxi stopped at a red light under an overpass. A train
roared by above us, its tiny square windows full of shapes.

"Look at her," Tata laughed from the front seat, "Negi's eyes
are popping out of her head."

"That's because the streets are not paved with gold, like she
thought," Mami teased.

The taxi driver grinned. I pressed my face to the window,
which was fogged all around except on the spot I'd rubbed so
that I could look out.

It was late. Few windows on the tall buildings flanking us
were lit. The stores were shuttered, blocked with crisscrossed
grates knotted with chains and enormous padlocks. Empty
buses glowed from within with eerie gray light, chugging slowly
from one stop to the next, their drivers sleepy and bored.

Mami was wrong. I didn't expect the streets of New York to

be paved with gold, but I did expect them to be bright and cheerful, clean, lively. Instead, they were dark and forbidding, empty, hard.

We stopped in front of a brick building. Here, too, battered trash cans were chained to a black lamppost, only these were filled with garbage, some of which had spilled out and lay scattered in puddles of pulpy hash. The door to the building was painted black, and there was a hole where the knob should have been.

Mami had to wake up Edna and Raymond. Tata picked one up, and Mami the other. Don Julio helped the taxi driver get our stuff.

"This way," Tata said.

We entered a hallway where a bare dim bulb shed faint blue light against green walls. Tata led us past many doors to the other end of the hall, where she pushed against another black door and led us into a cobblestoned courtyard with a tree in front of another, smaller building.

"Watch the puddles," Tata said, too late. Cold water seeped into my right shoe, soaking my white cotton socks. We went in another door without a knob, into a smaller hallway with steps leading up to a landing.

Tata pushed the first door on our left with her foot. We entered a small room with a window giving onto the courtyard. As we came in, a tall man got up from a cot near the window and weaved toward us. His long hair was gray. Round hazel eyes bulged from their sockets; the whites were streaked with red and yellow. He hugged Mami and helped her settle Raymond on the cot he'd just left. Tata lay Edna next to Raymond and tucked a blanket around them.

"So this is Negi," the tall man said.

"This is your uncle Chico, Tata's brother," Mami said. "You remember him, don't you?"

I remembered the name, but not this bony scarecrow with the stale smell of sweat and beer.

"She was just a little kid when I last saw her," he said, his hands on my shoulders. "How old are you now?"

"Thirteen," I croaked.

"Thirteen!" He whistled.

Don Julio came in. He took a key from a nail by the door and went out again.

"Give me a hand with this stuff, can you, Chico?"

"Oh, of course, of course." He shuffled off after Don Julio.

"How about something to eat?" Tata said. "Or a beer?" Mami shook her head. Tata took a Budweiser from the small refrigerator and opened it. She drank from the can.

"Are you hungry?" Mami asked me.

"Yes."

Tata put her beer down and turned on the hot plate next to the refrigerator.

"Chico made some *asopao*. I'll make some coffee."

"Where's the bathroom?" Mami asked.

"Across the hall." Tata pointed to the door. Next to it there was a curtained-off area. On her way out, Mami peeked inside. The curtain hid a large bed and clothes on wire hangers lining the wall.

"That's our bedroom," Tata said. "Your apartment is upstairs. Two big rooms. And you don't have to share a bathroom like we do."

"I'll go take a look." Mami stepped out then turned around to find me right behind her. "Negi, you wait right here."

"But I want to see too."

"Have something to eat and keep still. You'll have plenty of time later."

I leaned against the door and watched Tata.

Even though she was quite tall, Tata was not cramped by the small room. Her hands, with long tapered fingers and wide nails, grasped pots and cooking spoons from shelves above the stove and placed them soundlessly on the glowing hot-plate burner. Her back was wide, straight, and she carried her head as if she had something on it that she couldn't let fall. Her hair was black streaked with silver, cut short and curled away from her face. Her large brown eyes were outlined with long black lashes under arched brows. She smiled mischievously as she put a bowl of *asopao* on the table opposite the cot and dragged one of the two chairs from its place against the wall.

"Here you are," she said. "Chico makes good *asopao*, but not as good as mine."

It was delicious, thick with rice and chunks of chicken, cubed potatoes, green olives, and capers. She tore off a chunk of bread from a long loaf on top of the refrigerator, spread it thick with butter, and put the bread on a napkin in front of me.

"Monín told me you like bread. This is fresh from the bakery down the street."

It was crunchy on the outside and soft on the inside, just the way I liked it.

Don Julio and Chico came back, followed by Mami, her eyes bright.

"What a great place! Wait till you see it, Negi. It's twice the size of this one, with windows in the front and back. And there's a huge bathtub, and a gas stove with four burners!"

"And your school is only five blocks from here," Don Julio said. "Just beyond *la marketa*."

"What's a *marketa*?" I asked. Everyone laughed.

"It's a big building with stalls where you can buy anything," Mami said.

"Like the plaza in Bayamón," Tata added.

"Only much bigger," Chico said.

"Look at her. She's excited about it already," Tata said, and they all stared at me with broad smiles, willing me to give in to their enthusiasm. I ran into Mami's arms, unable to admit that a part of me was looking forward to the morning, to the newness of our life, and afraid to let the other part show, the part that was scared.

⟡ There were angels on the ceiling. Four fat naked cherubs danced in a circle, their hands holding ivy garlands, their round buttocks half covered by a cloth swirling around their legs. Next to me, Mami snored softly. At the foot of the bed,

Edna and Raymond slept curled away from each other, their
backs against my legs. The bedroom had very high ceilings
with braided molding all the way around, ending in a circle
surrounded by more braid above the huge window across from
the bed. The shade was down, but bright sunlight streaked in
at the edges. The cherubs looked down on us, smiling mys-
teriously, and I wondered how many people they had seen
come in and out of this room. Slowly I crawled over Mami,
out of bed.

"Where are you going?" she mumbled, half asleep.

"To the bathroom," I whispered.

The bed was pressed into the corner against the wall across
from the window, next to a wide doorway that led into the
next room. A long dresser stretched from the doorway to the
window wall, leaving an aisle just wide enough to open the
drawers halfway out.

It was six in the morning of my first day in Brooklyn. Our
apartment, on the second floor, was the fanciest place I'd ever
lived in. The stairs coming up from Tata's room on the first
floor were marble, with a landing in between, and a colored
glass window with bunches of grapes and twirling vines. The
door to our apartment was carved with more bunches of
grapes and leaves. From the two windows in the main room
we could look out on the courtyard we had come through the
night before. A tree with broad brown leaves grew from the
middle of what looked like a well, circled with the same stones
that lined the ground. Scraggly grass poked out between the
cracks and in the brown dirt around the tree. The building
across from ours was three stories high, crisscrossed by iron
stairs with narrow landings on which people grew tomatoes
and geraniums in clay pots. Our building was only two stories
high, although it was almost as tall as the one across the courtyard. We, too, had an iron balcony with a straight ladder
suspended halfway to the ground. It made me a little dizzy to
look down.

The main room of our apartment was large and sunny and
decorated with more braided molding. The whole apartment

was painted pale yellow, except for the ceilings, which were smoky gray. The floor was covered with a flat rug whose fringes had worn away into frayed edges where they met the wood floor. A fireplace had been blocked up with a metal sheet. More cherubs, grapes, and vines decorated the mantel. One of the cherubs was missing a nose; another had lost both hands and a foot. Next to the fireplace there was a small stove with four burners close together, a narrow counter with shelves underneath, and a deep sink. A door next to the sink led to the toilet, which was flushed by pulling a chain attached to a wooden box on the wall above the seat. On the other side of the toilet room door, on the wall opposite the windows, there was a huge, claw-foot bathtub covered by a metal sheet. In the middle of the room was a formica table and four chairs with plastic seats and backs that matched the tabletop. A lopsided couch and lumpy chair covered in a scratchy blue fabric faced the tub as if bathing were a special event to which spectators were invited.

The windows and door were locked, and Mami had warned the night before that I was not to leave the apartment without telling her. There was no place to go anyway. I had no idea where I was, only that it was very far away from where I'd been. Brooklyn, Mami had said, was not New York. I wished I had a map so that I could place myself in relation to Puerto Rico. But everything we owned was packed and stacked against the yellow walls. Not that there was a map in there, either.

There was nothing to do, nowhere to go, no one to talk to. The apartment was stifling. Inside the closed rooms, the air was still. Not even dust motes in the sunlight. Outside the windows, a steady roar was interrupted by sharp sirens or the insistent crash and clang of garbage cans, the whining motors of cars, and the faint sound of babies crying.

❧ *La marketa* took up a whole block. It was much bigger and more confusing than the plaza in Bayamón, although it carried pretty much the same types of things. It was a red brick building with skylights in the high ceiling, so that whatever sun made it in lit up the dusty beams and long fluorescent light fixtures suspended from them. The floor was a gritty cement and gravel mix, sticky in places, spotted with what looked like oil slicks. Stalls were arranged along aisles, the merchandise on deep shelves that slanted down.

On the way to *la marketa* we had passed two men dressed in long black coats, their faces bearded. Ringlets hung from under their hats alongside their faces.

"Don't stare," Mami pulled on my hand.

"Why are they dressed so strange?"

"They're Jewish. They don't eat pork."

"Why not?"

"I don't know. They all live in the same neighborhood and only buy food from each other."

In *la marketa* almost all the vendors were Jewish, only they didn't wear their coats and hats. They wore white shirts and little round doilies on their heads. Many of them spoke Spanish, which made it easy for Mami to negotiate the price of everything.

"You never pay the first price they tell you," she instructed. "They like to bargain."

We went from stall to stall, arguing about every item we picked out. The vendors always made it seem as if we were cheating them, even though Mami said everything was overpriced.

"Don't ever pay full price for anything," Mami told me. "It's always cheaper somewhere else."

It was a game: the vendors wanting more money than Mami was willing to spend, but both of them knowing that eventually, she would part with her dollars and they would get them. It made no sense to me. It took most of the day to buy the stuff we needed for our apartment. Had she spent less time shopping around, she might have bought more. As it was, she only had half the things we needed, and we were exhausted and irritable by the time we got home. I had spent my entire first day in New York hunting for bargains.

The second day was no different. "We have to buy your school clothes, and a coat," Mami said.

Winter would be coming soon, Tata said, and with it, chilly winds, snowstorms, and short days.

"The first winter is always the worst," Don Julio explained, "because your blood is still thin from living in Puerto Rico." I imagined my blood thickening into syrup but didn't know how that could make me warmer.

"I can't wait to see snow," Edna chirped.

"Me neither," said Raymond.

Two days in Brooklyn, and they already loved everything about it. Tata cared for them while Mami and I shopped. She sat them down in front of a black-and-white television set, gave each a chocolate bar, and they spent the entire day watching cartoons, while Tata smoked and drank beer.

"What good kids they are," she complimented Mami when we came back. "Not a peep out of them all day."

➣ Graham Avenue in Williamsburg was the broadest street I'd ever seen. It was flanked by three- and four-story apartment buildings, the first floors of which contained stores where you could buy anything. Most of these stores were also run by Jewish people, but they didn't speak Spanish like the ones in *la marketa*. They were less friendly, too, unwilling to negotiate prices. On Graham Avenue there were special restaurants where Mami said Jewish people ate. They were called delis, and there were foreign symbols in the windows, and underneath them the word *kosher*. I knew Mami wouldn't know what it meant, so I didn't bother asking. I imagined it was a delicacy that only Jewish people ate, which is why their restaurants so prominently let them know you could get it there. We didn't go into the delis because, Mami said, they didn't like Puerto Ricans in there. Instead, she took me to eat pizza.

"It's Italian," she said.

"Do Italians like Puerto Ricans?" I asked as I bit into hot cheese and tomato sauce that burned the tip of my tongue.

"They're more like us than Jewish people are," she said, which wasn't an answer.

In Puerto Rico the only foreigners I'd been aware of were *Americanos*. In two days in Brooklyn I had already encountered Jewish people, and now Italians. There was another group of people Mami had pointed out to me. *Morenos*. But they weren't foreigners, because they were American. They were black, but they didn't look like Puerto Rican *negros*. They dressed like *Americanos* but walked with a jaunty hop that made them look as if they were dancing down the street, only their hips were not as loose as Puerto Rican men's were. According to Mami, they too lived in their own neighborhoods, frequented their own restaurants, and didn't like Puerto Ricans.

"How come?" I wondered, since in Puerto Rico, all of the people I'd ever met were either black or had a black relative somewhere in their family. I would have thought *morenos* would like us, since so many of us looked like them.

"They think we're taking their jobs."

"Are we?"

"There's enough work in the United States for everybody," Mami said, "but some people think some work is beneath them. Me, if I have to crawl on all fours to earn a living, I'll do it. I'm not proud that way."

I couldn't imagine what kind of work required crawling on all fours, although I remembered Mami scrubbing the floor that way, so that it seemed she was talking about housework. Although, according to her, she wouldn't be too proud to clean other people's houses, I hoped she wouldn't have to do it. It would be too embarrassing to come all the way from Puerto Rico so she could be somebody's maid.

• The first day of school Mami walked me to a stone building that loomed over Graham Avenue, its concrete yard enclosed by an iron fence with spikes at the top. The front steps were wide but shallow and led up to a set of heavy double doors that slammed shut behind us as we walked down the shiny corridor. I clutched my eighth-grade report card filled with A's and B's, and Mami had my birth certificate. At the front office we were met by Mr. Grant, a droopy gentleman with thick glasses and a kind smile who spoke no Spanish. He gave Mami a form to fill out. I knew most of the words in the squares we were to fill in: NAME, ADDRESS (CITY, STATE), and OCCUPATION. We gave it to Mr. Grant, who reviewed it, looked at my birth certificate, studied my report card, then wrote on the top of the form "7–18."

Don Julio had told me that if students didn't speak English, the schools in Brooklyn would keep them back one grade until they learned it.

"Seven gray?" I asked Mr. Grant, pointing at his big numbers, and he nodded.

"I no guan seven gray. I eight gray. I teeneyer."

"You don't speak English," he said. "You have to go to seventh grade while you're learning."

"I have A's in school Puerto Rico. I lern good. I no seven gray girl."

Mami stared at me, not understanding but knowing I was being rude to an adult.

"What's going on?" she asked me in Spanish. I told her they wanted to send me back one grade and I would not have it. This was probably the first rebellious act she had seen from me outside my usual mouthiness within the family.

"Negi, leave it alone. Those are the rules," she said, a warning in her voice.

"I don't care what their rules say," I answered. "I'm not going back to seventh grade. I can do the work. I'm not stupid."

Mami looked at Mr. Grant, who stared at her as if expecting her to do something about me. She smiled and shrugged her shoulders.

"Meester Grant," I said, seizing the moment, "I go eight gray six mons. Eef I no lern inglish, I go seven gray. Okay?"

"That's not the way we do things here," he said, hesitating.

"I good studen. I lern queek. You see notes." I pointed to the A's in my report card. "I pass seven gray."

So we made a deal.

"You have until Christmas," he said. "I'll be checking on your progress." He scratched out "7–18" and wrote in "8–23." He wrote something on a piece of paper, sealed it inside an envelope, and gave it to me. "Your teacher is Miss Brown. Take this note upstairs to her. Your mother can go," he said and disappeared into his office.

"Wow!" Mami said, "you can speak English!"

I was so proud of myself, I almost burst. In Puerto Rico if I'd been that pushy, I would have been called *mal educada* by the Mr. Grant equivalent and sent home with a note to my mother. But here it was my teacher who was getting the note, I got what I wanted, and my mother was sent home.

"I can find my way after school," I said to Mami. "You don't have to come get me."

"Are you sure?"

"Don't worry," I said. "I'll be all right."

I walked down the black-tiled hallway, past many doors that were half glass, each one labelled with a room number in neat black lettering. Other students stared at me, tried to get my attention, or pointedly ignored me. I kept walking as if I knew where I was going, heading for the sign that said STAIRS with an arrow pointing up. When I reached the end of the hall and looked back, Mami was still standing at the front door watching me, a worried expression on her face. I waved, and she waved back. I started up the stairs, my stomach churning into tight knots. All of a sudden, I was afraid that I was about to make a fool of myself and end up in seventh grade in the middle of the school year. Having to fall back would be worse than just accepting my fate now and hopping forward if I proved to be as good a student as I had convinced Mr. Grant I was. "What have I done?" I kicked myself with the back of my right shoe, much to the surprise of the fellow walking behind me, who laughed uproariously, as if I had meant it as a joke.

→ Miss Brown's was the learning disabled class, where the administration sent kids with all sorts of problems, none of which, from what I could see, had anything to do with their ability to learn but more with their willingness to do so. They were an unruly group. Those who came to class, anyway. Half of them never showed up, or, when they did, they slept through the lesson or nodded off in the middle of Miss Brown's carefully parsed sentences.

We were outcasts in a school where the smartest eighth graders were in the 8-1 homeroom, each subsequent drop in number indicating one notch less smarts. If your class was in the low double digits, (8-10 for instance), you were smart, but not a pinhead. Once you got into the teens, your intelligence was in question, especially as the numbers rose to the high teens. And then there were the twenties. I was in 8-23, where the dumbest, most undesirable people were placed. My class was, in some ways, the equivalent of seventh grade, perhaps even sixth or fifth.

Miss Brown, the homeroom teacher, who also taught English composition, was a young black woman who wore sweat pads under her arms. The strings holding them in place sometimes slipped outside the short sleeves of her well-pressed white shirts, and she had to turn her back to us in order to adjust them. She was very pretty, with almond eyes and a hairdo that was flat and straight at the top of her head then dipped into tight curls at the ends. Her fingers were well manicured, the nails painted pale pink with white tips. She taught English composition as if everyone cared about it, which I found appealing.

After the first week she moved me from the back of the room to the front seat by her desk, and after that, it felt as if she were teaching me alone. We never spoke, except when I went up to the blackboard.

"Esmeralda," she called in a musical voice, "would you please come up and mark the prepositional phrase?"

In her class, I learned to recognize the structure of the English language, and to draft the parts of a sentence by the position of words relative to pronouns and prepositions without knowing exactly what the whole thing meant.

The school was huge and noisy. There was a social order that, at first, I didn't understand but kept bumping into. Girls and boys who wore matching cardigans walked down the halls hand in hand, sometimes stopping behind lockers to kiss and fondle each other. They were *Americanos* and belonged in the homerooms in the low numbers.

Another group of girls wore heavy makeup, hitched their skirts above their knees, opened one extra button on their blouses, and teased their hair into enormous bouffants held solid with spray. In the morning, they took over the girls' bathroom, where they dragged on cigarettes as they did their hair until the air was unbreathable, thick with smoke and hair spray. The one time I entered the bathroom before classes they chased me out with insults and rough shoves.

Those bold girls with hair and makeup and short skirts, I soon found out, were Italian. The Italians all sat together on one side of the cafeteria, the blacks on another. The two groups hated each other more than they hated Puerto Ricans. At least once a week there was a fight between an Italian and a *moreno*, either in the bathroom, in the school yard, or in an abandoned lot near the school, a no-man's-land that divided their neighborhoods and kept them apart on weekends.

The black girls had their own style. Not for them the big, pouffy hair of the Italians. Their hair was straightened, curled at the tips like Miss Brown's, or pulled up into a twist at the back with wispy curls and straw straight bangs over Cleopatra eyes. Their skirts were also short, except it didn't look like they hitched them up when their mothers weren't looking. They came that way. They had strong, shapely legs and wore knee socks with heavy lace-up shoes that became lethal weapons in fights.

It was rumored that the Italians carried knives, even the girls, and that the *morenos* had brass knuckles in their pockets and steel toes in their heavy shoes. I stayed away from both groups, afraid that if I befriended an Italian, I'd get beat up by a *morena*, or vice versa.

There were two kinds of Puerto Ricans in school: the newly arrived, like myself, and the ones born in Brooklyn of Puerto Rican parents. The two types didn't mix. The Brooklyn Puerto Ricans spoke English, and often no Spanish at all. To them, Puerto Rico was the place where their grandparents lived, a place they visited on school and summer vacations, a place which they complained was backward and mosquito-ridden. Those of us for whom Puerto Rico was still a recent memory were also split into two groups: the ones who longed for the island and the ones who wanted to forget it as soon as possible.

I felt disloyal for wanting to learn English, for liking pizza, for studying the girls with big hair and trying out their styles at home, locked in the bathroom where no one could watch. I practiced walking with the peculiar little hop of the *morenas*, but felt as if I were limping.

I didn't feel comfortable with the newly arrived Puerto Ricans who stuck together in suspicious little groups, criticizing everyone, afraid of everything. And I was not accepted by the Brooklyn Puerto Ricans, who held the secret of coolness. They walked the halls between the Italians and the *morenos*, neither one nor the other, but looking and acting like a combination of both, depending on the texture of their hair, the shade of their skin, their makeup, and the way they walked down the hall.

⮞ One day I came home from school to find all our things packed and Mami waiting.

"Your sisters and brothers are coming," she said. "We're moving to a bigger place."

Tata and I helped her drag the stuff out to the sidewalk. After it was all together, Mami walked to Graham Avenue and found a cab. The driver helped us load the trunk, the front seat, and the floor of the rear seat until we were sitting on our bundles for the short ride to Varet Street, on the other side of the projects.

I'd read about but had never seen the projects. Just that weekend a man had taken a nine-year-old girl to the roof of one of the buildings, raped her, and thrown her over the side, down twenty-one stories. *El Diario*, the Spanish newspaper, had covered the story in detail and featured a picture of the building facing Bushwick Avenue, with a dotted line from where the girl was thrown to where she fell.

But Mami didn't talk about that. She said that the new apartment was much bigger, and that Tata would be living with us so she could take care of us while Mami worked. I wouldn't have to change schools.

The air was getting cooler, and before Delsa, Norma, Héctor, and Alicia came, Mami and I went shopping for coats and sweaters in a secondhand store, so that the kids wouldn't get sick their first week in Brooklyn. We also bought a couch and two matching chairs, two big beds, a *chiforobe* with a mirror, and two folding cots. Mami let me pick out the stuff, and I acted like a rich lady, choosing the most ornate pieces I spotted, with gold curlicues painted on the wood, intricate carving, and fancy pulls on the drawers.

Our new place was a railroad-style apartment on the second floor of a three-story house. There were four rooms from front to back, one leading into the other: the living room facing Varet Street, then our bedroom, then Tata's room, then the kitchen. The tub was in the bathroom this time, and the kitchen was big enough for a table and chairs, two folding racks for drying clothes washed by hand in the sink, and a stack of shelves for groceries. The fireplace in the living room, with its plain marble mantel, was blocked off, and we put Tata's television in front of it. The wood floors were dark and difficult to clean because the mop strings caught in splinters and cracks. The ceilings were high, but no cherubs danced around garlands, and no braided molding curled around the borders.

On October 7, 1961, Don Julio, Mami, and I went to the airport to pick up Delsa, Norma, Héctor, and Alicia. Papi had sent them unescorted, with Delsa in charge. The first thing I noticed was that her face was pinched and tired. At eleven years old Delsa looked like a woman, but her tiny body was still that of a little girl.

In the taxi on the way home, I couldn't stop talking, telling Delsa about the broad streets, the big schools, the subway train. I told her about the Italians, the *morenos*, the Jewish. I described how in Brooklyn we didn't have to wear uniforms to school, but on Fridays there was a class called assembly in a big auditorium, and all the kids had to wear white shirts.

Tata prepared a feast: *asopao*, Drake's cakes, Coke, and potato chips. The kids were wide-eyed and scared. I wondered if that's the way I had looked two months earlier and hoped that if I had, it had worn off by now.

❧ All my brothers and sisters were sent back one grade so they could learn English, so I walked to the junior high school alone, and my sisters and brothers went together to the elementary school on Bushwick Avenue. Mami insisted that I take the long way to school and not cut across the projects, but I did it once, because I wanted to find the spot where the little girl had fallen. I wondered if she had been dead when she fell, or if she had been still alive. Whether she had screamed, or whether, when you fall from such a great height, you lose air and can't make a sound, as sometimes happened to me if I ran too fast. The broad concrete walkways curved in and around the massive yellow buildings that rose taller than anything else in the neighborhood. What would happen to the people who lived there in case of fire? I imagined people jumping out the windows, raining down onto the broad sidewalks and cement basketball courts.

The walls of the projects and the buildings nearby were covered with graffiti. I didn't know what LIKE A MOTHER FUCKER meant after someone's name. Sometimes the phrase would be abbreviated: SLICK L.A.M.F." or "PAPOTE L.A.M.F." I had heard kids say "shit" when something annoyed them, but when I tried it at home, Mami yelled at me for saying a bad word. I didn't know how she knew what it meant and I didn't, and she wouldn't tell me.

❧ "Mami, can I get a bra?"

"What for, you don't have anything up there." She laughed.

"Yes, I do. Look! All the girls in my school . . ."

"You don't need a bra until you're *señorita*, so don't ask again."

❧ "Mami," I said a couple of weeks later as she changed out of her work clothes. "I'm going to need that bra now."

"What?" she stared at me, ready to argue, and then her face lit up. "Really? When?"

"I noticed it when I came home from school."

"Do you know what to do?"

"*Sí.*"

"Who told you?" Her face was a jumble of disappointment and suspicion.

"We had a class about it in school."

"Ah, okay then. Come with me, and I'll show you where I keep my Kotex." We walked hand in hand to the bathroom. Tata was in the kitchen. "Guess what, Tata," Mami said. "Negi is a *señorita*!"

"Ay, that's wonderful!" She hugged and kissed me. She held me at arms length, her eyes serious. Her voice dropped to a grave tone. "Remember, when you're like that, don't eat pineapples."

"Why not?"

"It curdles the blood."

In the bathroom Mami showed me her Kotex, hidden on a high shelf under towels. "When you change them, wrap the soiled ones in toilet paper, so no one can see. Do you want me to help you put the first one on?"

"No!"

"Just asking." She left me alone, but I could hear her and Tata giggling in the kitchen. The next day Mami brought me a couple of white cotton bras with tiny blue flowers between the cups. "These are from the factory," she said. "I sewed the cups myself."

✎ While Mami worked in Manhattan, Tata watched us. As the days grew shorter and the air cooler, she began drinking wine or beer earlier in the day, so it wasn't unusual for us to come home from school and find her drunk, although she still would make supper and insist that we eat a full helping of whatever she had cooked.

"My bones hurt," she said. "The beer makes the pain less."

Her blood had never thickened, Don Julio explained, and she had developed arthritis. Tata had been in Brooklyn more than fifteen years, and if her blood hadn't thickened by then, I worried about how long it would take.

We complained about being cold all the time, but Mami couldn't do anything about it. She called *"el lanlor"* from work, so that he would turn on the heat in the building, but he never did.

On the coldest days, Tata lit up the oven and the four burners on the stove. She left the oven door open, and we took turns sitting in front of it warming up.

One evening as we all sat grouped around the stove I told the kids a fairy tale I'd just read. Don Julio crouched in the corner listening. Like my sisters and brothers, he frequently interrupted the story to ask for more details, like what color was the Prince's horse, and what did the fairy godmother wear? The more they asked, the more elaborate the story became until, by the end, it was nothing like what I had started with. When it was over, they applauded.

"Tell us another one," Héctor demanded.

"Tomorrow."

"If you tell it now," Don Julio said, "I'll give you a dime."

"For a dime, *I'll* tell a story," Delsa jumped in.

"I'll do it for a nickel," challenged Norma.

"Everyone quiet! It's my dime. I'll tell it."

Edna and Raymond huddled closer to my feet. Delsa and Norma, who had sprawled on the linoleum floor wrapped in a blanket, argued about who had to move to give the other more room.

"Let me get another beer," Don Julio said, and he lumbered to the refrigerator.

Tata lay on her bed in the next room. "Get me one too, will you Julio?" she called out. "Negi, talk louder so I can hear the story."

"Would anyone like some hot chocolate and bread with butter?" Mami offered.

There was a chorus of "Me, me, me, me."

"Do you want me to tell the story or not?"

"Yes, of course," Don Julio said. "Let's just get comfortable."

"Go ahead and start, Negi," Mami said. "The milk takes a while to heat up, and I have to melt the chocolate bar first."

"All right. Once upon a time . . ."

"One minute," Alicia interrupted. "I have to go to the bathroom. Don't nobody take my place," she warned.

The fluorescent fixture overhead buzzed and flickered, its blue-gray light giving our faces an ashen color, as if we were dead. Don Julio's face looked menacing in that light, although his small green eyes and childlike smile were reassuring. My sisters and brothers were huddled together as close to the open oven door as they could manage without getting in Mami's way as she melted a bar of Chocolate Cortés and kept adjusting the flame on the pan of milk so that it wouldn't boil over. The room looked larger when we were all together like this, leaning toward the warmth. The walls seemed higher and steeper, the ceilings further away, the sounds of the city, its constant roar, disappeared behind the clink of Mami's spoon stirring chocolate, the soft, even breathing of my sisters and brothers, the light thump each time Don Julio set his beer can on the formica table. Brooklyn became just a memory as I led them to distant lands where palaces shimmered against desert sand and paupers became princes with the whush of a magic wand.

Every night that first winter we gathered in the kitchen around the oven door, and I embellished fairy tales in which the main characters were named after my sisters and brothers, who, no matter how big the odds, always triumphed and always went on to live happily ever after.

❧ "Come kids, come look. It's snowing!" Mami opened the window wide, stuck out her hand, and let the snow collect on her palm. It looked like the coconut flakes she grated for *arroz con dulce*. The moment it fell onto our hands, it melted into shimmering puddles, which we licked in slurpy gulps.

"Can we go down and play in it, Mami?" we begged, but she wouldn't let us because it was dark out, and the streets were never safe after dark. We filled glasses with the snow clumping on the fire escape then poured tamarind syrup on it to make *piraguas* Brooklyn-style. But they tasted nothing like the real thing because the snow melted in the cup, and we missed the crunchy bits of ice we were used to.

The next day schools were closed, and we went out bundled in all the clothes Mami could get on us. The world was clean and crisp. A white blanket spread over the neighborhood, covering garbage cans and the hulks of abandoned cars, so that the street looked fresh and full of promise.

When schools opened again, kids ran in groups and made snowballs, which they then threw at passing buses, or at each other. But as beautiful as it was, and as cheerful as it made everyone for a while, in Brooklyn, even snow was dangerous. One of my classmates had to be rushed to the hospital when another kid hit him in the eye with a rock tightly packed inside a clump of snow.

❧ Every day after school I went to the library and took out as many children's books as I was allowed. I figured that if American children learned English through books, so could I, even if I was starting later. I studied the bright illustrations and learned the words for the unfamiliar objects of our new life in the United States: A for Apple, B for Bear, C for Cabbage. As my vocabulary grew, I moved to large-print chapter books.

Mami bought me an English-English dictionary because that way, when I looked up a word I would be learning others.

By my fourth month in Brooklyn, I could read and write English much better than I could speak it, and at midterms I stunned the teachers by scoring high in English, History, and Social Studies. During the January assembly, Mr. Grant announced the names of the kids who had received high marks in each class. My name was called out three times. I became a different person to the other eighth graders. I was still in 8-23, but they knew, and I knew, that I didn't belong there.

❧ That first winter, Mami fell in love with Francisco, who lived across the street. He had straight black hair combed into a pompadour, black eyes, and very pale skin. He looked at Mami the way I imagined Prince Charming looked at Cinderella, and she blushed when he was around. When he came to visit, he brought us candy, and once he brought Mami flowers.

We teased her. "Mami has a boyfriend. Mami has a boyfriend."

"Stop that nonsense," she'd say. "You're being disrespectful." But there was a secret smile on her face, and we knew she wasn't angry.

Tata didn't like Francisco. "He's younger than you are," she told Mami. "You should be ashamed."

But Mami wasn't. Evenings, after work, she visited across the street, where Francisco lived with his parents and brother. After dinner they played cards around the dining room table. Mami never stayed long, but she always came back from his house happy. That put Tata in a dark mood, especially when she'd been drinking.

"Everyone's talking," she'd say.

"I don't care," Mami would answer. "It's my life."

Once, Tata and Don Julio had been drinking all afternoon. We knew to stay away from the kitchen, where they argued about politics, the price of ham hocks, whether or not his daughters were uppity, and which horse had won the trifecta. When Mami came home from work, she took her dinner to the living room and ate in front of the television while we did our homework.

There was a knock on the door and when Mami opened it, Francisco stood in the hall, a shy smile on his lips.

"Who's there?" Tata called from the kitchen in a challenging tone.

Mami didn't answer, but stepped aside to let Francisco in. As soon as she saw him, Tata flew out of the kitchen like a witch toward the full moon and screamed insults at Francisco.

"Tata, please," Mami begged, "behave yourself. He's a guest. Don't embarrass me."

But Tata pushed against Don Julio, who held her back, as if she wanted to jump on Francisco and beat the daylights out of him. In tears, Mami let Francisco out, then she gathered us for bed while Don Julio dragged Tata back to the kitchen. We turned the lights out in our part of the apartment, but we could still hear Tata and Don Julio arguing about whether a thirty-year-old woman with seven children should encourage a man in his twenties.

"And what about your daughters?" Tata yelled. "What kind of an example are you giving them?" Mami just pulled the covers over her head.

A week later we moved down the street to a two-room apartment in front of a bottling company. Francisco came to visit every day. He could be counted on to play gin rummy and dominoes, to bring us candy and soda, and to make Mami smile like she hadn't done in a long time. One day he came for dinner, and the next morning he was still there. After that, he lived with us.

❧ That summer, Marilyn Monroe killed herself.

Across the street from our apartment trucks idled in the loading zone of the soft-drink warehouse at all hours while men loaded crates of cola, grape, and orange soda in to the backs of the trucks. I often leaned on the window sill and watched the huge garage doors groaning up and down, the forklifts whizzing in and out with pallets stacked with crates of delicious fizzy drinks.

I listened to the radio anecdotes about Marilyn and watched the activity across the street and down the block, where someone had opened a hydrant and children squealed in and out of the rushing water. No matter how hot it got, Mami wouldn't allow us to cool off in the hydrant with the neighborhood kids, whom she considered a bad influence.

A truck pulled up, the driver went into the building across the street, came out, sat in his truck, and waited for it to be loaded. He waved at me, and when I looked, he dove his hand into his crotch and pulled out what looked like a pale salami. I couldn't take my eyes off it as his hand pumped rhythmically to the loud rock and roll on his radio. He was at it a long time, and I lost interest, closed the venetian blind, and joined my sisters and brothers in front of the television set. But after a while I was curious, so I went back and lifted one of the blinds. He still sat there, but his hand now toyed around his crotch as if he'd lost something. He saw me and began rubbing again, a grimace on his face.

I'd changed enough diapers to know what happened if a boy was touched a certain way, but this man, touching himself and only coming to life if I watched, added a new dimension to my scanty knowledge of sex.

The fact that his penis had grown when I was looking meant something. I hadn't done any of the things women did to get men interested. I'd been minding my own business at home, hadn't dressed up, had not acted provocatively, had not flirted, had not, I was sure, smiled when he waved for me to look. It was alarming, and at once I realized why Mami always told me to be *más disimulada* when I stared at people, which meant that I should pretend I wasn't interested.

Men only want one thing, I'd been told. A female's gaze was enough to send them groping for their *huevos*. That was why

Marilyn Monroe always looked at the camera and smiled. Men only want one thing, and until then, I thought it was up to me to give it up. But that's not the way it was. A little girl leaning out a window watching the world fulfilled the promises Marilyn Monroe made with her eyes. I who had promised nothing, who knew even less, whose body was as confusing as the rock and roll lyrics accompanying the trucker's hand pumping up and down to words yelled, not sung.

I left the window and looked for Mami in the kitchen. She was in her at-home clothes, her hair not curled, her eyebrows not drawn in.

"What's the matter?" she asked. "Why do you look so scared?"

"Nothing," I said.

It had all been my fault. Somehow, my just being at the window had made it happen. I went back, opened the blinds all the way, and watched openly. He was having a great time, while I vacillated between fear and curiosity, between embarrassment and the knowledge that, like it or not, I was having my first sexual experience.

I smiled at him then, a wide, seductive, Marilyn Monroe smile that took him by surprise. His eyes veiled suspiciously, and he leaned over to see if anyone else was hanging out from the other windows in the building. But it was just the two of us, me smiling brazenly while inside I quaked in terror, and him, flustered beyond comprehension.

I wondered what I'd done, why he stuffed his now limp penis back into his pants, zipped himself up, leaned his left elbow on his window, and parked his chin on his hand, his eyes focused on the warehouse full of soft drinks, the bald circle on the back of his head as vulnerable as a baby's soft spot. Whatever he'd wanted from me he didn't want anymore, and I was certain it was because I'd been too willing to give it to him.

YOU DON'T
WANT TO
KNOW

Dime con quien andas, y te diré quién eres.

❧

Tell me who you walk with, and I'll tell you who you are.

At about the same time that Mami started looking pregnant Francisco was rushed to the emergency room with a stomachache. We thought he had appendicitis, but after many tests and operations Mami told Tata that Francisco had cancer. We moved, for the fourth time in twelve months, to a bigger apartment in the building next door, so that Tata could live with us again. Every day Mami went from work straight to the hospital. She stayed with Francisco until visiting hours were over then came home, exhausted, hungry, her eyes red. She was very thin, but her belly grew high and round, and everyone knew she was having a boy.

Francisco was in and out of the hospital. When he was home, Tata was nice to him, prepared him special broths, cooked him creamy rice with milk. But when she drank, she was still nasty.

We steered clear of the bedroom Francisco shared with Mami, kept the television low, and did our homework and fighting in the kitchen, where he couldn't hear us as well. Every once in a while he came out of the room dressed in his pajamas, a cotton robe wrapped around his slight body, his hands large and bony, holding the front of the robe as if he didn't trust the knot he had tied at his waist. Even with all those clothes on he looked like a skeleton. His elbows were pointy, and the skin on his face, hands, and feet was translucent. Bones stuck out of his back like truncated wings. His black hair, over which he couldn't trouble as much anymore, grew long and lanky, so that it often covered his eyes, making him look younger.

Mami and Francisco's baby was born in March. Francisco was in the hospital, but he came home the same day that Mami did. For days he lay in bed with Franky on his chest, singing *jíbaro* songs in a soft voice.

Francisco's family didn't want him living with us. Every time he went in for another operation, they argued with Mami that he should be with them. It was embarrassing to hear his family bickering right over his bed, as if he couldn't hear them.

One time Mami and I went to see him at King's County Hospital. He was in a huge ward with waxed floors, beds lined up against the walls, each with a small night table to its right and a pale yellow curtain to separate it from the other beds. There was a green metal chair next to his bed.

Mami sent me out to get water in a basin. She then bathed and powdered Francisco, changed his johnny, shaved him, and brushed his hair. His eyes had grown larger and settled deep into his skull. His pale skin had turned gray and smooth. He looked as serene as the dead baby whose eyes I had closed in El Mangle.

"I saw an angel last night," he told Mami.

"Don't talk such nonsense," Mami said, but she gave me a fearful look.

"It was dressed in white and floated inside a ball of light."

"It was a nurse, probably."

When we came home, Mami cried when she told Tata about Francisco's vision.

A few days later he was released from the hospital to his parents' house. The next day he was dead. Tata said they fed him peanuts, which killed him.

Mami cried for days. Tata took care of her, cooked special treats, and took Franky to bed with her so that Mami could rest.

Mami was in mourning for over a year, and for that whole time she kept white novena candles lit on her dresser, their flame throwing ghostly shapes on the ceiling, where we all could see them.

❧ I had corresponded with Papi for the first few weeks after our arrival in Brooklyn. I described our apartments, *la marketa*, the Jewish people, the Italian girls, and the books I was reading. He wrote back with remembrances from Abuela and newspaper clippings. But when my sisters and brother came, they brought stories with them that he hadn't included in his letters.

Papi, Delsa said, had married shortly after Mami left with me, Edna, and Raymond. He had scattered Delsa, Norma, Héctor, and Alicia among relatives, hadn't visited them regularly, and hadn't seemed to care what happened to them. He had, in fact, seemed relieved to be rid of them so that he could start his new life, just as we were starting ours.

I asked Mami about this. She said that yes, Papi had another wife, and there was no chance we would ever live with him again. I wrote him a letter asking why he hadn't told me, and I told him that from now on he was as good as dead to me. He wrote to Mami accusing her of turning his children against him. Mami yelled at me for lying to Papi about what she said about him. It was all mixed up. Mami blamed me. Papi blamed Mami. I blamed Papi. But none of us said we were sorry.

Still Mami insisted that we keep in touch with him.

"You must never forget your father," she reminded us at Christmas, Father's Day, and his birthday. "You're his flesh and blood, and even if he has another family now, he still loves you."

We didn't believe her. Grudgingly, we sent him cards on special days, copied out our best compositions, stayed in touch, knowing it was all show. Because in Brooklyn, after Francisco's death, Mami became, even more than before, both mother and father to us. We could count on her in a way we had never been able to count on Papi, Tata, or Francisco, who had made everyone happy for such a short time before dying and becoming a ghost that haunted us all for the rest of our lives.

❧ Mornings, Mami left the house while it was still dark for the subway ride into Manhattan. She dressed "for work" in clothes that she changed out of the minute she came home, so that they wouldn't get stained with oil, *achiote*, or tomato sauce. She began as a thread cutter, even though in Puerto Rico she had been a machine operator.

"Here you have to prove yourself all over again," she said. She tried hard, which impressed her supervisors, and was moved up quickly to the stitching work she loved.

She bought a special pair of scissors for work. When she walked across the projects on her way home from the subway, she put them in her pocket and held them tight until she was safely inside the house. She then wiped the sweat off them and put them in a special quilted case she had made.

We joked about her handbag, which we worried was an inducement for muggers, since it was big and bulging. In it she carried our birth certificates, immunization records, and school papers. She also kept a small notebook in which she wrote the hours she worked, so that *el bosso* wouldn't cheat her on payday. She kept her makeup (pressed powder, eyebrow pencil, rouge, and lipstick) in its own small pouch. If a mugger were to steal her purse, he wouldn't get any money, because she carried that in a wallet in her skirt pocket under her coat.

When she worked, Mami was happy. She complained about sitting at a machine for hours, or about the short coffee breaks, or about *el bosso*. But she was proud of the things she made. Often she brought home samples of the bras and girdles she worked on and showed us how she had used a double-needle machine, or how she had figured out that if you stitched the cup a certain way, it would fit better. But even though she was proud of her work, she didn't want us to follow in her footsteps.

"I'm not working this hard so that you kids can end up working in factories all your lives. You study, get good grades, and graduate from high school so that you can have a profession, not just a job."

She never asked to see our homework, but when we brought home report cards, she demanded that we read her the grades and then translate the teachers' comments so that she would know exactly how we were doing in school. When the reports were good, she beamed as if she herself had earned the good marks.

"That's what you have to do in this country," she'd say. "Anyone willing to work hard can get ahead."

We believed her and tried to please her as best we could. Since we'd come to Brooklyn, her world had become full of new possibilities, and I tried very hard to share her excitement about the good life we were to have somewhere down the road. But more and more I suspected Mami's optimism was a front. No one, I thought, could get beat down so many times and still come up smiling.

Sometimes I lay in bed, in the unheated rooms full of beds and clothes and the rustle of sleeping bodies, terrified that what lay around the corner was no better than what we'd left behind, that being in Brooklyn was not a new life but a continuation of the old one. That everything had changed, but nothing had changed, that whatever Mami had been looking for when she brought us to Brooklyn was not there, just as it wasn't in Puerto Rico.

❧ Tata's brother Chico didn't live with us, but he spent a lot of time in our apartment. He, Tata, and Don Julio split whatever money they made at their jobs, or playing the numbers, to buy cheap wine and six-packs of beer. Unlike Tata and Don Julio, who only drank in the afternoon, Chico drank all the time. Once, when we were trying out new English words, one of us called him a bum. Mami smacked whoever it was and warned us never to say that word again.

Chico's pockets jingled with coins, which he handed out if we did him small favors.

"Get me another beer," he'd say, and we'd scramble to the refrigerator.

"Light my cigarette," and three or four matches would be struck at the same time. He paid us all.

While Tata tended to get loud and angry when she drank, Chico was quiet and morose. Mami said he was a harmless drunk, "like a kid," and always made sure he ate something when he was at our house.

"At least he knows how to hold his liquor," she'd tell us.

*   *   *

❧ I was on my way to school. Chico was coming in from his night job to sleep on our couch.

"Show me and I'll give you a quarter."

"Show you what?"

"Open your blouse," Chico said, "and let me see. I'll pay you."

"No!"

He blocked the hallway with his long arms. "I won't touch you. I just want to look." His eyes were teary.

"If you don't let me by I'll scream."

"Come on, Negi . . . I'm family." Sharp white stubble covered his chin. He smacked his lips.

"You'd better not bother me again, or I'm telling Mami." I pushed past him and ran down the stairs and out into the street.

The next day I was brushing my hair in front of the dresser in the bedroom of our railroad-style apartment. Chico lay on the couch, watching television with the kids, but every once in a while I noticed his eyes fixed on me. I turned my back, face burning, goose bumps rising. Tata called him to the kitchen. His bones creaked when he got up. As he passed behind me, he slipped his hand under my raised arms and pinched my left nipple.

"Don't tell anyone," he mumbled into my ear.

I collapsed on the bed, holding myself against the pain and humiliation, but I didn't scream. On his way back he threw a dollar at me. It was wrinkled and dirty, its edges ragged. I stretched it out and flattened it with my palm. George Washington, I had just learned, was the Father of our country. I put him inside my thick history book. The next day, on the way home from school, I ate my very first sundae with three kinds of ice cream, pineapples, nuts, chocolate sauce, and marshmallows.

❧ "Tomorrow," Mami said, "you're not going to school. I need you to come with me to the welfare office."

"Ay, Mami, can't you take Delsa?"

"No, I can't."

When Mami was laid off, we had to go on welfare. She took me with her because she needed someone to translate. Six months after we landed in Brooklyn, I spoke enough English to explain our situation.

"My mother she no spik inglish. My mother she look for work evree day, and nothin. My mother she say she don't want her children suffer. My mother she say she want work bot she lay off. My mother she only need help a leetle while."

I was always afraid that if I said something wrong, if I mispronounced a word or used the wrong tense, the social workers would say no, and we might be evicted from our apartment, or the electricity would be shut off, or we'd freeze to death because Mami couldn't pay for heating fuel.

The welfare office was in a brick building with wire covering the windows. The waiting room was always packed with people, and the person at the front desk never knew when we would be helped or where the social workers were. It was a place where you went and waited for hours, with nothing to do but sit and stare at the green walls. Once there, you couldn't even go out to get a bite to eat, because your name might be called any time, and if you were gone, you'd lose your turn and have to come back the next day.

On the way there, Mami bought the paper, and I brought along the thickest library book I could find. The first couple of hours usually went by fast, since there were forms to fill out and interesting conversations going on around us as the women told each other their stories. There were never any men, just tired-looking women, some with their children, as if bringing children there would make the social workers talk to them.

Mami dressed nicely for the welfare office and insisted that I do too.

"We're not going there looking like beggars," she said, and while we waited she kept reminding me to sit up, to stay alert, to look as neat and dignified as the women on the other side of the partition, phones at their ears, pens poised over the forms

handed to them by the receptionist with the dour expression
who wouldn't smile if her life depended on it.

Occasionally there were fights. Women beat up on the clerks
who refused them help, or who made them wait in line for
days, or who wouldn't see them at all after they'd waited for
hours. Once Mami punched a social worker who was rude
to her.

"They treat us like animals," she cried after she'd been re-
strained. "Don't they care that we're human beings, just like
them?"

Her makeup streaked, her hair dishevelled, she left the welfare office with her back slumped and her eyes cast down and
furtive. I was sure everyone on the bus knew that we had spent
the day in the welfare office and that Mami had just hit a social worker. That night as she told Tata and Don Julio what
had happened, Mami made it sound like it was a joke, no big
deal. I added my own exaggerated details of how many people
had to restrain her, without any mention of how frightened I'd
been, and how ashamed I'd felt when she lost control in front
of everybody.

Often I would be asked to translate for other women at the
welfare office, since Mami told everyone I spoke good English.
Their stories were no different from Mami's. They needed just
a little help until they could find a job again.

Every once in a while I could tell that the people I translated
for were lying.

"What do you think?" they'd ask. "Should I say my husband
has disappeared, or that he's a *sinvergüenza* who refuses to
help with the kids?"

Women with accents that weren't Puerto Rican claimed they
were so that they could reap the benefits of American citizen-
ship. A woman I was translating for once said, "These *gringos*
don't know the difference anyway. To them we're all spiks."

I didn't know what to do. To tell the interviewer that I knew
the woman was lying seemed worse than translating what the
woman said as accurately as I could and letting the interviewer
figure it out. But I worried that if people from other countries

passed as Puerto Ricans in order to cheat the government, it reflected badly on us.

I never knew if my translations helped, but once an old *jíbara* took my hands in hers and kissed them, which made me feel like the best person in the world.

➥ "Where have you been?" Mami screamed one day when I came home after school later than usual.

"In the library." I showed her the stack of books.

"You know I don't want you out after dark. The streets are dangerous. What if something were to happen?"

"Nothing happened . . ."

"Don't you talk back!"

"I'm not talking . . ."

My sisters and brothers scurried away. Tata, Don Julio, and Chico left their domino game in the kitchen to see what was going on.

"Monín, leave her alone," Tata said, her hand on Mami's shoulder.

"Don't you tell me how to raise my children!" Mami screamed, backing away from her.

My knees shook. What if Mami knew that I hitched my skirt up so I wouldn't look so dumb? What if she knew that I sometimes wore eye makeup and washed it off before I came home? What if some nosy neighbor had told her that a boy had once walked me halfway home from the library?

I stood by the door, arms laden with books, my winter coat still on, too terrified to move. I knew I must have done something to cause her rage, but I didn't know what it could be. I wasn't about to admit to anything before she accused me.

"You think just because you can speak a little English you can do anything you like!"

"That's not true."

She came at me, her hands raised, ready to strike. My b dropped to the floor, and before I knew it I was holdi her hands, gripping the wrists tight. I didn't know I was that strong, and Mami was surprised too, because she backed off, her face startled.

"Hit me, go ahead. You can kill me if that makes you feel better," I screamed loud enough for the world to hear. I stood in front of her, shaking all over, hands at my sides, martyrlike, fully aware of the dramatic moment that might backfire but willing to take the chance.

"What?" she croaked and then came at me again. I didn't move. She stopped just short of a blow. I kept my eyes on hers. She must have seen the fear in them, and the defiance. "Get out of my sight," she snarled, and Tata grabbed me and dragged me into the kitchen.

Mami and I didn't speak for days. But she never, ever, hit me again.

⮎ After we came to Brooklyn, all our time was spent indoors. We lived cooped up because our neighborhood was filled with "*gente mala*," bad people. The little girl who was raped and thrown over the side of a twenty-one-story building in the projects was only one of the gory crimes I read about in *El Diario*. Every day there were murders, rapes, muggings, knifings, and shootings. In Puerto Rico the crimes had always happened somewhere else, in cities far from Macún. But in Brooklyn bad things happened on our block.

One day Don Julio, who already looked like a boxer who had taken too many hits, came home bloodied and bruised, his eyes lost behind swollen cheeks and nose.

"*¡Ay, Señor, Dios Santo!*" Mami cried. "What happened to you?"

jumped me as I came out of the subway station."
ed bats, pipes, and chains. Once they had him
they stole his wallet, which Don Julio claimed
llars in it, and his Timex watch, a gift from
er.

"They didn't see my gold chain with the medallion of the Holy Virgin." He pulled it out from inside his shirt and kissed it. "I guess She was looking out for me, or they would have killed me."

It was still early, around 7:30 P.M., when Don Julio was attacked in the same subway station where Mami took the train every day. From that day forward I sat pretending to read by the window, watching for Mami to come down the street when she was supposed to. Every minute that went by and she wasn't home added fuel to the images from the newspapers of women lying in pools of blood on cracked sidewalks, their handbags torn from their arms, split open, the contents spilled over them like garbage.

The men they beat up; the women, they raped. I couldn't stop thinking about it as I walked to school, or home from the library: every man was a potential rapist, and every dark doorway was a potential hiding place for someone waiting to hurt me.

There were gangs, whose slogans and names were painted in bold letters on the sides of buildings or on sidewalks.

"Don't ever walk down that side of the street," a classmate told me once. "It's not our turf."

"What does that mean, *turf*?"

"It's a part of the neighborhood that belongs to a gang."

"But what if I have to visit someone on that side of the street?"

"Believe me, you don't want to know anyone over there," she claimed.

Mami said that at night gangs roamed the streets doing all sorts of mischief.

"Like what?" I asked.

"You don't want to know," she warned.

When the days became shorter and night came earlier, we were only allowed out to go to school. We couldn't even go to the *bodega* across the street. When the weather was warm and people sat out on their stoops, Mami insisted we stay inside, unless she could come out to watch us. Not even Tata was trusted with keeping an eye on us, and least of all me, since I'd already proved an unreliable baby-sitter.

If I told Mami exactly where I was going, who I was going to see, how long I would be there, and when I'd be back, she'd sometimes let me go off alone on a Saturday afternoon.

"Don't walk on any of the side streets," she'd warn. "Keep to the avenues. Don't talk to anyone. Don't accept any rides. If there are too many people milling around a sidewalk, cross the street and walk on the other side."

In Puerto Rico when Mami had laid out the same general rules, I'd found ways of, if not completely ignoring them, at least bending them to suit my curiosity. Her caution then seemed to have more to do with keeping us from hurting ourselves. Now it was directed at preventing other people from hurting us.

I couldn't imagine why neighbors would harm me or my sisters and brothers. But I also couldn't imagine how they could help us if we needed them. We lived separated by thick doors with several bolts, windows with iron grates, peepholes. No one dropped in unannounced to chat. An unexpected knock would set our hearts thumping, and we'd look at one another with questions in our eyes before peeping through the pinhole on the door, or opening it a crack, with the chain secured across the narrow gap.

"I can't depend on anyone," Mami often told us, and we knew that to be true. *El Bosso* could lay her off any minute. The welfare workers never believed a strong-looking woman like Mami couldn't find work. Tata was sometimes dependable, but just as often she was incoherent, or laid up with aches and pains. Our neighbors were strangers, or worse, *gente mala*. There was an extended family, Mami's aunts, uncles, and cousins, who dropped in and out of our lives with warm clothes, advice, and warnings. But Mami was too proud to ask them for more than they volunteered, and we were all developing the same stubborn pride, behind which our frightened selves hid, pretending everything was all right.

A SHOT
AT IT

Te conozco bacalao, aunque vengas disfrazao.

❧

I recognize you salted codfish, even if you're in disguise.

While Francisco was still alive, we had moved to Ellery Street. That meant I had to change schools, so Mami walked me to P.S. 33, where I would attend ninth grade. The first week I was there I was given a series of tests that showed that even though I couldn't speak English very well, I read and wrote it at the tenth-grade level. So they put me in 9-3, with the smart kids.

One morning, Mr. Barone, a guidance counsellor, called me to his office. He was short, with a big head and large hazel eyes under shapely eyebrows. His nose was long and round at the tip. He dressed in browns and yellows and often perched his tortoiseshell glasses on his forehead, as if he had another set of eyes up there.

"So," he pushed his glasses up, "what do you want to be when you grow up?"

"I don't know."

He shuffled through some papers. "Let's see here . . . you're fourteen, is that right?"

"Yes, sir."

"And you've never thought about what you want to be?"

When I was very young, I wanted to be a *jíbara*. When I was older, I wanted to be a cartographer, then a topographer. But since we'd come to Brooklyn, I'd not thought about the future much.

"No, sir."

He pulled his glasses down to where they belonged and shuffled through the papers again.

"Do you have any hobbies?" I didn't know what he meant. "Hobbies, hobbies," he flailed his hands, as if he were juggling, "things you like to do after school."

"Ah, yes." I tried to imagine what I did at home that might qualify as a hobby. "I like to read."

He seemed disappointed. "Yes, we know that about you."
He pulled out a paper and stared at it. "One of the tests we
gave you was an aptitude test. It tells us what kinds of things
you might be good at. The tests show that you would be good
at helping people. Do you like to help people?"

I was afraid to contradict the tests. "Yes, sir."

"There's a high school we can send you where you can study
biology and chemistry which will prepare you for a career in
nursing."

I screwed up my face. He consulted the papers again.

"You would also do well in communications. Teaching
maybe."

I remembered Miss Brown standing in front of a classroom
full of rowdy teenagers, some of them taller than she was.

"I don't like to teach."

Mr. Barone pushed his glasses up again and leaned over the
stack of papers on his desk. "Why don't you think about it and
get back to me," he said, closing the folder with my name
across the top. He put his hand flat on it, as if squeezing something out. "You're a smart girl, Esmeralda. Let's try to get you
into an academic school so that you have a shot at college."

On the way home, I walked with another new ninth grader,
Yolanda. She had been in New York for three years but knew
as little English as I did. We spoke in Spanglish, a combination
of English and Spanish in which we hopped from one
language to the other depending on which word came first.

"*Te preguntó el* Mr. Barone, you know, *lo que querías hacer*
when you grow up?" I asked.

"*Sí, pero*, I didn't know. *¿Y tú?*"

"*Yo tampoco*. He said, *que* I like to help people. *Pero*, you
know, *a mí no me gusta mucho la gente.*" When she heard me
say I didn't like people much, Yolanda looked at me from the
corner of her eye, waiting to become the exception.

By the time I said it, she had dashed up the stairs of her
building. She didn't wave as she ducked in, and the next day
she wasn't friendly. I walked around the rest of the day in embarrassed isolation, knowing that somehow I had given myself

away to the only friend I'd made at Junior High School 33. I had to either take back my words or live with the consequences of stating what was becoming the truth. I'd never said that to anyone, not even to myself. It was an added weight, but I wasn't about to trade it for companionship.

A few days later, Mr. Barone called me back to his office.

"Well?" Tiny green flecks burned around the black pupils of his hazel eyes.

The night before, Mami had called us into the living room. On the television "fifty of America's most beautiful girls" paraded in ruffled tulle dresses before a tinsel waterfall.

"Aren't they lovely?" Mami murmured, as the girls, escorted by boys in uniform, floated by the camera, twirled, and disappeared behind a screen to the strains of a waltz and an announcer's dramatic voice calling their names, ages, and states. Mami sat mesmerized through the whole pageant.

"I'd like to be a model," I said to Mr. Barone.

He stared at me, pulled his glasses down from his forehead, looked at the papers inside the folder with my name on it, and glared. "A model?" His voice was gruff, as if he were more comfortable yelling at people than talking to them.

"I want to be on television."

"Oh, then you want to be an actress," in a tone that said this was only a slight improvement over my first career choice. We stared at one another for a few seconds. He pushed his glasses up to his forehead again and reached for a book on the shelf in back of him. "I only know of one school that trains actresses, but we've never sent them a student from here."

Performing Arts, the write-up said, was an academic, as opposed to a vocational, public school that trained students wishing to pursue a career in theater, music, and dance.

"It says here that you have to audition." He stood up and held the book closer to the faint gray light coming through the narrow window high on his wall. "Have you ever performed in front of an audience?"

"I was announcer in my school show in Puerto Rico," I said. "And I recite poetry. There, not here."

He closed the book and held it against his chest. His right index finger thumped a rhythm on his lower lip. "Let me call them and find out exactly what you need to do. Then we can talk some more."

I left his office strangely happy, confident that something good had just happened, not knowing exactly what.

❧ "I'm not afraid . . . I'm not afraid . . . I'm not afraid." Every day I walked home from school repeating those words. The broad streets and sidewalks that had impressed me so on the first day we had arrived had become as familiar as the dirt road from Macún to the highway. Only my curiosity about the people who lived behind these walls ended where the façades of the buildings opened into dark hallways or locked doors. Nothing good, I imagined, could be happening inside if so many locks had to be breached to go in or step out.

It was on these tense walks home from school that I decided I had to get out of Brooklyn. Mami had chosen this as our home, and just like every other time we'd moved, I'd had to go along with her because I was a child who had no choice. But I wasn't willing to go along with her on this one.

"How can people live like this?" I shrieked once, desperate to run across a field, to feel grass under my feet instead of pavement.

"Like what?" Mami asked, looking around our apartment, the kitchen and living room crisscrossed with sagging lines of drying diapers and bedclothes.

"Everyone on top of each other. No room to do anything. No air."

"Do you want to go back to Macún, to live like savages, with no electricity, no toilets . . ."

"At least you could step outside every day without somebody trying to kill you."

"Ay, Negi, stop exaggerating!"

"I hate my life!" I yelled.

"Then do something about it," she yelled back.

Until Mr. Barone showed me the listing for Performing Arts High School, I hadn't known what to do.

➥ "The auditions are in less than a month. You have to learn a monologue, which you will perform in front of a panel. If you do well, and your grades here are good, you might get into the school."

Mr. Barone took charge of preparing me for my audition to Performing Arts. He selected a speech from *The Silver Cord*, a play by Sidney Howard, first performed in 1926, but whose action took place in a New York drawing room circa 1905.

"Mr. Gatti, the English teacher," he said, "will coach you. . . . And Mrs. Johnson will talk to you about what to wear and things like that."

I was to play Christina, a young married woman confronting her mother-in-law. I learned the monologue phonetically from Mr. Gatti. It opened with "You belong to a type that's very common in this country, Mrs. Phelps—a type of self-centered, self-pitying, son-devouring tigress, with unmentionable proclivities suppressed on the side."

"We don't have time to study the meaning of every word," Mr. Gatti said. "Just make sure you pronounce every word correctly."

Mrs. Johnson, who taught Home Economics, called me to her office.

"Is that how you enter a room?" she asked the minute I came in. "Try again, only this time, don't barge in. Step in slowly, head up, back straight, a nice smile on your face. That's it." I took a deep breath and waited. "Now sit. No, not like that. Don't just plop down. Float down to the chair with your knees together." She demonstrated, and I copied her. "That's better. What do you do with your hands? No, don't hold your chin like that; it's not ladylike. Put your hands on your lap, and leave them there. Don't use them so much when you talk."

I sat stiff as a cutout while Mrs. Johnson and Mr. Barone asked me questions they thought the panel at Performing Arts would ask.

"Where are you from?"

"Puerto Rico."

"No," Mrs. Johnson said, "Porto Rico. Keep your *r*'s soft. Try again."

"Do you have any hobbies?" Mr. Barone asked. Now I knew what to answer.

"I enjoy dancing and the movies."

"Why do you want to come to this school?"

Mrs. Johnson and Mr. Barone had worked on my answer if this question should come up.

"I would like to study at Performing Arts because of its academic program and so that I may be trained as an actress."

"Very good, very good!" Mr. Barone rubbed his hands together, twinkled his eyes at Mrs. Johnson. "I think we have a shot at this."

"Remember," Mrs. Johnson said, "when you shop for your audition dress, look for something very simple in dark colors."

Mami bought me a red plaid wool jumper with a crisp white shirt, my first pair of stockings, and penny loafers. The night before, she rolled up my hair in pink curlers that cut into my scalp and made it hard to sleep. For the occasion, I was allowed to wear eye makeup and a little lipstick.

"You look so grown up!" Mami said, her voice sad but happy, as I twirled in front of her and Tata.

"*Toda una señorita,*" Tata said, her eyes misty.

We set out for the audition on an overcast January morning heavy with the threat of snow.

"Why couldn't you choose a school close to home?" Mami grumbled as we got on the train to Manhattan. I worried that even if I were accepted, she wouldn't let me go because it was so far from home, one hour each way by subway. But in spite of her complaints, she was proud that I was good enough to be considered for such a famous school. And she actually seemed excited that I would be leaving the neighborhood.

"You'll be exposed to a different class of people," she assured me, and I felt the force of her ambition without knowing exactly what she meant.

&ℰ Three women sat behind a long table in a classroom where the desks and chairs had been pushed against a wall. As I entered I held my head up and smiled, and then I floated down to the chair in front of them, clasped my hands on my lap, and smiled some more.

"Good morning," said the tall one with hair the color of sand. She was big boned and solid, with intense blue eyes, a generous mouth, and soothing hands with short fingernails. She was dresssed in shades of beige from head to toe and wore no makeup and no jewelry except for the gold chain that held her glasses just above her full bosom. Her voice was rich, modulated, each word pronounced as if she were inventing it.

Next to her sat a very small woman with very high heels. Her cropped hair was pouffed around her face, with bangs brushing the tips of her long false lashes, her huge dark brown eyes were thickly lined in black all around, and her small mouth was carefully drawn in and painted cerise. Her suntanned face turned toward me with the innocent curiosity of a lively baby. She was dressed in black, with many gold chains around her neck, big earrings, several bracelets, and large stone rings on the fingers of both hands.

The third woman was tall, small boned, thin, but shapely. Her dark hair was pulled flat against her skull into a knot in back of her head. Her face was all angles and light, with fawnlike dark brown eyes, a straight nose, full lips painted just a shade pinker than their natural color. Silky forest green cuffs peeked out from the sleeves of her burgundy suit. Diamond studs winked from perfect earlobes.

I had dreamed of this moment for several weeks. More than anything, I wanted to impress the panel with my talent, so that I would be accepted into Performing Arts and leave Brooklyn every day. And, I hoped, one day I would never go back.

But the moment I faced these three impeccably groomed women, I forgot my English and Mrs. Johnson's lessons on how to behave like a lady. In the agony of trying to answer their barely comprehensible questions, I jabbed my hands here and there, forming words with my fingers because the words refused to leave my mouth.

"Why don't you let us hear your monologue now?" the woman with the dangling glasses asked softly.

I stood up abruptly, and my chair clattered onto its side two feet from where I stood. I picked it up, wishing with all my strength that a thunderbolt would strike me dead to ashes on the spot.

"It's all right," she said. "Take a breath. We know you're nervous."

I closed my eyes and breathed deeply, walked to the middle of the room, and began my monologue.

"Ju bee lonh 2 a type dats berry cómo in dis kuntree, Mees-sees Felps. A type off selfcent red self pee tee in sun de boring tie gress wid on men shon ah ball pro klee bee tees on de side."

In spite of Mr. Gatti's reminders that I should speak slowly and enunciate every word, even if I didn't understand it, I recited my three-minute monologue in one minute flat.

The small woman's long lashes seemed to have grown with amazement. The elegant woman's serene face twitched with controlled laughter. The tall one dressed in beige smiled sweetly.

"Thank you, dear," she said. "Could you wait outside for a few moments?"

I resisted the urge to curtsy. The long hallway had narrow wainscotting halfway up to the high ceiling. Single bulb lamps hung from long cords, creating yellow puddles of light on the polished brown linoleum tile. A couple of girls my age sat on straight chairs next to their mothers, waiting their turn. They looked up as I came out and the door shut behind me. Mami stood up from her chair at the end of the hall. She looked as scared as I felt.

"What happened?"

"Nothing," I mumbled, afraid that if I began telling her about it, I would break into tears in front of the other people, whose eyes followed me and Mami as we walked to the EXIT sign. "I have to wait here a minute."

"Did they say anything?"

"No. I'm just supposed to wait."

We leaned against the wall. Across from us there was a bulletin board with newspaper clippings about former students. On the ragged edge, a neat person had printed in blue ink, "P.A." and the year the actor, dancer, or musician had graduated. I closed my eyes and tried to picture myself on that bulletin board, with "P.A. '66" across the top.

The door at the end of the hall opened, and the woman in beige poked her head out.

"Esmeralda?"

"*Sí*, I mean, here." I raised my hand.

She led me into the room. There was another girl in there, whom she introduced as Bonnie, a junior at the school.

"Do you know what a pantomime is?" the woman asked. I nodded. "You and Bonnie are sisters decorating a Christmas tree."

Bonnie looked a lot like Juanita Marín, whom I had last seen in Macún four years earlier. We decided where the invisible Christmas tree would be, and we sat on the floor and pretended we were taking decorations out of boxes and hanging them on the branches.

My family had never had a Christmas tree, but I remembered how once I had helped Papi wind colored lights around the eggplant bush that divided our land from Doña Ana's. We started at the bottom and wound the wire with tiny red bulbs around and around until we ran out; then Papi plugged another cord to it and we kept going until the branches hung heavy with light and the bush looked like it was on fire.

Before long I had forgotten where I was, and that the tree didn't exist and Bonnie was not my sister. She pretended to hand me a very delicate ball, and just before I took it, she made like it fell to the ground and shattered. I was petrified that Mami would come in and yell at us for breaking her favorite decoration. Just as I began to pick up the tiny fragments of nonexistent crystal, a voice broke in. "Thank you."

Bonnie got up, smiled, and went out.

The elegant woman stretched her hand out for me to shake. "We will notify your school in a few weeks. It was very nice to meet you."

I shook hands all around then backed out of the room in a fog, silent, as if the pantomime had taken my voice and the urge to speak.

On the way home Mami kept asking what had happened, and I kept mumbling, "Nothing. Nothing happened," ashamed that, after all the hours of practice with Mrs. Johnson, Mr. Barone, and Mr. Gatti, after the expense of new clothes and shoes, after Mami had to take a day off from work to take me into Manhattan, after all that, I had failed the audition and would never, ever, get out of Brooklyn.

EPILOGUE:
ONE OF
THESE DAYS

El mismo jíbaro con diferente caballo.

❧❧

Same jíbaro, different horse.

A decade after my graduation from Performing Arts, I visited the school. I was by then living in Boston, a scholarship student at Harvard University. The tall, elegant woman of my audition had become my mentor through my three years there. Since my graduation, she had married the school principal.

"I remember your audition," she said, her chiseled face dreamy, her lips toying with a smile that she seemed, still, to have to control.

I had forgotten the skinny brown girl with the curled hair, wool jumper, and lively hands. But she hadn't. She told me that the panel had had to ask me to leave so that they could laugh, because it was so funny to see a fourteen-year-old Puerto Rican girl jabbering out a monologue about a possessive mother-in-law at the turn of the century, the words incomprehensible because they went by so fast.

"We admired," she said, "the courage it took to stand in front of us and do what you did."

"So you mean I didn't get into the school because of my talent, but because I had chutzpah?" We both laughed.

"Are any of your sisters and brothers in college?"

"No, I'm the only one, so far."

"How many of you are there?"

"By the time I graduated from high school there were eleven of us."

"Eleven!" She looked at me for a long time, until I had to look down. "Do you ever think about how far you've come?" she asked.

"No." I answered. "I never stop to think about it. It might jinx the momentum."

"Let me tell you another story, then," she said. "The first day of your first year, you were absent. We called your house. You said you couldn't come to school because you had nothing to wear. I wasn't sure if you were joking. I asked to speak to your mother, and you translated what she said. She needed you to go somewhere with her to interpret. At first you wouldn't tell me where, but then you admitted you were going to the welfare office. You were crying, and I had to assure you that you were not the only student in this school whose family received public assistance. The next day you were here, bright and eager. And now here you are, about to graduate from Harvard."

"I'm glad you made that phone call," I said.

"And I'm glad you came to see me, but right now I have to teach a class." She stood up, as graceful as I remembered. "Take care."

Her warm embrace, fragrant of expensive perfume, took me by surprise. "Thank you," I said as she went around the corner to her classroom.

I walked the halls of the school, looking for the room where my life had changed. It was across from the science lab, a few doors down from the big bulletin board where someone with neat handwriting still wrote the letters "P.A." followed by the graduating year along the edges of newspaper clippings featuring famous alumni.

"P.A. '66," I said to no one in particular. "One of these days."

GLOSSARY

A otro perro con ese hueso (Ah au-troh peh-rroh cun ess-eh oo-eh-soh): Literally, another dog for that bone. Used to dismiss a story one knows to be untrue.

Abuela (Ah-boo-eh-lah): Grandmother

Abuelo (Ah-boo-eh-loh): Grandfather

acerola (ah-ceh-ro-lah): West Indian cherry

achiote (ah-chee-oh-teh): A bright orange seasoning made from an-natto seeds

agua Florida (ah-goo-ah flo-ree-dah): Flower scented water from Florida

aguinaldos (ah-ghee-nal-doss): Traditional Christmas songs

alcapurrias (al-kah-poo-rhee-ass): Ground plantain and green ba-nanas stuffed with meat then fried

alcoholado (al-coh-lah-doh): Eucalyptus alcohol

Aleluya (ah-leh-loo-yah): Hallelujah

Americanitos (ah-mer-ee-can-ee-tohs): Little Americans

Americanos (ah-mer-ee-can-ohs): Americans

arroz con dulce (ah-rrohz cohn dool-seh): Sweetened rice spiced with ginger, coconut milk, and cinnamon

artesanías (art-eh-san-ee-ass): Crafts

asopao (ah-soh-pah-oh): Meat or fish soup thickened with rice and potatoes

Ay bendito (I behn-dee-toh): Exclamation that literally means "Blessed be"

Ay Dios mío (I dee-oss mee-oh): Oh, my God

Ay Santo Dios, bendícemela (I sahn-toh Dee-óhs, ben-dee-seh-meh-lah): Oh, dear God, bless her for me

batatas (bah-tah-tahss): Sweet potatoes

bodega (boh-deh-gah): Neighborhood grocery store

bohío (boh-ee-oh): Typical dwelling of Puerto Rican jíbaros

bolero (boh-leh-ro): Ballad

Borinquen (Boh-reen-ken): Pre-Columbian name for Puerto Rico

botánica (boh-tah-nee-cah): Shop that specializes in herbs, icons, and materials used in African-Caribbean religions

bueno (boo-eh-noh): Well or good

cafetín (kah-feh-teen): Open air coffee shop

caldero (kahl-deh-roh): A special heavy pot for cooking rice

carajo (kah-rah-ho): Swear word

charamanbiche (chah-rah-man-bee-cheh): Son of a bitch

chiforobe (chee-foh-roh-beh): Chest of drawers

cocotazos (koh-koh-tah-ssos): Hits on the head with knuckles

colibrí (koh-lee-brée): Hummingbird

coquí (koh-kee): Tiny tree frog, native to Puerto Rico, named after its distinctive song

cuatro (koo-ah-troh): A typical Puerto Rican stringed instrument, smaller than a guitar

curandera (coo-rahn-deh-rah): A woman healer

dignidad (deeg-nee-dad): Dignity

el bosso (ehl boss-oh): The boss

El Cura (el koo-rah): The priest

escupidera (ess-coo-pee-deh-rah): Literally, cuspidor. Chamber pot.

fiambreras (fee-am-breh-rahs): Portable covered dishes used to carry meals to and from work

finca (feen-kah): Farm

fogón (foh-góhn): Cooking fire

gallería (gah-yeh-ree-ah): Place where cocks fight

gente mala (hen-teh mah-lah): Bad people

guanimes (goo-ah-nee-mess): Cornmeal dumplings wrapped in plantain or banana leaves then boiled. Often stuffed.

guarachas (goo-ah-rah-chahs): A type of dance music popular in the Caribbean

guayabera (goo-ah-yah-berr-ah): Embroidered light cotton shirt

güiro (goo-ee-roh): Musical instrument made out of dried gourd across which metal tines are rubbed to produce a scratchy sound

hijas de la gran puta (ee-hass deh lah grahn poo-tah): Daughters of a great whore

huevos (oo-eh-voss): Eggs. Also, men's testicles

jamona (hah-móh-nah): Woman who has never married

jíbaro (hee-bah-roh): Rural Puerto Rican with distinctive dialect and customs

Jurutungo (Hoo-roo-toon-goh): Somewhere that's nowhere

La Colorá (Lah Koh-loh-rah): The red girl

los nervios (loss ner-vee-oss): Nervous attack

Macún (Mah-coon): Place where Esmeralda grew up

mal educada (mahl eh-doo-cah-dah): Poorly educated, rude

mancha de plátano (man-cha deh pláh-tah-noh): Plantain stain

marido (mah-ree-do): Husband or live-in-lover

maví (mah-vee): Bark beer

mercado (mer-kah-doh): Market

m'hija (mee-hah): Short for *mi hija*, my daughter

montes (mohn-tess): Woodsy hills

morcillas (mohr-cee-yass): Blood sausages

morivivi (mohr-ee-vee-vee): (L) *Mimosa pudica*, sensitive plant

muchachas (moo-cha-chas): Young women

muchacho (moo-cha-cho): Young man

muñequita (moo-nyeh-kee-tah): Little doll

nada (nah-dah): Nothing

negrita (o) (neh-gree-tah): Endearment, little black one

nena (neh-nah): Girl

novena (no-veh-nah): Prayer repeated for nine nights

pan de agua (pahn deh agoo-ah): French style bread

pan de manteca (pahn deh man-teh-cah): Lard bread

Papa Dios (pah-pah deeoss): Father God

parcela (par-seh-lah): Small farm

parrandas (pah-ran-dahs): Christmas tradition in which groups of people go from house to house singing and dancing

pasita (pah-see-tah): Raisin. Also used to describe the texture of African hair, said to resemble little raisins.

pasteles (pass-teh-less): Ground plantain, green bananas, and yucca stuffed with seasoned meat, wrapped in a roasted banana leaf, then boiled

piraguas (peer-ah-goo-ass): Shaved ice sweetened with fruit syrups
piropos (pee-roh-poss): Flirtatious comments men make to women as they pass
plaza del mercado (plah-ssah dell mer-kah-doh): Marketplace
pocavergüenza (pock-ah-ver-gwenn-zah): Shameless actions
pomarrosa (poh-mah-roh-ssa): Rose apple
purgante (poor-gahn-teh): Purge
puta (poo-tah): Whore
público (poo-blee-coh): Public car

qué lindos (keh leen-doss): So pretty
queso del país (keh-soh dell pah-ees): Cheese made in Puerto Rico
quinqué (keen-kéh): Kerosene lamp

salchichas (sahl-chee-chahs): Sausages
salsa (sahl-sah): A type of modern Caribbean dance music. Also, sauce.
sancocho (sahn-kóh-choh): Vegetable stew
señorita (se-nyo-ree-tah): A girl who has begun menstruating. Also, Miss.
sinvergüenza (seen-ver-gwenn-zah): Shameless person
sofrito (soh-free-toh): Vegetables, herbs, and spices ground up and combined. Used to season Puerto Rican food.
solitaria (soh-lee-tah-ree-ah): Alone. Also, tapeworm.

tembleque (tem-bleh-keh): Cornstarch pudding made with coconut milk
toda una señorita (toh-dah oo-nah seh-nyo-ree-tah): All a young lady should be

vaguadas (vah-goo-ah-dahs): Heavy rains
velorio (veh-loh-ree-oh): Wake

An excerpt from

Almost a Woman

by Esmeralda Santiago

Now available in hardcover from Perseus Books
Coming this fall in a Vintage Books trade paperback edition

"Martes, ni te cases, ni te embarques, ni de tu familia te apartes."

In the twenty-one years I lived with my mother, we moved at least twenty times. We stuffed our belongings into ragged suitcases, boxes with bold advertising on the sides, pillowcases, empty rice sacks, cracker tins that smelled of flour and yeast. Whatever we couldn't carry, we left behind: dressers with missing drawers, refrigerators, lumpy sofas, the fifteen canvases I painted one summer. We learned not to attach value to possessions because they were as temporary as the walls that held us for a few months, as the neighbors who lived down the street, as the sad-eyed boy who loved me when I was thirteen.

We moved from country to city to country to small town to big city to the biggest city of all. Once in New York, we moved from apartment to apartment, in search of heat, of fewer cockroaches, of more rooms, of quieter neighbors, of more privacy, of nearness to the subway or the relatives. We moved in loops around the neighborhoods we wanted to avoid, where there were no Puerto Ricans, where graffiti warned of gang turfs, where people dressed better than we did, where landlords didn't accept welfare, or didn't like Puerto Ricans, or looked at our family of three adults, eleven children and shook their heads.

We avoided the neighborhoods with too few stores, or too many stores, or the wrong kind of store, or no stores at all. We circled around our first apartment the way animals circle the place where they will sleep, and after ten years of circling, Mami returned to where we began the journey, to Macún, the Puerto Rican barrio where everyone knew each other and each other's business, where what we left behind was put to good use by people who moved around less.

By the time she returned to Macún, I'd also moved. Four days after my twenty-first birthday, I left Mami's house, the rhyme I sang as a child forgotten: "*Martes, ni te cases, ni te embarques, ni de tu familia te apartes.*" On a misty Tuesday, I didn't marry, but I did travel, and I did leave my family. I stuffed in the mailbox a letter addressed to Mami in which I said goodbye, because I didn't have the courage to say goodbye in person.

I went to Florida, to begin my own journey from one city to another. Each time I packed my belongings, I left a little of myself in the rooms that sheltered me, never home, always just the places I lived. I congratulated myself on how easy it was to leave them, how well I packed everything I owned into a couple of boxes and a suitcase.

Years later, when I visited Macún, I went to the spot where my childhood began and ended. I stepped on what was left of our blue tiled floor and looked at the wild greenness around me, at what had been a yard for games, at the corner where an eggplant bush became a Christmas tree, at the spot where I cut my foot and blood seeped into the dust. It was no longer familiar, nor beautiful, nor did it give a clue of who I'd been there, or who I might become wherever I was going next. The *morivivi* weeds and the *culantro* choked the dirt yard, creepers had overgrown the cement floor, pinakoop climbed over what was left of the walls and turned them into soft green mounds that sheltered drab olive lizards and chameleons, *coquí* and hummingbirds. There was no sign we'd ever been there, except for the hillock of blue cement tile on which I stood. It gleamed in the afternoon sun, its color so intense that I wondered if I had stepped onto the wrong floor because I didn't remember our floor being that blue.

"Something could happen to you."

We came to Brooklyn in 1961, in search of medical care for my youngest brother, Raymond, whose toes were nearly severed by a bicycle chain when he was four. In Puerto Rico, doctors wanted to amputate the often red and swollen foot, because it wouldn't heal. In New York, Mami hoped, doctors could save it.

The day we arrived, a hot, humid afternoon had splintered into thunderstorms as the last rays of the sun dipped into the rest of the United States. I was thirteen and superstitious enough to believe thunder and lightning held significance beyond the meteorological. I stored the sights and sounds of that dreary night into memory as if their meaning would someday be revealed in a flash of insight to transform my life forever. When the insight came, nothing changed, for it wasn't the weather in Brooklyn that was important, but the fact that I was there to notice it.

One hand tightly grasped by Mami, the other by six-year-old Edna, we squeezed and pushed our way through the crowd of travelers. Five-year-old Raymond clung to Mami's other hand, his unbalanced gait drawing sympathetic smiles from people who moved aside to let us walk ahead of them.

At the end of the tunnel waited Tata, Mami's mother, in black lace and high heels, a pronged rhinestone pin on her left shoulder. When she hugged me, the pin pricked my cheek, pierced subtle flower-shaped indentations that I rubbed rhythmically as our taxi hurtled through drenched streets banked by high, angular buildings.

New York was darker than I expected, and, in spite of the cleansing rain, dirtier. Used to the sensual curves of rural Puerto Rico, my eyes had to adjust to the regular, aggressive two-dimensionality of Brooklyn. Raindrops pounded the hard streets, captured the dim silver glow of street lamps, bounced against sidewalks in glistening sparks, then disappeared, like tiny ephemeral jewels, into the darkness. Mami and Tata teased that I was disillusioned because the streets were not paved with gold. But I had no such vision of New York. I was disappointed by the darkness and fixed my hopes on the promise of light deep within the sparkling raindrops.

~

Two days later, I leaned against the wall of our apartment building on McKibbin Street wondering where New York ended and the rest of the world began. It was hard to tell. There was no horizon in Brooklyn. Everywhere I looked, my eyes met a vertical maze of gray and brown straight-edged buildings with sharp corners and deep shadows. Every few blocks there was a cement playground surrounded by chain-link fence. And in between, weedy lots mounded with garbage and rusting cars.

A girl came out of the building next door, a jump rope in her hand. She appraised me shyly; I pretended to ignore her. She stepped on the rope, stretched the ends overhead as if to measure their length, and then began to skip, slowly, grunting each time she came down on the sidewalk. Swish splat grunt swish, she turned her back to me; swish splat grunt swish, she faced me again and smiled. I smiled back, and she hopped over.

"*¿Tú eres hispana?*" she asked, as she whirled the rope in lazy arcs.

"No, I'm Puerto Rican."

"Same thing. Puerto Rican, Hispanic. That's what we are here." She skipped a tight circle, stopped abruptly, and shoved the rope in my direction. "Want a turn?"

"Sure." I hopped on one leg, then the other. "So, if you're Puerto Rican, they call you Hispanic?"

"Yeah. Anybody who speaks Spanish."

I jumped a circle, as she had done, but faster. "You mean, if you speak Spanish, you're Hispanic?"

"Well, yeah. No . . . I mean your parents have to be Puerto Rican or Cuban or something."

I whirled the rope to the right, then the left, like a boxer. "Okay, your parents are Cuban, let's say, and you're born here, but you don't speak Spanish. Are you Hispanic?"

She bit her lower lip. "I guess so," she finally said. "It has to do with being from a Spanish country. I mean, you or your parents, like, even if you don't speak Spanish, you're Hispanic, you know?" She looked at me uncertainly. I nodded and returned her rope.

But I didn't know. I'd always been Puerto Rican, and it hadn't occurred to me that in Brooklyn I'd be someone else.

Later, I asked. "Are we Hispanics, Mami?"

"Yes, because we speak Spanish."

"But a girl said you don't have to speak the language to be Hispanic."

She scrunched her eyes. "What girl? Where did you meet a girl?"

"Outside. She lives in the next building."

"Who said you could go out to the sidewalk? This isn't Puerto Rico. *Algo te puede suceder.*"

"Something could happen to you" was a variety of dangers outside the locked doors of our apartment. I could be mugged. I could be dragged into any of the dark, abandoned buildings on the way to or from school and be raped and murdered. I could be accosted by gang members into whose turf I strayed. I could be seduced by men who preyed on unchaperoned girls too willing to talk to strangers. I listened to Mami's lecture with downcast eyes and the necessary, respectful expression of humility. But inside, I quaked. Two days in New York, and I'd already become someone else. It wasn't hard to imagine that greater dangers lay ahead.

Our apartment on McKibbin Street was more substantial than any of our houses in Puerto Rico. Its marble staircase, plaster walls, and tiled floors were bound to the earth, unlike the wood and zinc rooms on stilts where I'd grown up. Chubby angels with bare buttocks danced around plaster wreaths on the ceiling. There was a bathtub in the kitchen with hot and cold running water, and a toilet inside a closet with a sink and a medicine chest.

An alley between our bedroom window and the wall of the next building was so narrow that I stretched over to touch the bricks and left my mark on the greasy soot that covered them. Above, a sliver of sky forced vague yellow light into the ground below, filled with empty detergent boxes, tattered clothes, un-paired shoes, bottles, broken glass.

Mami had to go look for work, so Edna, Raymond, and I went downstairs to stay with Tata in her apartment. When we knocked on her door, she was just waking up. I sat at the small table near the cooking counter to read the newspapers that Don Julio, Tata's boyfriend, had brought the night before. Edna and Raymond stood in the middle of the room and stared at the small television on a low table. Tata switched it on, fiddled with the knobs and the antenna until the horizontal lines disappeared and black-and-white cartoon characters chased each other across a flat landscape. The kids sank to the floor cross-legged, their eyes on the screen. Against the wall, under the window, Tata's brother, Tío Chico, slept with his back to us. Every so often, a snore woke him, but he chewed his drool, mumbled, slept again.

While Tata went to wash up in the hall bathroom, I tuned in to the television. A dot bounced over the words of a song being performed by a train dancing along tracks, with dogs, cats, cows, and horses dangling from its windows and caboose. I was hypno-tized by the dot skipping over words that looked nothing like they sounded. "Shilbee cominrun demuntin wenshecoms, toot-toot" sang the locomotive, and the ball dipped and rose over "She'll be coming 'round the mountain when she comes," with no toots. The animals, dressed in cowboy hats, overalls, and bandannas, waved pickaxes and shovels in the air. The toot-toot was replaced by a bow-wow or a miaow-ow, or a moo-moo. It was joyous and silly, and made Edna and Raymond laugh. But it was hard for me to enjoy it as I focused on the words whizzing by, on the dot jumping rhythmically from one syllable to the next, with barely enough time to connect the letters to the sounds, with the added distraction of an occasional neigh, bark, or kid's giggle.

When Tata returned from the bathroom, she made coffee on the two-burner hot plate. Fragrant steam soon filled the small room, and as she strained the grounds through a well-worn flannel filter, Tío Chico rose as if the aroma were an alarm louder and more insistent than the singing animals on the television screen, the clanking of pots against the hot plate and counter, the screech of the chair legs as I positioned myself so that I could watch both Tata and the cartoons.

"Well, look who we have here," Tío Chico said, as he stretched until his long, bony fingers scraped the ceiling. He wore the same clothes as on the day before: a faded pair of dark pants and a short-sleeved undershirt, both wrinkled and giving off a pungent, sweaty smell. He stepped over Edna and Raymond, who barely moved to let him through. In two long-legged strides, he slipped out to the bathroom. As he shut the door, the walls closed in, as if his lanky body added dimension to the cramped room.

Tata hummed the cartoon music. Her big hands reached for a pan, poured milk, stirred briskly as it heated and frothed. I was mesmerized by her grace, by how she held her head, by the disheveled, ash-colored curls that framed her high cheekbones. She looked up with mischievous caramel eyes and grinned without breaking her rhythm.

Tío Chico returned showered and shaved, wearing a clean shirt and pants as wrinkled as the ones he'd taken off. He dropped the dirty clothes in a corner near Tata's bed and made up his cot.

Tata handed me a cup of sweetened *café con leche* and, with a head gesture, indicated that I should vacate the chair for Tío Chico.

"No, no, that's okay," he said, "I'll sit here."

He perched on the edge of the cot, elbows on knees, his fingers wrapped around the mug Tata gave him. Steam rose from inside his hands in a transparent spiral. Tata served Edna and Raymond, then sat with her coffee in one hand and a cigarette in the other, talking softly to Tío Chico, who also lit up. I brought my face to the steaming coffee to avoid the mentholated smoke that curled from their corner of the room to ours, settling like a soft, gray blanket that melted into our clothes and hair.

I couldn't speak English, so the school counselor put me in a class for students who'd scored low on intelligence tests, who were behavior problems, who were marking time until their sixteenth birthday, when they could drop out. The teacher, a pretty black woman only a few years older than her students, pointed to a seat in the middle of the room. I didn't dare look anyone in the eyes. Grunts and mutters followed me, and although I had no idea what they meant, they didn't sound friendly.

The desk surface was elaborately carved. There were many names, some followed by an apostrophe and a year. Several carefully rendered obscenities meant nothing to me, but I appreciated the workmanship of the shadowed letters, the fastidious edges around the *f* and *k*. I guessed a girl had written the cursive message whose *i*s were dotted with hearts and daisies. Below it, several lines of timid, chicken-scratch writing alternated with an aggressive line of block letters.

I pressed my hands together under the desk to subdue their shaking, studied the straight lines and ragged curves chiseled into the desktop by those who had sat there before me. Eyes on the marred surface, I focused on the teacher's voice, on the unfamiliar waves of sound that crested over my head. I wanted to float up and out of that classroom, away from the hostile air that filled every corner of it, every crevice. But the more I tried to disappear, the more present I felt, until, exhausted, I gave in, floated with the words, certain that if I didn't, I would drown in them.

On gym days, girls had to wear grass green, cotton, short-sleeved, bloomer-leg, one-piece outfits that buttoned down the front to an elastic waistband covered with a sash too short to tie into anything but a bulky knot. Grass green didn't look good on anyone, least of all adolescent girls whose faces broke out in red pimples. The gym suit had elastic around the bottom to prevent the sight of panties when we fell or sat. On those of us with skinny legs, the elastic wasn't snug enough, so the bloomers hung limply to our knees, where they flapped when we ran.

The uniform, being one piece, made it impossible to go to the bathroom in the three minutes between classes. Instead of wearing it all day, we could bring it to school and change before gym, but no one did, since boys periodically raided the locker room to see our underwear. With the gym suit on, proper hygiene during "the curse" was difficult, as we needed at least three hands, so most girls brought notes from their mothers. The problem was that if you didn't wear the uniform on gym days, everyone knew you were menstruating.

One girl bought two gym suits, chopped off the bottom of one, seamed around the selvage, and wore the top part under her blouse so that no one could tell if she had her period or not. I asked Mami to do that for me, but she said we didn't have money to waste on such foolishness.

Friday mornings we had Assembly. The first thing we did was to press our right hands to our breasts and sing "The Star-Spangled Banner." We were encouraged to sing as loudly as we could, and within a couple of weeks I had learned the entire song by heart.

Ojo sé. Can. Juice. ¿Y?
Bye de don surly lie.
Whassoprowow we hell
Add debt why lie lass gleam in.
Whosebrods tripe sand bye ¿Stars?
True de perro los ¡Ay!
Order am parts we wash,
Wha soga lang tree streem in.

I had no idea what the song said or meant, and no one bothered to teach me. It was one of the things I was supposed to know, and like the daily recitation of the pledge of allegiance, it had to be done with enthusiasm, or teachers gave out demerits. The pledge was printed in ornate letters on a poster under the flag in every classroom. "The Star-Spangled Banner," however, remained a mystery for years, its nonsense words the only song I could sing in English from beginning to end.

⁓

On a chill October afternoon, Mami, Don Julio, and I went to the airport to pick up the rest of my sisters and brothers, who'd stayed in Puerto Rico with our father until Mami could afford their plane fare. Delsa, Norma, Héctor, and Alicia were smaller than I remembered them, darker, more foreign. They huddled close to one another, holding hands. Their eyes darted from corner to corner of the enormous terminal, to the hundreds of people waving, hugging, kissing, to the luggage that banged into them. Birdlike, they lifted their heads, mouths open, toward the magnified, disembodied voices bleating orders from the ceilings. I wondered if I had looked that frightened and vulnerable only two months earlier.

We'd moved to a new, larger apartment on Varet Street. Tata and Tío Chico had been cooking all morning, and as we entered the apartment, the fragrance of roasting *achiote*, garlic, and oregano, the family milling around, laughing and talking, made it like Christmas.

We had many relatives in Brooklyn. Paco, Tío Chico's son, was short and muscular. His arms and face were always bruised, his eyes swollen and bloodshot, his nose bandaged, the result of his work as a wrestler. His professional name was El Santo. In the ring, he wore white tights and boots, a white leather belt, a white mask, a milky satin cape with a stand-up collar studded with rhinestones. He was one of the good guys, but although he usually won his fights, he always received a beating from the guys in black.

Paco's brother, Jalisco, worked in a factory. He was tall and lean like his father and groomed his mustache into a black, straight fuzz over his lips, like Jorge Negrete, the Mexican singer and movie star. Whenever Jalisco came over, I circled him like a febrile butterfly — offering drinks or food, or reminding him he'd promised to sing *"Cielito Lindo"* after supper. Mami never left me alone with him.

Tata's two sisters lived within a few blocks of our apartment. Tía Chía and her daughters — Margot, Gury, and La Muda — were close to my mother. They came dragging bags full of clothes and shoes they no longer wore. Gury, the youngest, was slender and soft-spoken. Her clothes fit me, although Mami said that the straight skirts, sheer blouses, and high heels Gury favored were not appropriate for a girl my age.

Her sister La Muda was deaf and mute. According to Mami, La Muda had been born with perfect hearing but as a toddler she got sick, and when she recovered, she was deaf.

"Then why don't they call her La Sorda . . ." I began, and Mami warned I was disrespectful.

La Muda read lips. If we spoke with our faces away from her, she shook our shoulders and made us repeat what we'd said while her eyes focused on our mouths. We quickly learned to interpret her language, a dance of gestures enhanced with hums, gurgles, and grunts that didn't seem to come from her throat but from a deeper source, inside her belly. Her hands were large, well manicured, bedecked with numerous gold and stone rings that shimmered as her fingers flew here and there.

La Muda liked us to read the paper to her. That is, Mami or Don Julio read it aloud, while we kids acted out the news. La Muda's eyes darted from Mami's lips to our portrayals of that day's murders, car crashes, and results at the track, enacted race by race around the kitchen table. Her laugh, frequent and contagious, was deep but flat, as if, unable to hear herself laugh, she couldn't get the tone.

Her boyfriend was someone we'd known in Puerto Rico. He was a thin, laconic, dark-haired man who dressed in a beige suit. When we first met him, my six sisters and brothers and I were afraid of him, but he took a deck of cards from his pocket, performed some tricks, and after that we called him Luigi, which sounded like the perfect name for a magician.

Tata's other sister, Titi Ana, had two daughters who were closer to my age than La Muda, Margot, or Gury. Alma was a year older, and Corazón a year younger. They spoke English to each other, and when they talked to us or to their mother, their Spanish was halting and accented. Mami said they were Americanized. The way she pronounced the word *Americanized,* it sounded like a terrible thing, to be avoided at all costs, another *algo* to be added to the list of "somethings" outside our door.

When they walked into the apartment, my sisters and brother submitted to hugs and kisses from people who were strangers to them but who introduced themselves as Cousin this or Auntie that. Delsa was on the verge of tears. Norma held on to Alicia as if afraid they'd get lost in the confusion. Héctor circulated among the men, followed by Raymond, who chattered about Paco's exploits in the ring or about Don Julio's generosity with pocket change.

Luigi, his usually solemn face lit by the hint of a smile, performed new tricks, and the kids relaxed somewhat, as if this reminder of our life in Puerto Rico were enough to dissolve their fears. Margot had brought a portable record player and records, which played full blast in the kitchen, while in the front room the television was tuned to the afternoon horror movie. The kids shuffled from room to room in a daze, overdosed on the Twinkies, Yodels, and potato chips Don Julio had brought for us.

The welcome party lasted into the night. Don Julio and Jalisco went to the *bodega* several times for more beer, and Tío Chico found a liquor store and came back with jugs of Gallo wine. Mami ran from the adults to the kids, reminding the men that there were children in the house, that they should stop drinking.

One by one the relatives left, and the kids once more surrendered to hugs and kisses. Our pockets jingled with pennies that the aunts, uncles, and cousins had handed out as if to pay for the party. Luigi escorted La Muda from the apartment. His pale fingers pressed against her waist, his too-big suit flapped around his scarecrow frame. As they walked out, the adults exchanged mysterious smiles.

Tío Chico and his sons were the last to leave. Tata and Don Julio went into her room and drew the curtain that separated their part of the apartment from ours. "It's time for bed," Mami reminded us. We got ready, Delsa and I on the top bunk, Norma and Alicia on the bottom, Héctor on the sofa, Raymond in the upholstered chairs pushed together, Edna and Mami in the double bed. She turned out the light, and the soft rustles of my sisters and brothers settling into their first night in Brooklyn filled me with a secret joy, which I never admitted but which soothed and reassured me in a way nothing had since we'd left Puerto Rico.

LAS CHRISTMAS

Escritores Latinos Recuerdan Las Tradiciones Navideñas
edited by Esmeralda Santiago and Joie Davidow

From Julia Alvarez's tale of how Santicló delivered a beloved uncle from political oppression to Junot Díaz's story of his own uneasy assimilation on his first Christmas in America, to Sandra Cisnero's poignant memories of her late father's holiday dinners, *Las Christmas* gives us true stories from writers of many traditions—memories of Christmas and Hanukkah that vividly capture the pride and pain, joy and heartbreak, that so often accompany the holidays in the Americas.

Antologia/Festivas/0-375-70169-9

LAS CHRISTMAS

Favorite Latino Authors Share Their Holiday Memories
Anthology/Holidays/0-375-40151-2